THE H.M.S. BAD IDEA
AN ANTI-SELF-HELP COMIC COLLECTION

PETER CHIYKOWSKI
**ROCKPAPERCYNIC.COM**

Distributed in Canada by:

HarperCollins Canada Ltd.
1995 Markham Road
Scarborough, ON M1B 5M8
Toll Free: 1-800-387-0117
e-mail: hcorder@harpercollins.com

Distributed in the U.S. by:

Diamond Comic Distributors, Inc.
10150 York Road, Suite 300
Hunt Valley, MD 21030
Phone: (443) 318-8500
e-mail: books@diamondbookdistributors.com

Printed in PRC.

CIP data available upon request.

ROCK, PAPER, CYNIC
Toronto, Canada
www.rockpapercynic.com
peter@rockpapercynic.com

CHIGRAPHIC
An imprint of ChiZine Publications
Toronto, Canada
www.chizinepub.com
info@chizinepub.com

FIRST EDITION
ISBN 978-1-77148-369-8 (tpb) / 978-1-77148-372-8 (hardcover) / 978-1-77148-370-4 (pdf)

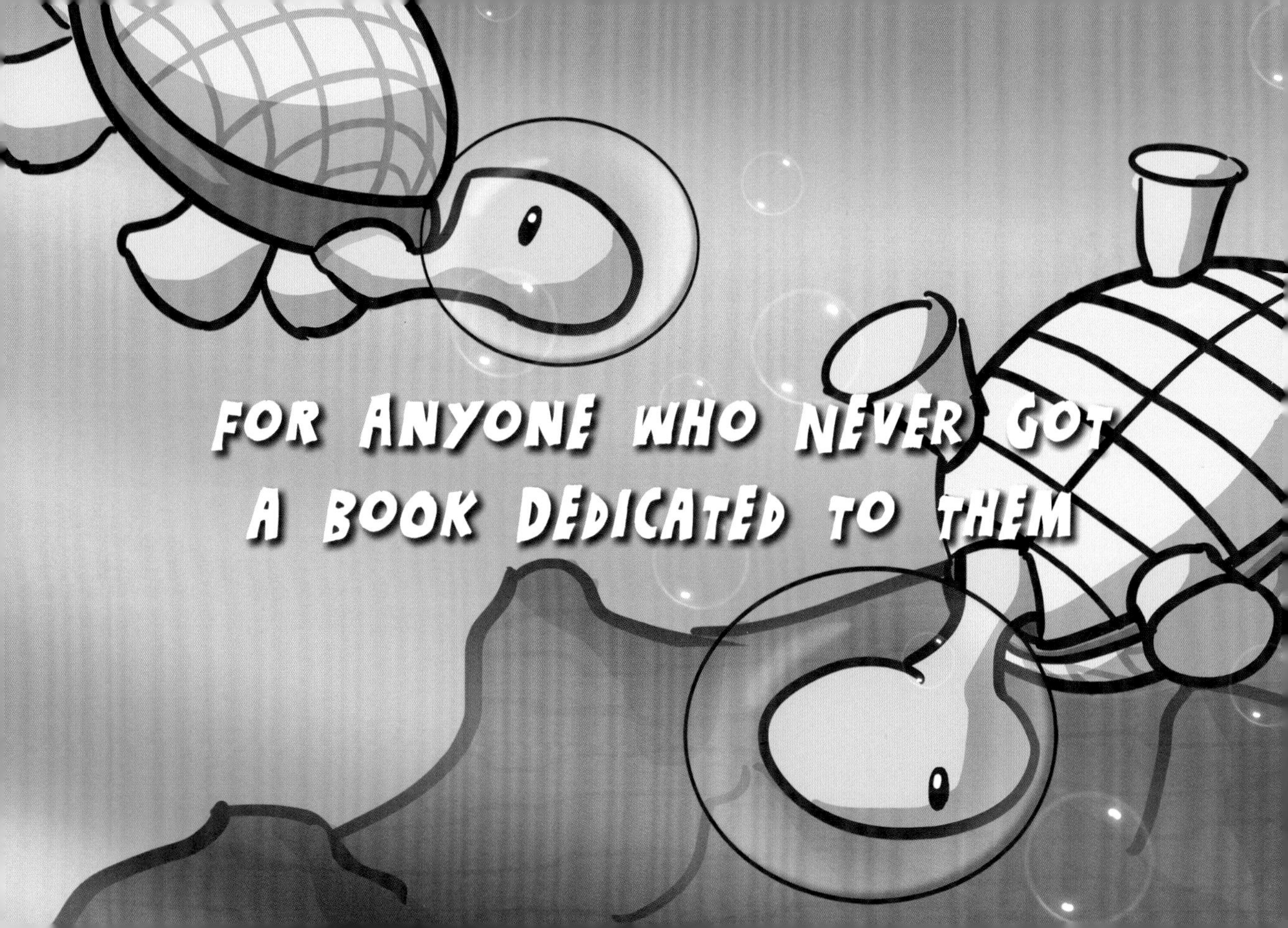

FOR ANYONE WHO NEVER GOT
A BOOK DEDICATED TO THEM

THE FOREWORD

NOW YOU'VE GONE AND DONE IT!

YOU STARTED READING THE FOREWORD. WHO DOES THAT? WHO READS *THE FOREWORD?*

ALRIGHT, GREAT. NOW I HAVE TO WRITE ONE. BUT SINCE THIS IS YOUR FAULT, YOU HAVE TO HELP ME.

I'LL WRITE, LIKE, 90% OF IT, BUT I'M GONNA LEAVE A BUNCH OF BLANKS THAT YOU HAVE TO FILL IN.

JUST DON'T TURN THE PAGE YET! I'M STILL WORKING ON IT.

OKAY, COOL. I THINK IT'S READY. YOU CAN TURN NOW.

OKAY, THIS IS HOW IT'S GONNA GO DOWN.

HERE ARE THE BLANKS YOU'RE GOING TO HAVE TO FILL IN TO MAKE THIS WORK.

MADE-UP SOVIET REPUBLIC

OLD-SCHOOL BRITISH LAST NAME

RANDOM NUMBER BETWEEN 1 AND 20

TERRIBLE NAME FOR A DOG

FAKE MYTHICAL CREATURE

NAME OF A CLEARLY HAUNTED FOREST

ANTIQUATED EXCLAMATION OF SURPRISE

FANTASTICAL MACHINE PART

BLACK MARKET TRADE ITEM

OUTLANDISH ARTICLE OF CLOTHING

IRRATIONAL NUMBER

ILLEGAL-SOUNDING LIQUOR

SKETCHY-SOUNDING GOD

ADJECTIVE DESCRIBING THIS BOOK

ADJECTIVE DESCRIBING YOUR OWN HANDWRITING

MADE-UP NOUN MEANING "MOST MYSTERIOUS MAN"

ADVERB FOR HOW A MADMAN LAUGHS

RIDICULOUS TIME-TRAVEL PARADOX

MONSTER THAT LIVES IN THE TIME STREAM

YOUR NAME

OKAY, NOW TURN THE PAGE! ↗

Dear reader,

I first met Peter in _____ in 1863. We were both there on time-travel business,
made-up Soviet republic

him in his beat-up old _____ chrono-transference machine, and I in the newer,
old-school British last name

sleeker version. He wore a ____-foot tall stovepipe hat and was accompanied by his trusty dog
random no.

_____ as he hunted for the elusive _____ of _____.
terrible name for a dog   *fake mythical creature*   *name of a clearly haunted forest*

"_____!" he exclaimed. "I require your assistance, friend! The _____
antiquated exclamation of surprise   *fantastical machine part*

in my time machine is totally borked! In exchange for your aid in fixing it, I will give you three crates

of _____ and a magical book of sagely life advice that was given to me by a mysterious
black market trade item

traveler wearing a _____!"
outlandish article of clothing

I took pity on the poor devil and decided to help him on his way back to the year _____,
irrational number

which he claimed was a real year, but totally isn't. Anyway, it turned out nothing was wrong with his

time machine. Drunk on _____, he had forgotten to flick the "on" switch.
illegal-sounding liquor

With his machine functioning again, he turned to me and said, "Thank you, friend! May

_____ smile upon you!" And then he handed me a _____ book.
sketchy-sounding god   *adjective describing this book*

As his machine prepared to launch, I scanned the pages and saw that the foreword to the book

contained blanks filled in by my own _____ handwriting.
adjective describing your own handwriting

"Wait, you most mysterious _____," I cried! "Who gave you this book?"
made-up noun meaning "most mysterious man"

"What a strange question, dear reader!" he replied, laughing _____. "YOU DID!"
adverb for how a madman laughs

I looked at myself and realized that I was wearing a _____ and that I had written
REPEAT: article of outlandish clothing

the very foreword of the fiendish text!

That's right, dear reader. *YOU ARE ME AND I AM YOU.* Because of Peter, this impossible

book, and the _____, we are trapped in a time loop. I hope this book will help
ridiculous time-travel paradox

you/me/us escape, or, if nothing else, provide paper for starting fires with which to ward off the mighty

_____ that guards the year 1863.
monster that lives in the time stream

Godspeed,

_____
your name

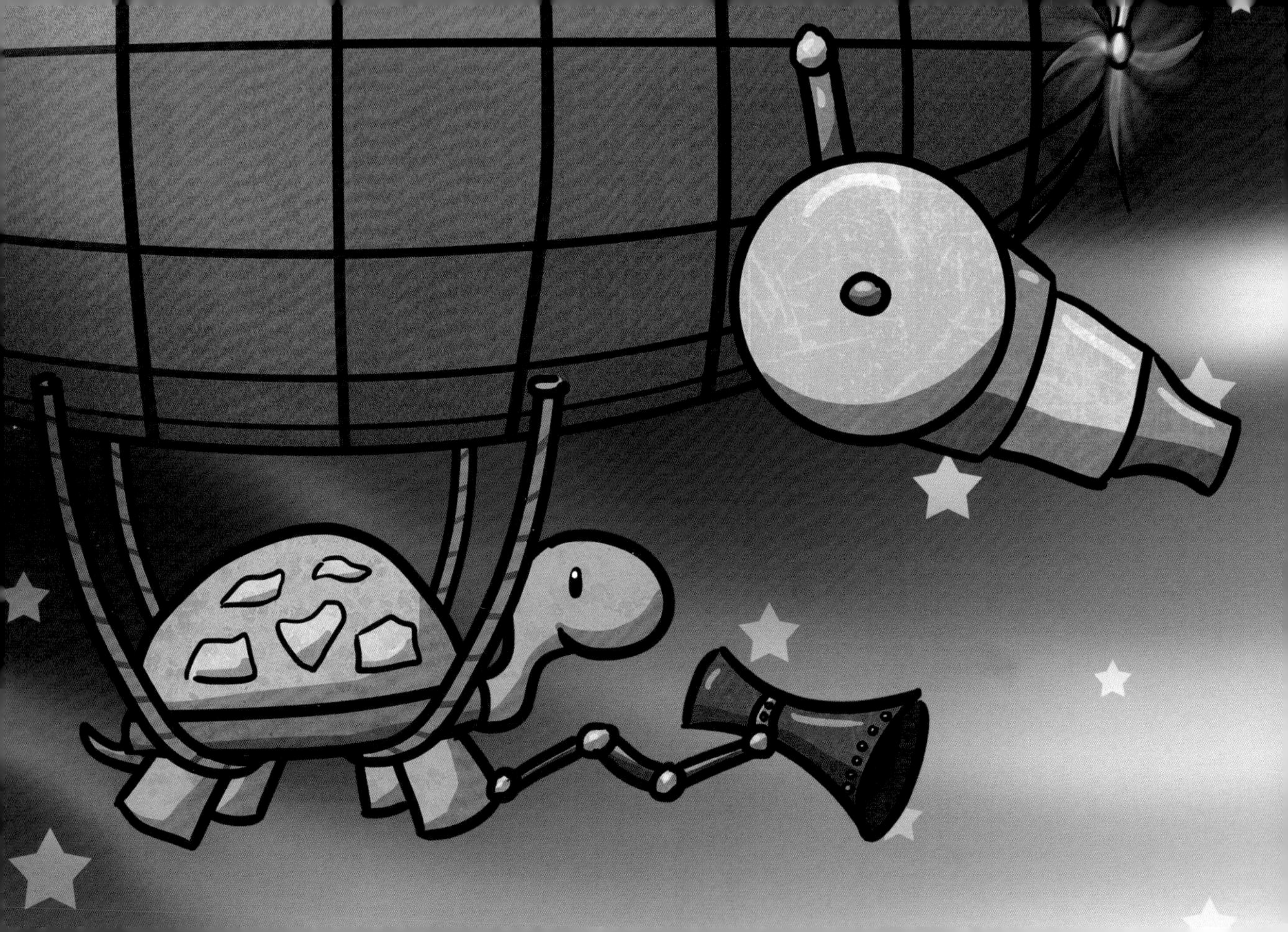

LIFE IS AN AIRSHIP FULL OF REGRETS AND BAD DECISIONS.

YOU CAN LET THEM WEIGH YOU DOWN, OR YOU CAN CHUCK 'EM IN THE FURNACE AND SET COURSE FOR SOMEPLACE AWESOME.

AND IF YOU EVER RUN OUT, YOU CAN ALWAYS MAKE MORE.

DID I NEED TO STEAL AN ATTACK WALRUS IN ORDER TO WIN MY FREEDOM FROM THAT GOVERNMENT RESEARCH FACILITY?
NO.
BUT AT SOME POINT WE ALL MUST CHOOSE BETWEEN WHAT IS RIGHT AND WHAT IS AWESOME.

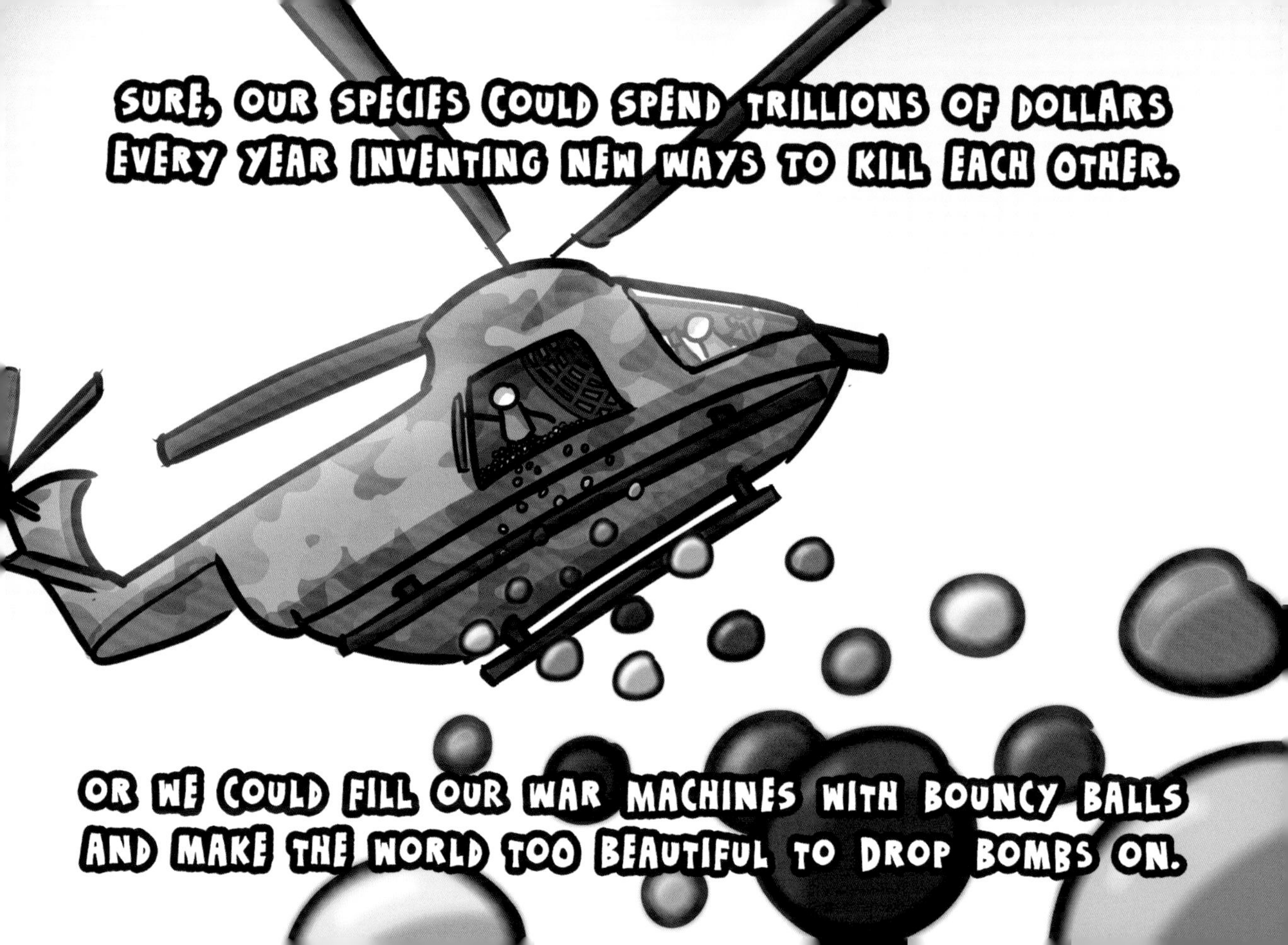
SURE, OUR SPECIES COULD SPEND TRILLIONS OF DOLLARS EVERY YEAR INVENTING NEW WAYS TO KILL EACH OTHER.
OR WE COULD FILL OUR WAR MACHINES WITH BOUNCY BALLS AND MAKE THE WORLD TOO BEAUTIFUL TO DROP BOMBS ON.

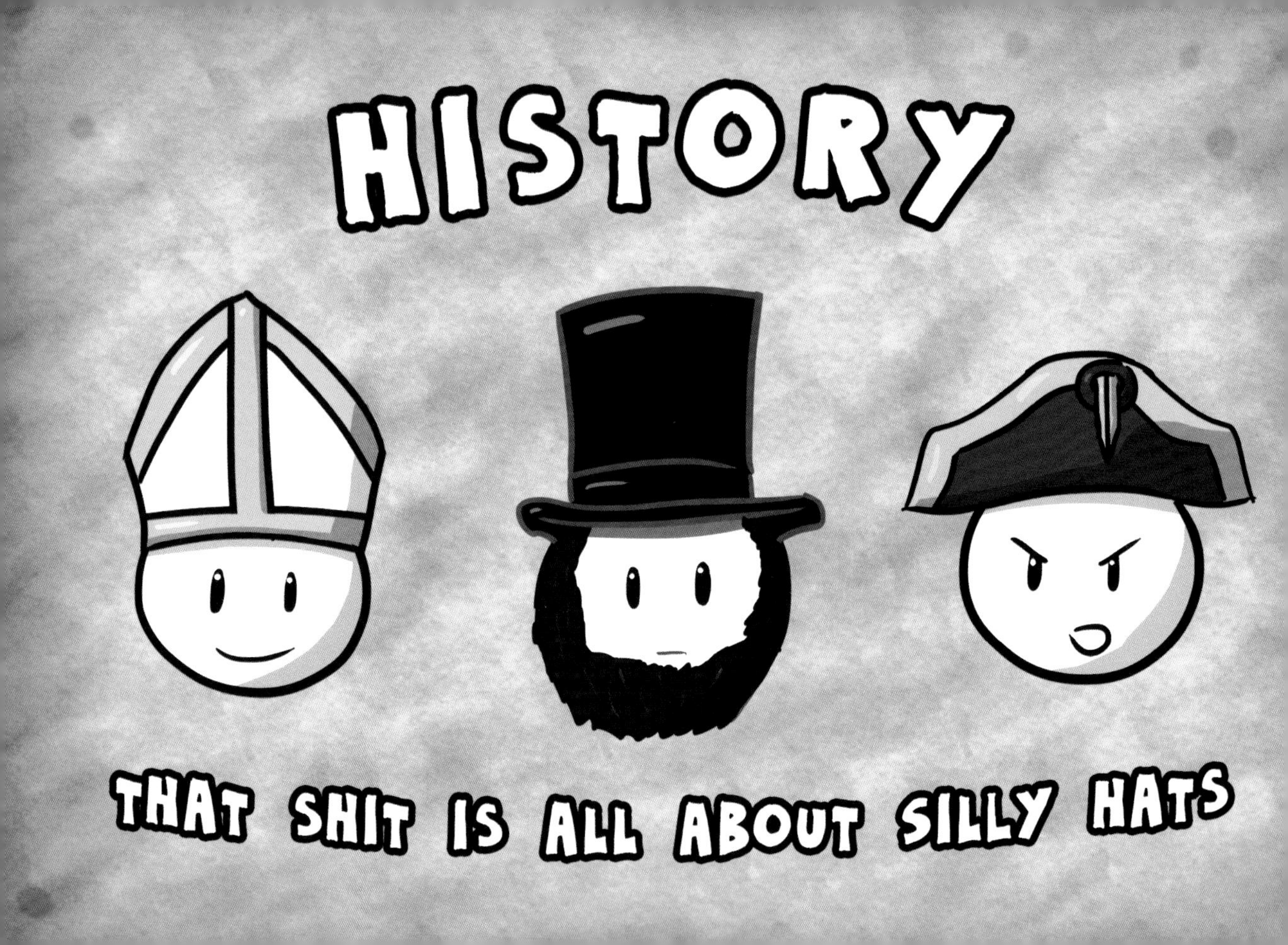
HISTORY
THAT SHIT IS ALL ABOUT SILLY HATS

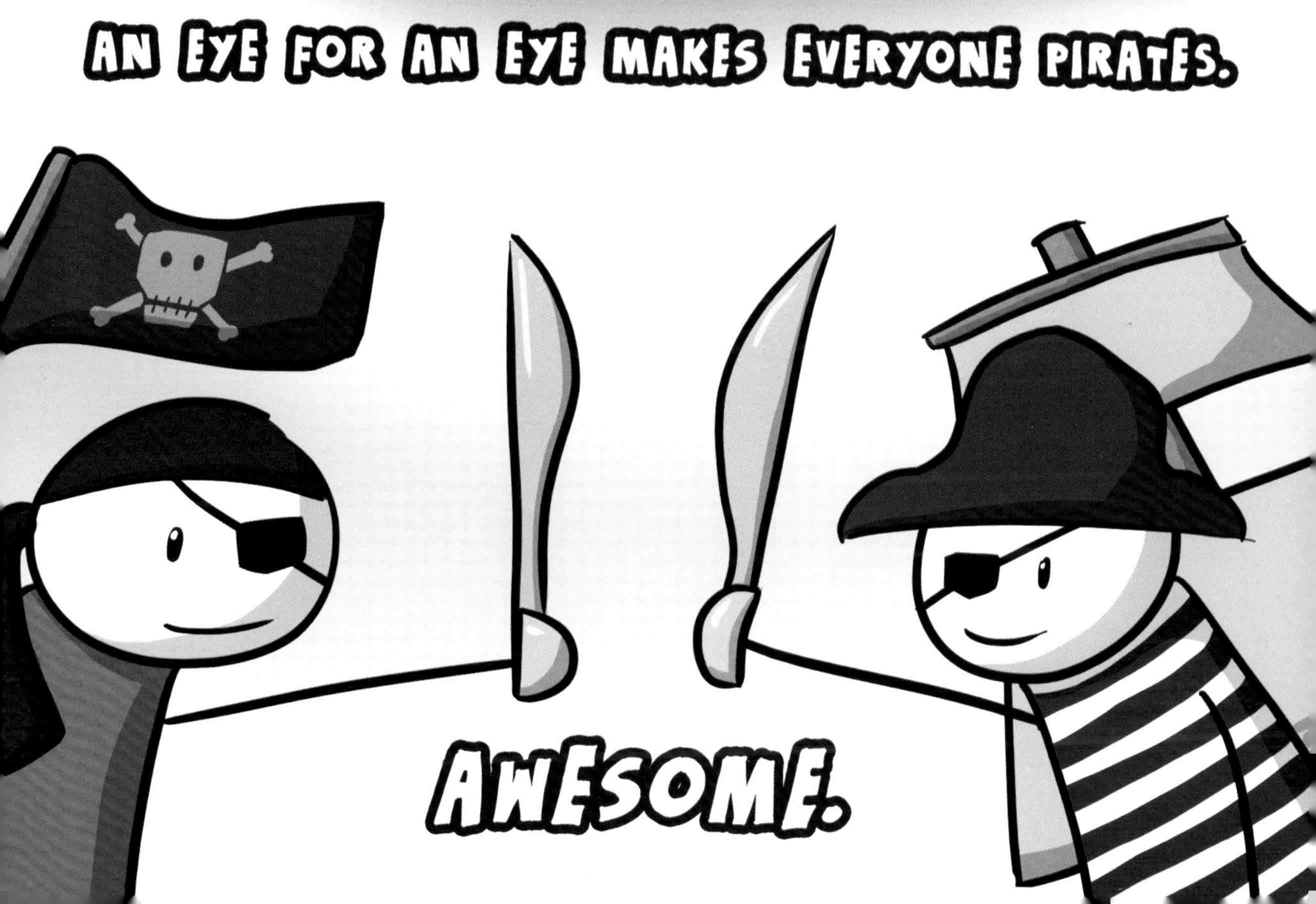
AN EYE FOR AN EYE MAKES EVERYONE PIRATES.
AWESOME.

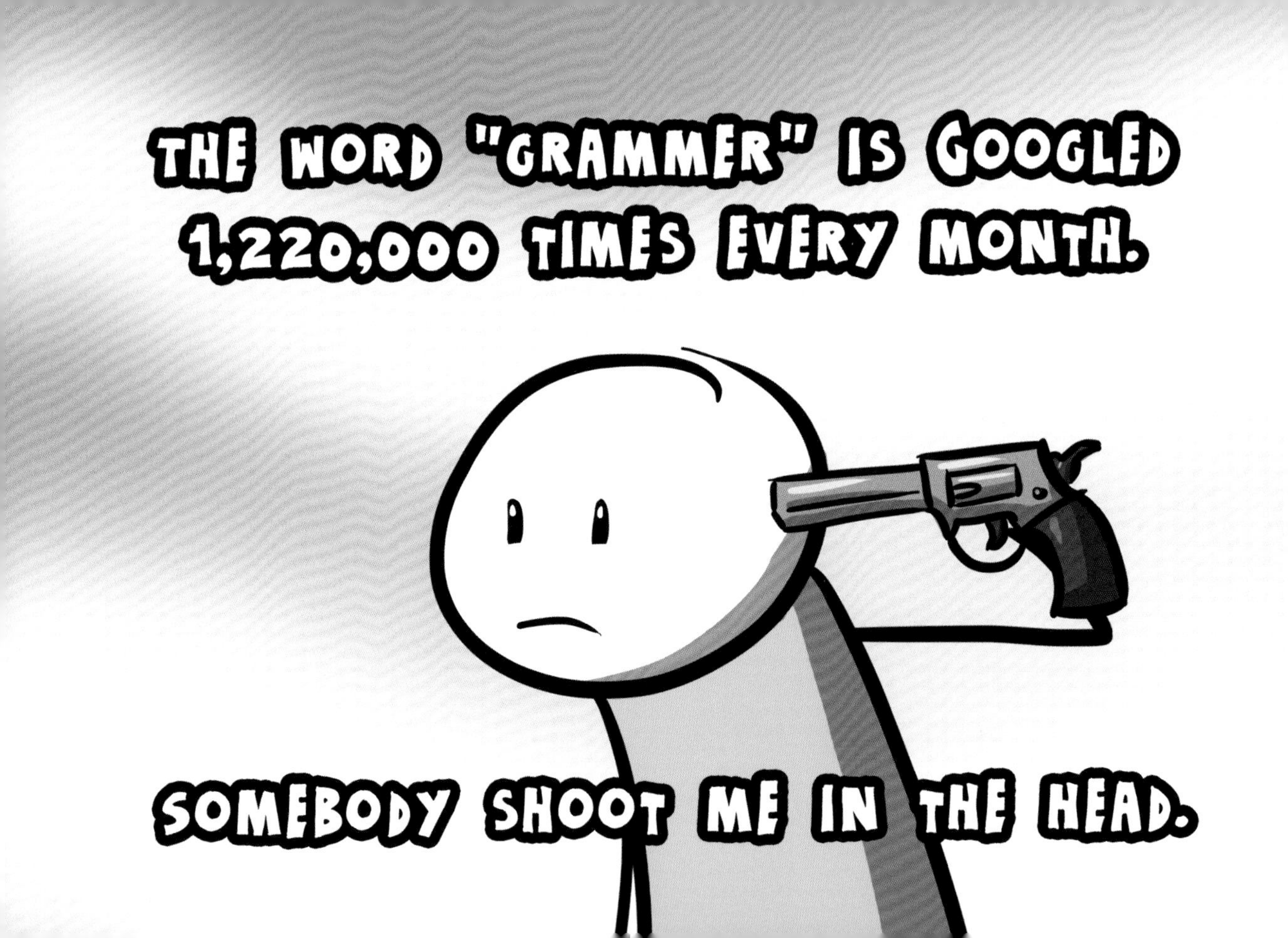
THE WORD "GRAMMER" IS GOOGLED 1,220,000 TIMES EVERY MONTH.
SOMEBODY SHOOT ME IN THE HEAD.

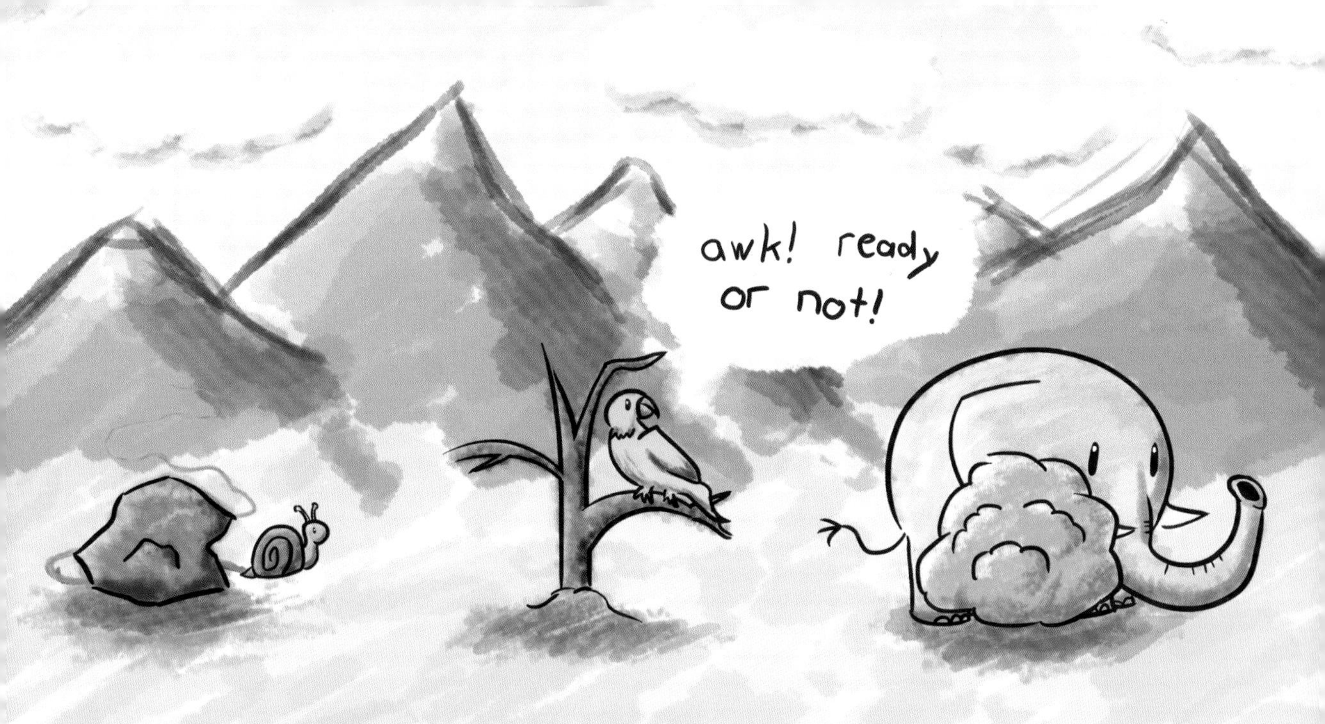
awk! ready or not!

FIRST ANNUAL MEETING OF THE "ANIMALS THAT ARE BAD AT HIDE-AND-SEEK" CLUB

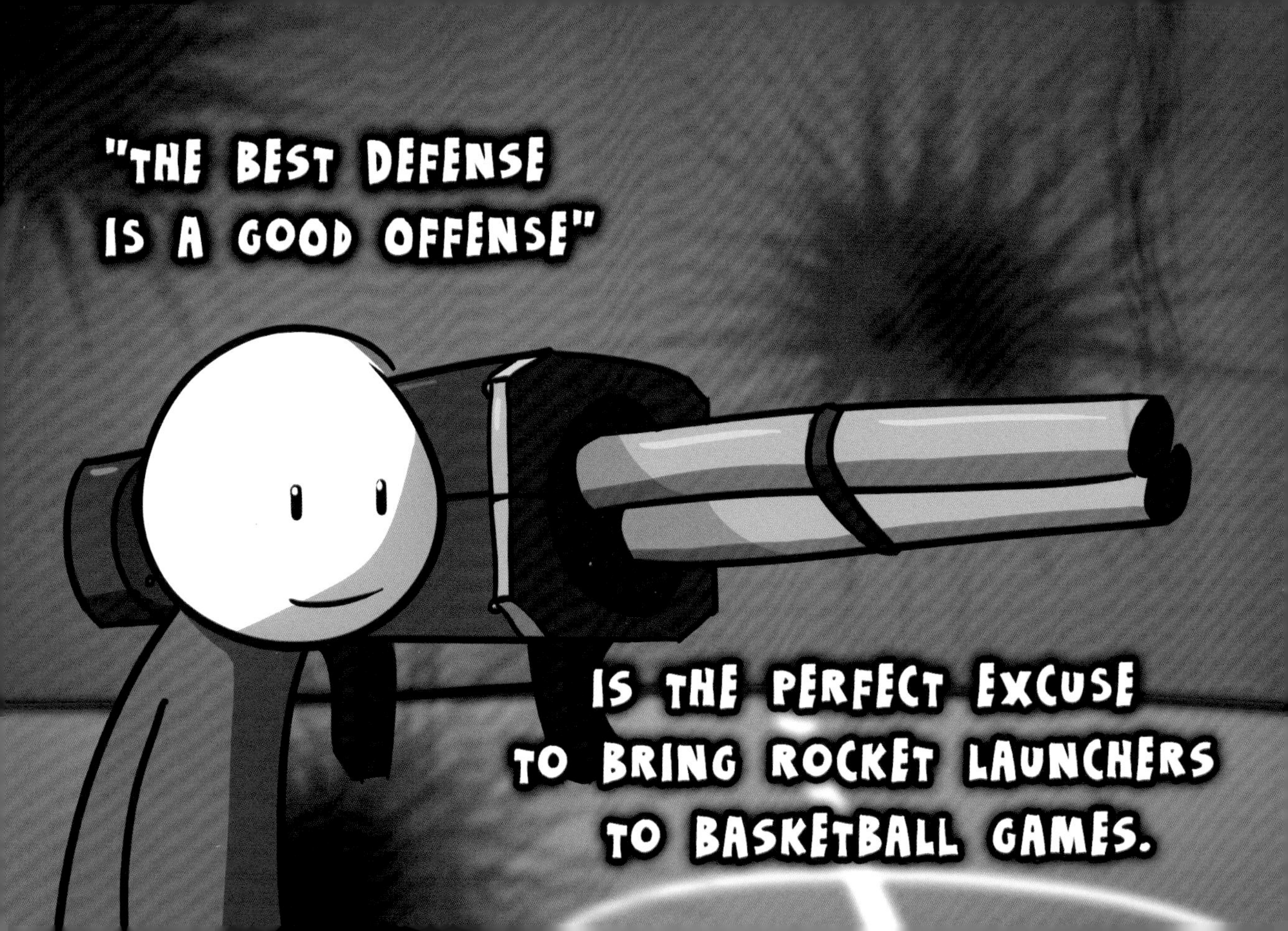
"THE BEST DEFENSE IS A GOOD OFFENSE"
IS THE PERFECT EXCUSE TO BRING ROCKET LAUNCHERS TO BASKETBALL GAMES.

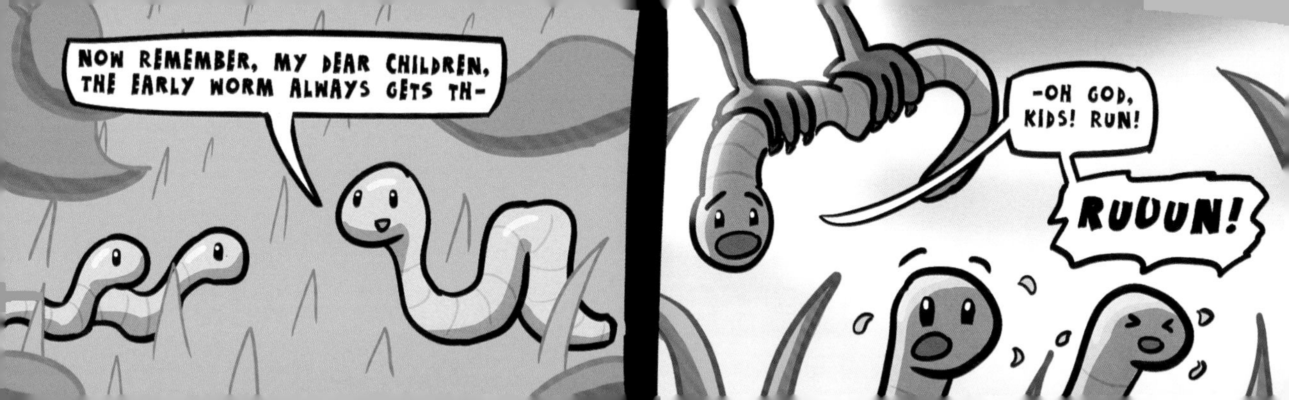
NOW REMEMBER, MY DEAR CHILDREN, THE EARLY WORM ALWAYS GETS TH-
-OH GOD, KIDS! RUN!
RUUUN!

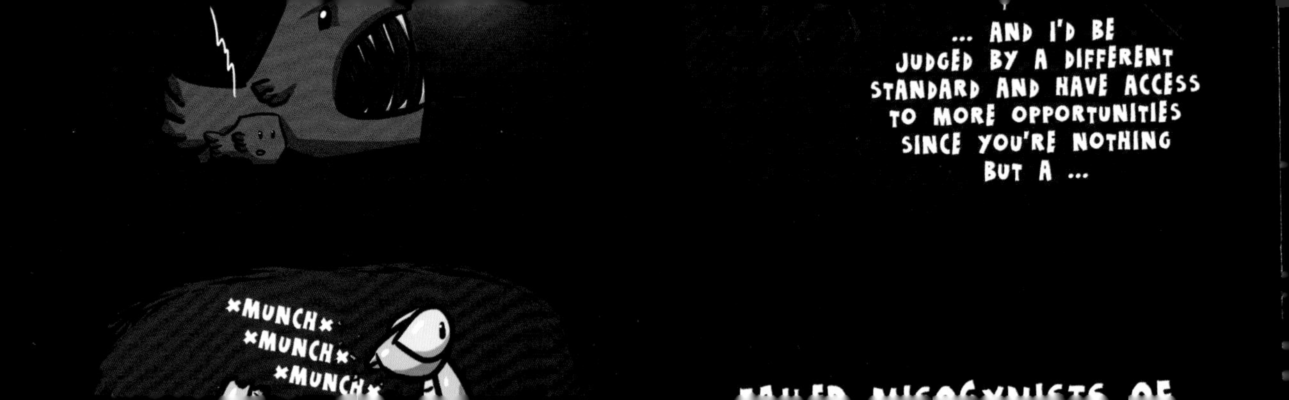
... AND I'D BE JUDGED BY A DIFFERENT STANDARD AND HAVE ACCESS TO MORE OPPORTUNITIES SINCE YOU'RE NOTHING BUT A ...
MUNCH
MUNCH
MUNCH

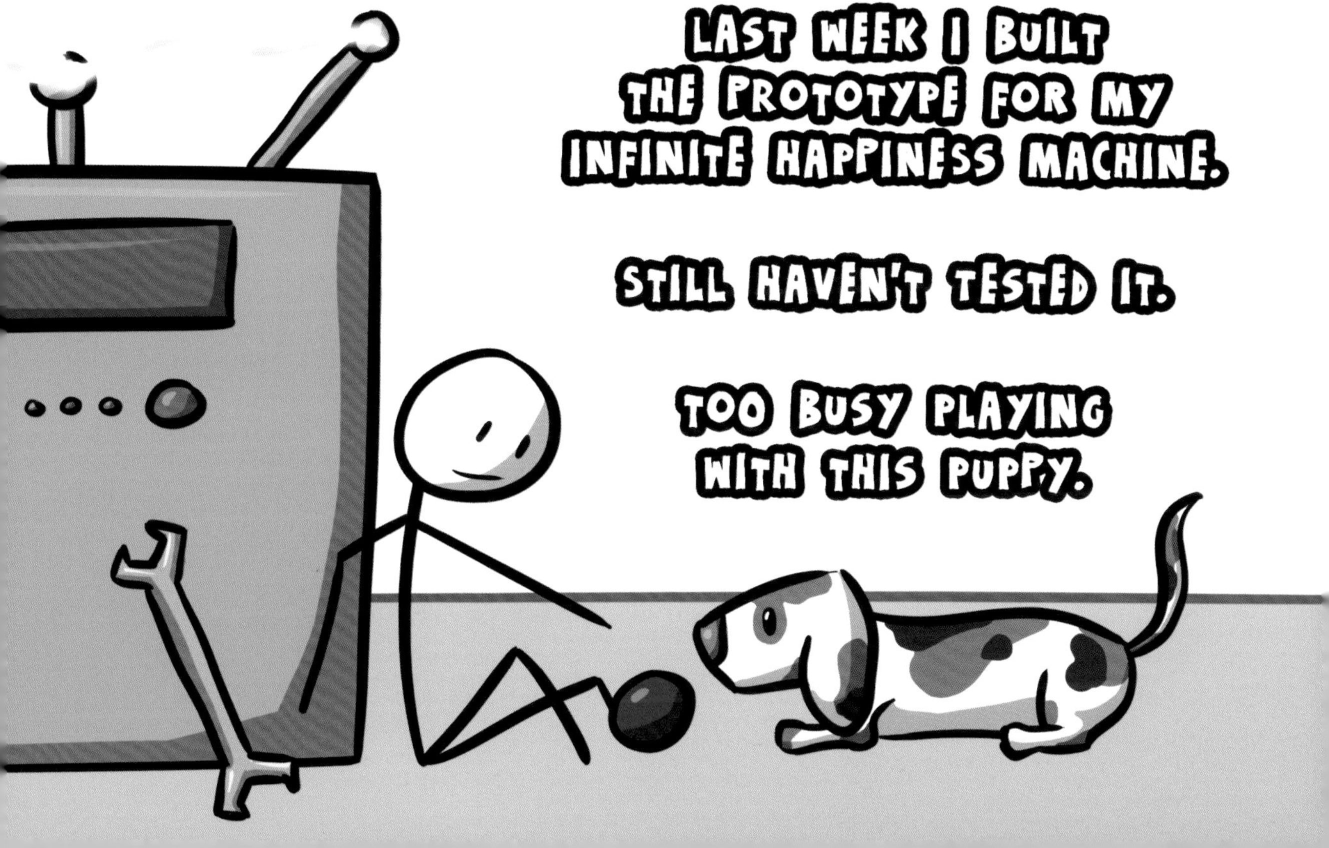
LAST WEEK I BUILT THE PROTOTYPE FOR MY INFINITE HAPPINESS MACHINE.
STILL HAVEN'T TESTED IT.
TOO BUSY PLAYING WITH THIS PUPPY.

EVERY CIRCLE IS ACTUALLY A PIE CHART OF HOW AWESOME PIES ARE.

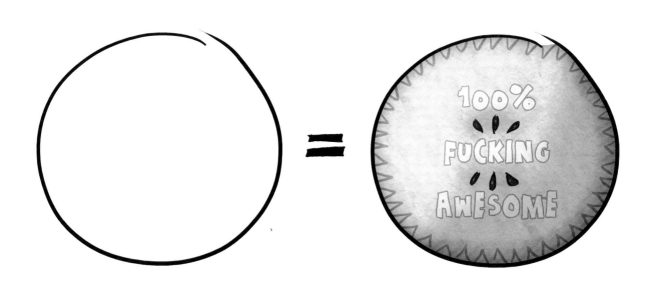

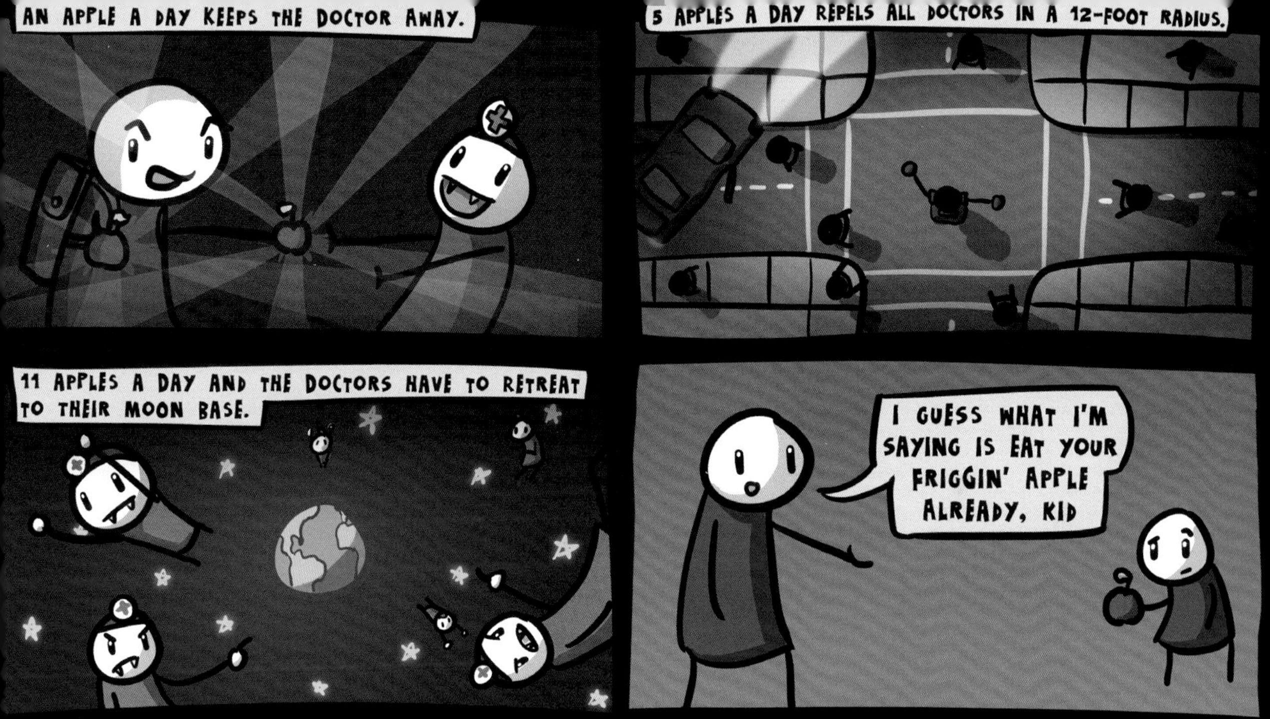
AN APPLE A DAY KEEPS THE DOCTOR AWAY.
5 APPLES A DAY REPELS ALL DOCTORS IN A 12-FOOT RADIUS.
11 APPLES A DAY AND THE DOCTORS HAVE TO RETREAT TO THEIR MOON BASE.
I GUESS WHAT I'M SAYING IS EAT YOUR FRIGGIN' APPLE ALREADY, KID

PARENTING

10% KNOWING WHAT YOU'RE DOING. 90% CREATIVE BULLSHIT

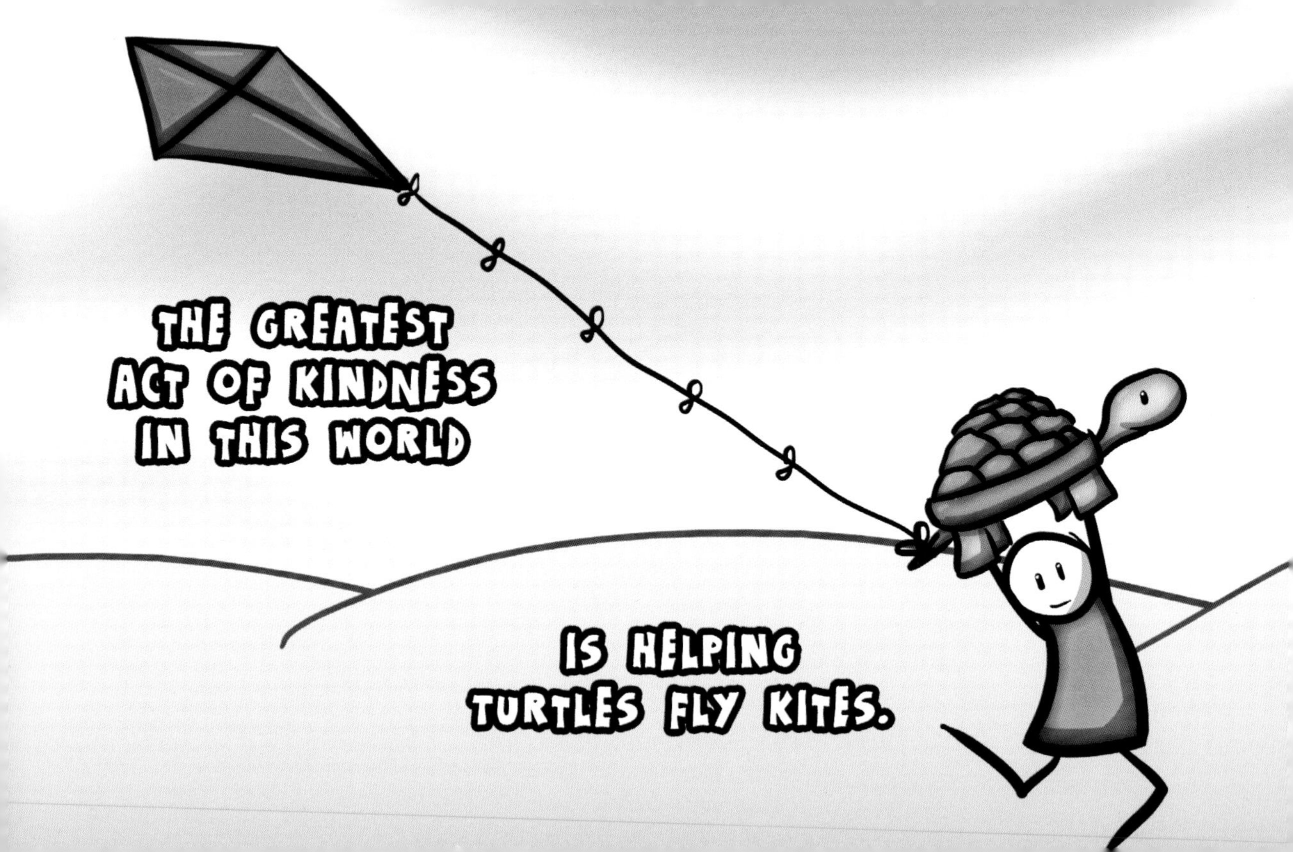
THE GREATEST
ACT OF KINDNESS
IN THIS WORLD
IS HELPING
TURTLES FLY KITES.

STEP 1: SET UP
SO A SHEEP AND A LANDLUBBER WALK INTO A BAR...
STEP 2: BUILD UP
...AND THE SHEEP SAYS TO THE LANDLUBBER...
STEP 3: BURN AND PILLAGE
I DON'T GET IT.

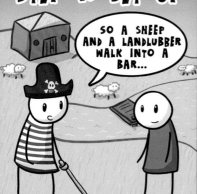

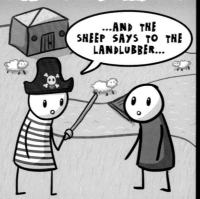

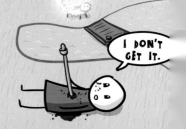

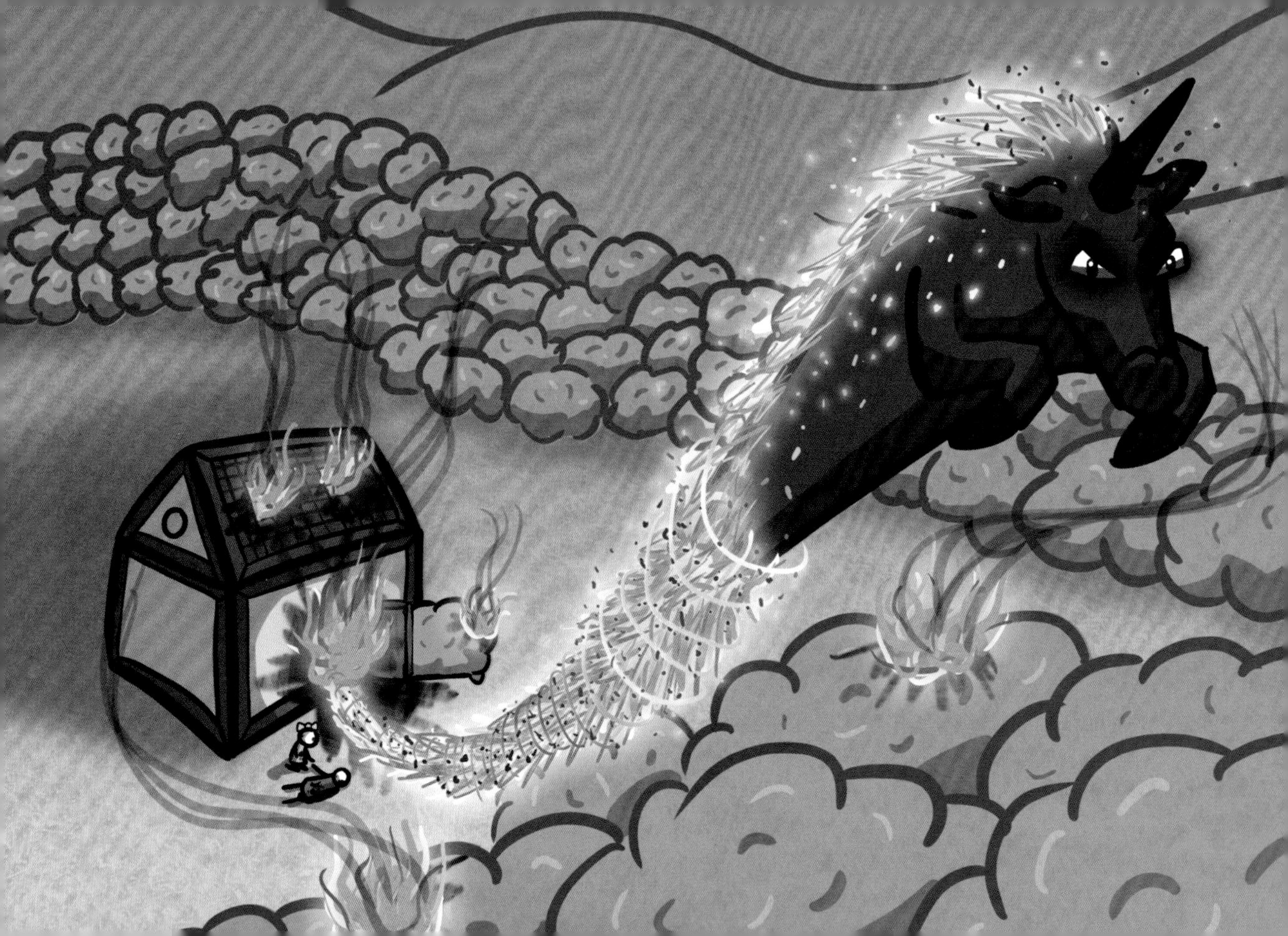

ACID BALLOON FIGHT. * GET AN AORTA PIERCING. * TEACH CHILDREN TO JUGGLE WITH CHAINSAWS. * PLAY TENNIS WITH GRENADES. * HOST A HEAD-BUTTING CONTEST AGAINST A YAK. * WAKE UP ON THE WRONG SIDE OF THE BED ON THE PRECIPICE OF AN ACTIVE VOLCANO. * BUILD AN ELABORATE HUMAN TESTING FACILITY AND GIVE EVERY SUBJECT A POWERFUL TELEPORTATION GUN. * WEAR RED TO A BULL'S WEDDING.

BAD IDEA #1: RELEASE LORD SPARKLEMANE, KING OF THE DOOMICORNS, FROM HIS RAINBOW PRISON.

MEDDLE IN THE AFFAIRS OF WIZARDS. * "OUTRUN THE LIVE CHEETAHS" MASCOT RACE. * GIVE DARTH VADER A BREATHALYZER TEST. * BECOME SURROGATE MOTHER TO A LITTER OF BABY HONEY BADGERS. * BUY A MUG WITH "FUTURE URINE" PRINTED ON IT. * PLAY "GOT YOUR NOSE" WITH A PYTHON. * USE A CAT AS A BACKSCRATCHER. * BECOME A COLORED-WIRE BOMB DEFUSAL AGENT WHEN YOU'RE COLOR-BLIND

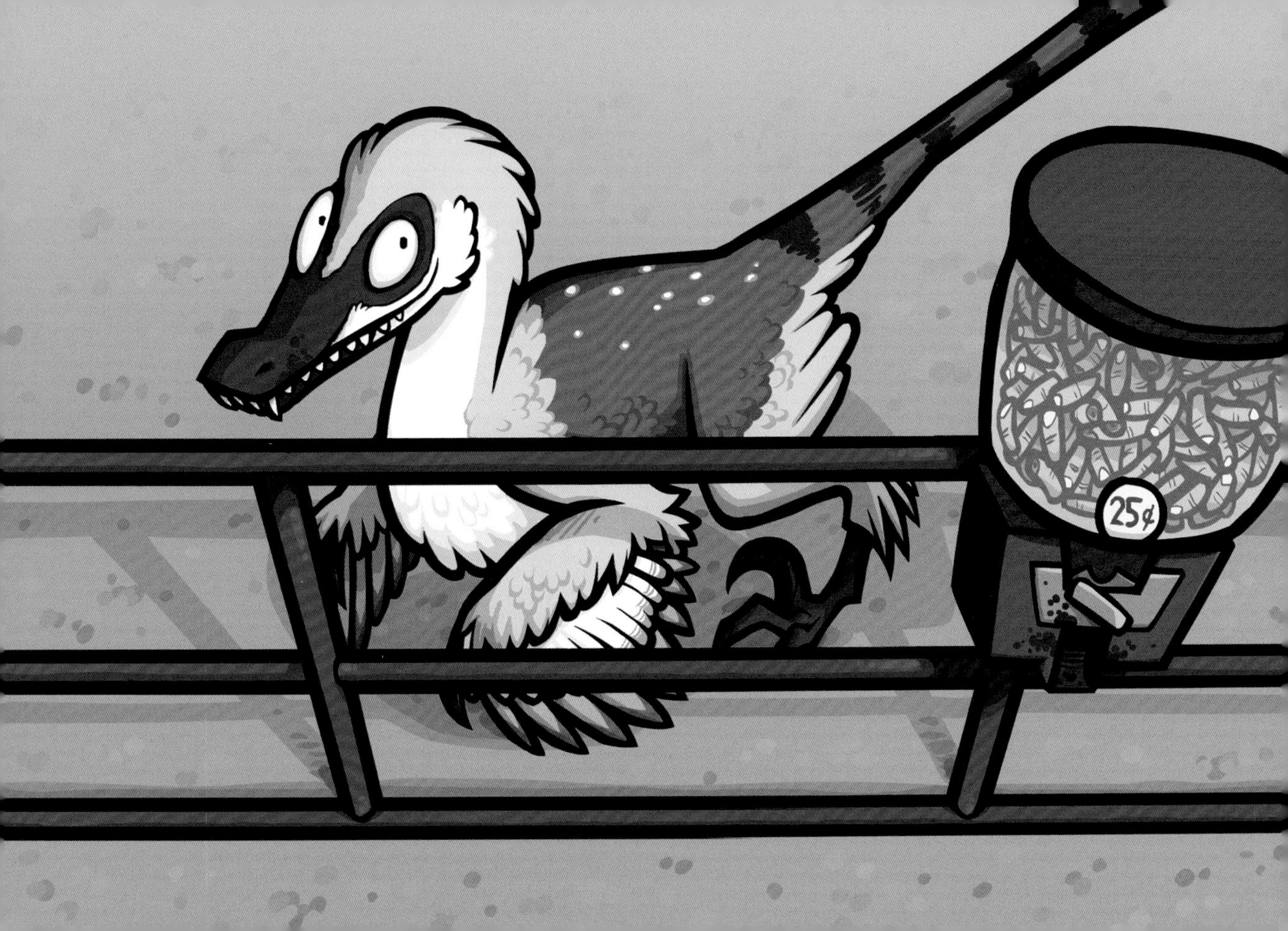
25¢

EAT YOUR WEIGHT IN BLOWFISH MEAT. * SHOW OFF YOUR HAND GRENADE AND SKI-MASK COLLECTION TO AIRPORT SECURITY. * BUTT-SLAP A BULL IN A GESTURE OF SPORTSMANSHIP. * CLEAN A FORMALDEHYDE SPILL WITH BLEACH. * FORGET ABOUT DRE. ON HIS BIRTHDAY. * THE BEFORE-AND-AFTER DRINK: LOOKS AND TASTES THE SAME GOING DOWN AS IT DOES COMING UP! * BABY GLADIATORS * TODDLER GLADIATORS.

BAD IDEA #285:
DINOSAUR PETTING ZOO.

THROW YOUR BABY IN SELF-DEFENSE. * LACTOSE INTOLERANT COWS. SUNDIAL WRISTWATCHES. * GENETICALLY ENGINEERED SNAKES THAT WILL GENETICALLY ENGINEER HUMANS. * DO PRETTY MUCH ANYTHING WITH SNAKES. * PAY A $7.00 LIBRARY FINE WITH UNROLLED NICKELS. * "GOTTA CATCH 'EM ALL" S.T.D.S. * PUT RABID ANIMALS IN OLYMPIC STADIUMS TO MOTIVATE RUNNERS. * TRAVEL BACK IN TIME TO BECOME HITLER'S GRANDFATHER

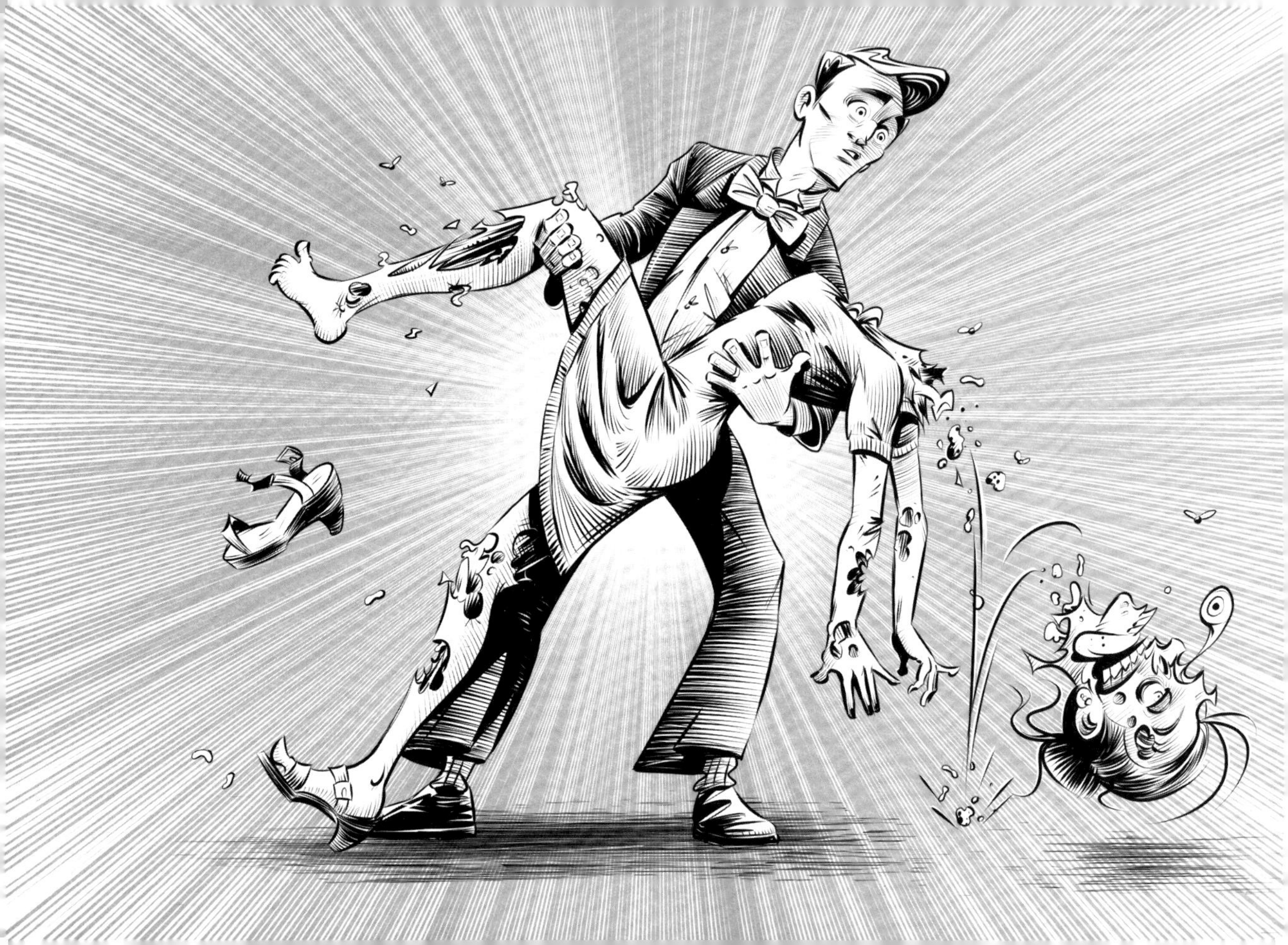

* START A WEBCOMIC. * PUT A SLINKY ON AN ESCALATOR.* NICKNAME YOUR PENIS "PLAGUEBEARER." * PLAY HIDE-AND-SEEK IN THE FOREST WHILE WEARING YOUR BOAR COSTUME DURING HUNTING SEASON. * TRIM NOSE HAIR WITH FIRE. * ENTER A COMPETITIVE GLASS-EATING CONTEST. * ASBESTOS CONFETTI. * NARRATE YOUTUBE COMMENTS.

BAD IDEA #363: TEACH A ZOMBIE HOW TO WALTZ.

WALK A MILE IN THE SHOES OF SOMEONE WHO JUST HAD THEIR SHOES STOLEN. * WRITE THAT YOU "HATE GRAMMAR" BUT "LOVE BARBEQUING KIDS AND DOGS" ON YOUR ONLINE DATING PROFILE. * ALL-BAGPIPE MARCHING BAND. * POISON NERF DARTS. * CIRCUMCISE YOURSELF WITH A GUILLOTINE. * ATTEMPT WORLD DOMINATION WITH AN ARMY OF CATS. * HAVE STARING CONTEST WITH A BEHOLDER. * GUN VIOLENCE.

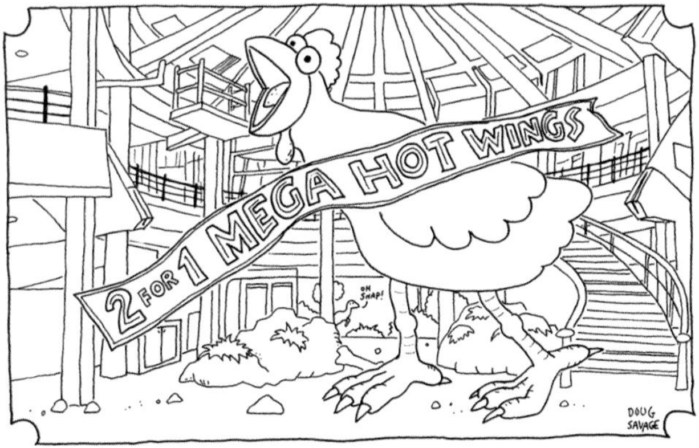
2 FOR 1 MEGA HOT WINGS
OH SNAP!
DOUG SAVAGE

FEND OFF ZOMBIES USING A YARD OF WEAPONIZED PLANTS. * BUILD A SNOW-POWERED LAWNMOWER. * INFORM YOUR BOSS OF THE TRUE VALUE OF HIS IDEAS. * TAKE A DEEP-SEA ANGLERFISH AS YOUR WIFE. * SKI THROUGH A FOREST WHILE PLAYING SOUSAPHONE.

BAD IDEA #421: PLAY "NAME THAT TASTE" AT THE BIOWEAPONS LAB.

ANTAGONIZE DRAGONS. * CANDLES MADE OF PURE KEROSENE. * HAMMER ON THE PILOT'S DOOR MID-FLIGHT WITH A PAPER BAG IN YOUR HAND. THEN EXPLAIN TO THE MAN SITTING ON YOUR CHEST THAT THE PILOT FORGOT HIS LUNCH. * LAND MINE HOPSCOTCH.

LIST ALL THE POKEMON YOU'VE CAUGHT IN A JOB INTERVIEW. * PORCUPINE ACUPUNCTURE. * PLAY TWISTER WITH A SUMO WRESTLER. * PLAY RED ROVER WITH GODZILLA. * INVENT THE HORNET'S NEST MASSAGER. * LOCKPICK AN AIRLOCK.

BAD IDEA #414: BREED A CHICKEN THE SIZE OF A T-REX.

ADD A SMARTPHONE ATTACHMENT TO A SWISS ARMY KNIFE. * GO TO A GOVERNMENT OFFICE IN AN UNBELIEVABLE HURRY. * BUILD A SENTIENT HOUSE AND GET INTO A FIGHT WITH IT. * ATTEMPT TO STOP SPEEDING BULLETS WITH SHEER WILLPOWER.

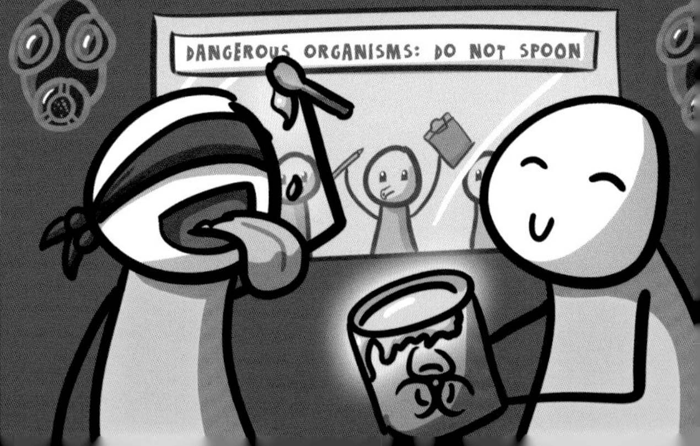
DANGEROUS ORGANISMS: DO NOT SPOON

BAD IDEA # 451: ZERBIL, THE ZOMBIE GERBIL! "GIVE YOUR KIDS THE PET THAT CAN'T DIE... BUT SHOULD."

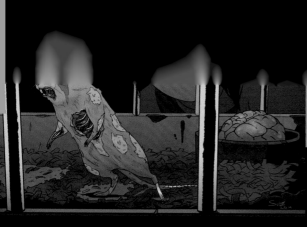

STEAL A WRITER'S COFFEE. GO ON, I DARE YOU. * CHALLENGE A DOUBLE AMPUTEE TO A THUMB WAR. * GET INTO A FENCING MATCH WITH THE HIGHLANDER. * LIST "ZYGOTE" UNDER "PREVIOUS POSITIONS" ON YOUR RESUME. * ROMANTIC CANDLELIGHT GASOLINE BATH.

PURCHASE THE EXTENDED WARRANTY. * OFFER TO SHIP DIRT ACROSS INTERNATIONAL BORDERS AS CONTEST PRIZE. * ROUND UP THE "USUAL" SUSPECTS. * INVITE A CANNIBAL TO YOUR MEET AND GREET. * AUTOMATIC STAPLE GUN. * COW POLO.

BAD IDEA #463: BUTTHOLE ARCHERY.

ANYTHING INVOLVING DIOXYGEN DIFLUORIDE. * TRY THE NEW SCOTCH BONNET CHILI-BASED INTIMATE LUBRICANT. * FIGHT FIRE WITH FIRE. UNLESS YOU ARE A FIREFIGHTER. * MICROWAVE YOUR LAUNDRY. * GIVE A BAT AN ULTRASOUND. * NAPALM RAVES.

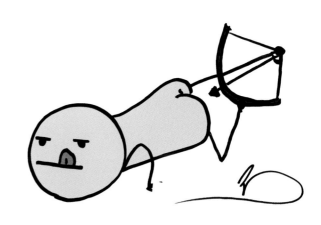

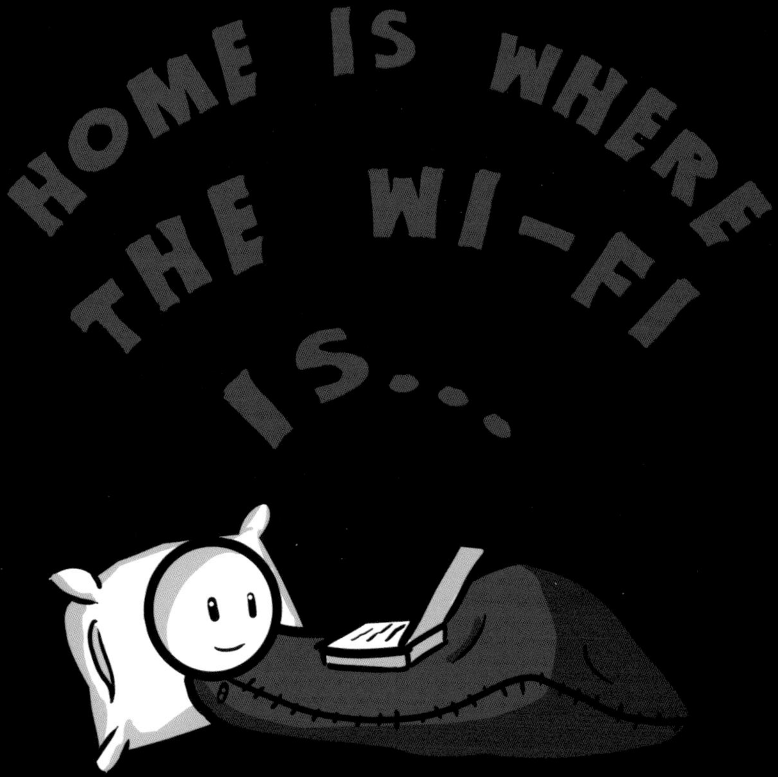
HOME IS WHERE THE WI-FI IS...

IN A WORLD OF SHOCK MEDIA AND MASS-MARKETED CHE GUEVARA T-SHIRTS, THE GREATEST ACT OF REBELLION IS JUST BEING HAPPY MOST OF THE TIME

DEAR T-REX,

I'M SORRY EVERYONE MAKES FUN OF YOUR TINY ARMS.

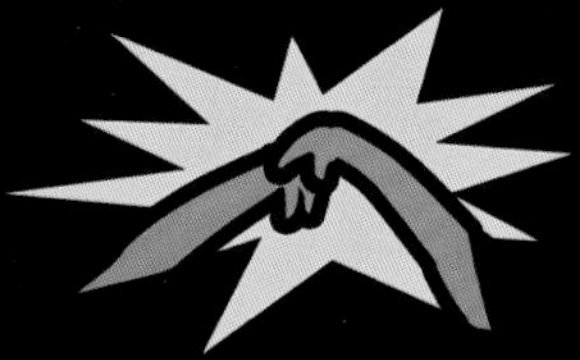

BUT YOU DON'T NEED BIG LIMBS TO HIGH-FIVE YOURSELF FOR BEING APEX PREDATOR FOR ONE AND A HALF MILLION YEARS, AM I RIGHT?

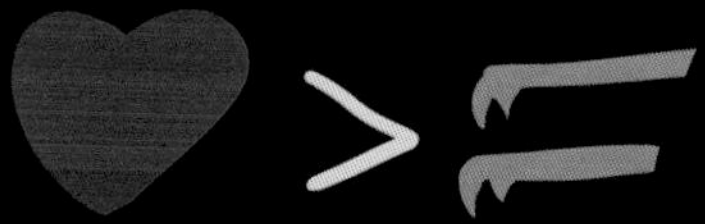

BESIDES, IT'S THE SIZE OF YOUR HEART, NOT YOUR FORELIMBS, THAT MATTERS.

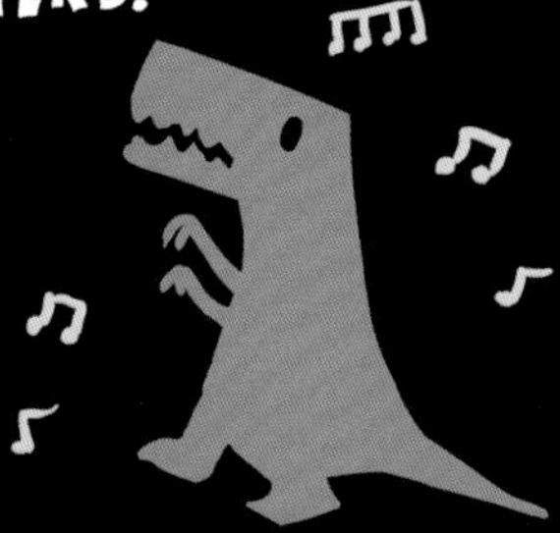

AND I KNOW WHEN NO ONE'S LOOKING, YOU USE THOSE STUBS TO HUG SHORTER T-REXES AND HOLD AIRPORT TAXI SIGNS FOR LOST TRAVELERS AND DO THAT ZOMBIE DANCE FROM THRILLER.

DEAR T-REX, I'M SORRY THIS IS COMING 65 MILLION YEARS TOO LATE, BUT LET'S GIVE YOU A NEW LOOK. LET'S SHOW THE WORLD THAT WITH TINY CLAWS, YOU CAN STILL LIVE LARGE.

INTRODUCING

BOW-TIE-RANNOSAURUS

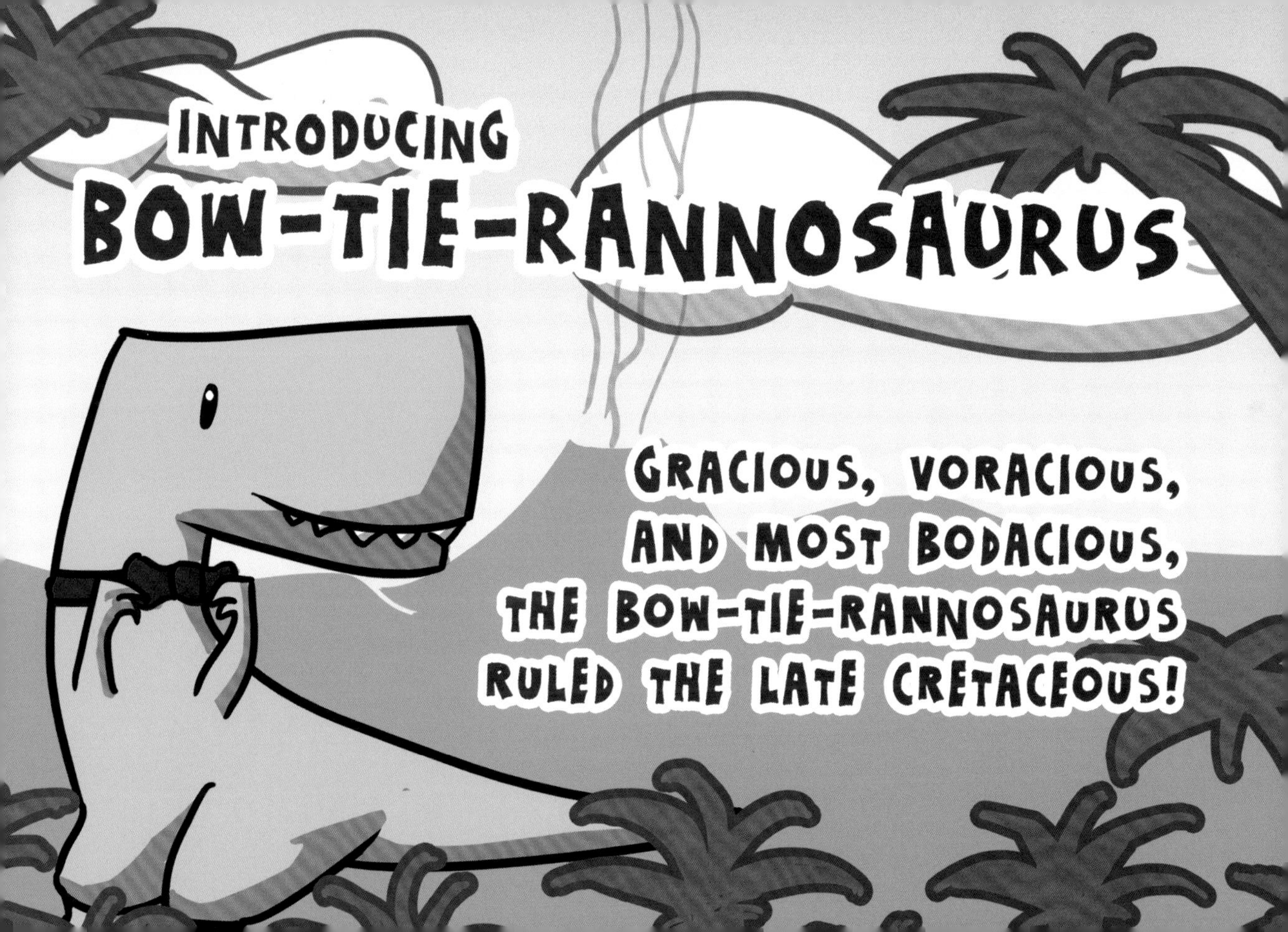

GRACIOUS, VORACIOUS, AND MOST BODACIOUS, THE BOW-TIE-RANNOSAURUS RULED THE LATE CRETACEOUS!

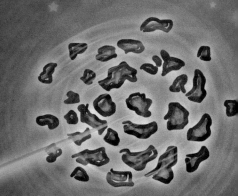

MY ROBOT LOVER'S HEART CAN'T UNDERSTAND EMOTIONS, BUT IT CAN SHOOT LASERS,

WHICH, IN MY BOOKS, IS THE FOUNDATION OF ANY MEANINGFUL RELATIONSHIP.

I WANTED TO TELL YOU HOW YOU'RE
AN AMAZING PERSON AND I LIKE YOU
A LOT, BUT INSTEAD I GOT SCARED AND
DREW YOU THIS PICTURE OF A CLAM.

I HOPE YOU
LIKE IT.

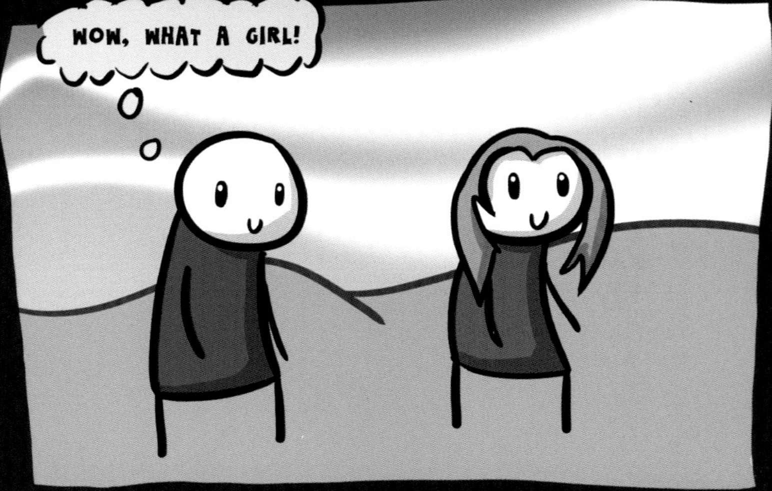
WOW, WHAT A GIRL!

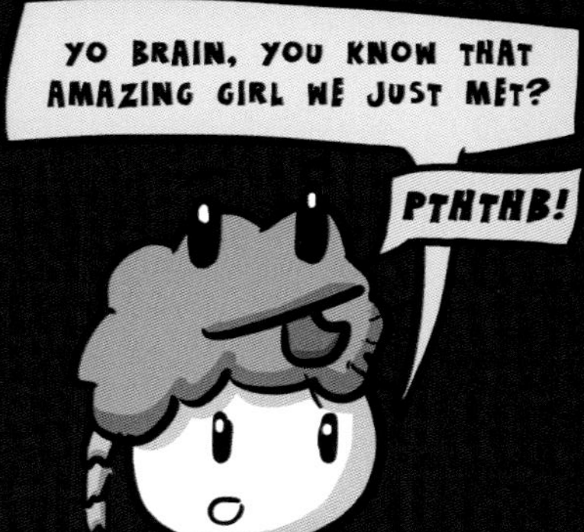
YO BRAIN, YOU KNOW THAT AMAZING GIRL WE JUST MET?
PTHTHB!

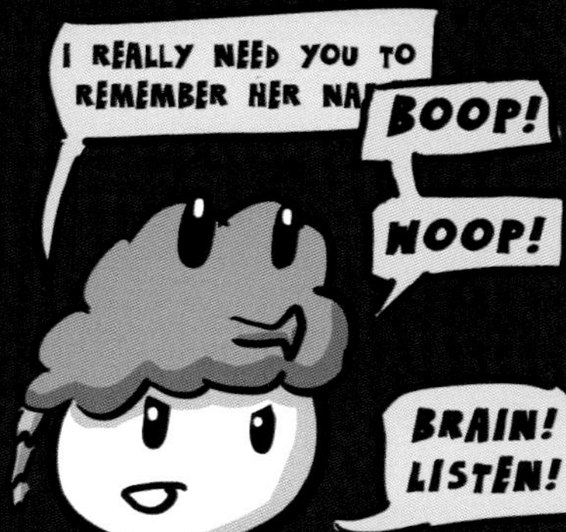
I REALLY NEED YOU TO REMEMBER HER NA
BOOP!
WOOP!
BRAIN! LISTEN!

HEY, REMEMBER WHEN YOUR LAST GIRLFRIEND LEFT YOU AND BROKE YOUR HEART AND SMASHED YOUR CONFIDENCE?
LET'S THINK ABOUT THAT...
FOREVER.

SHAKESPEAREAN HUMOUR

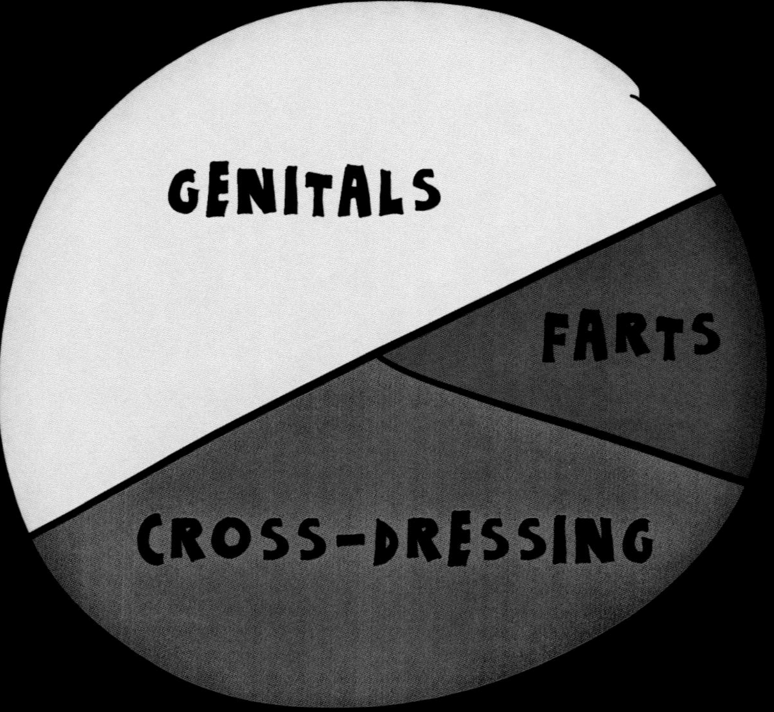
GENITALS
FARTS
CROSS-DRESSING

GENIUS.

Two-Reality Laundry Hamper

Now you can fold reality alongside your laundry! Contains superimposed compartments for clean and dirty clothes at the same time. Extra dimensions optional.

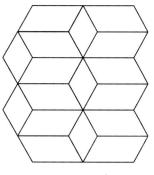

Impossible Realities Picture Frame

Now you can display all of your M. C. Escher lithographs the way they were meant to be seen!

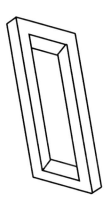

Dimensionally Collapsible Privacy Screen

Do you ever worry that you're being watched from a location beyond space and time? This screen protects you from all possible worlds and can be folded into nothingness for storage convenience.

WARNING: This product may collapse reality as you know it.

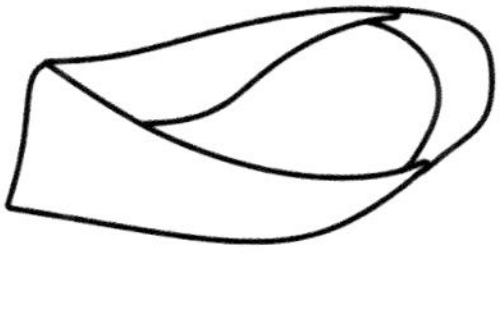

Mobius Napkin

If it gets dirty, you can always turn it over and... oh, wait... No. Never mind.

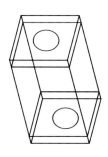

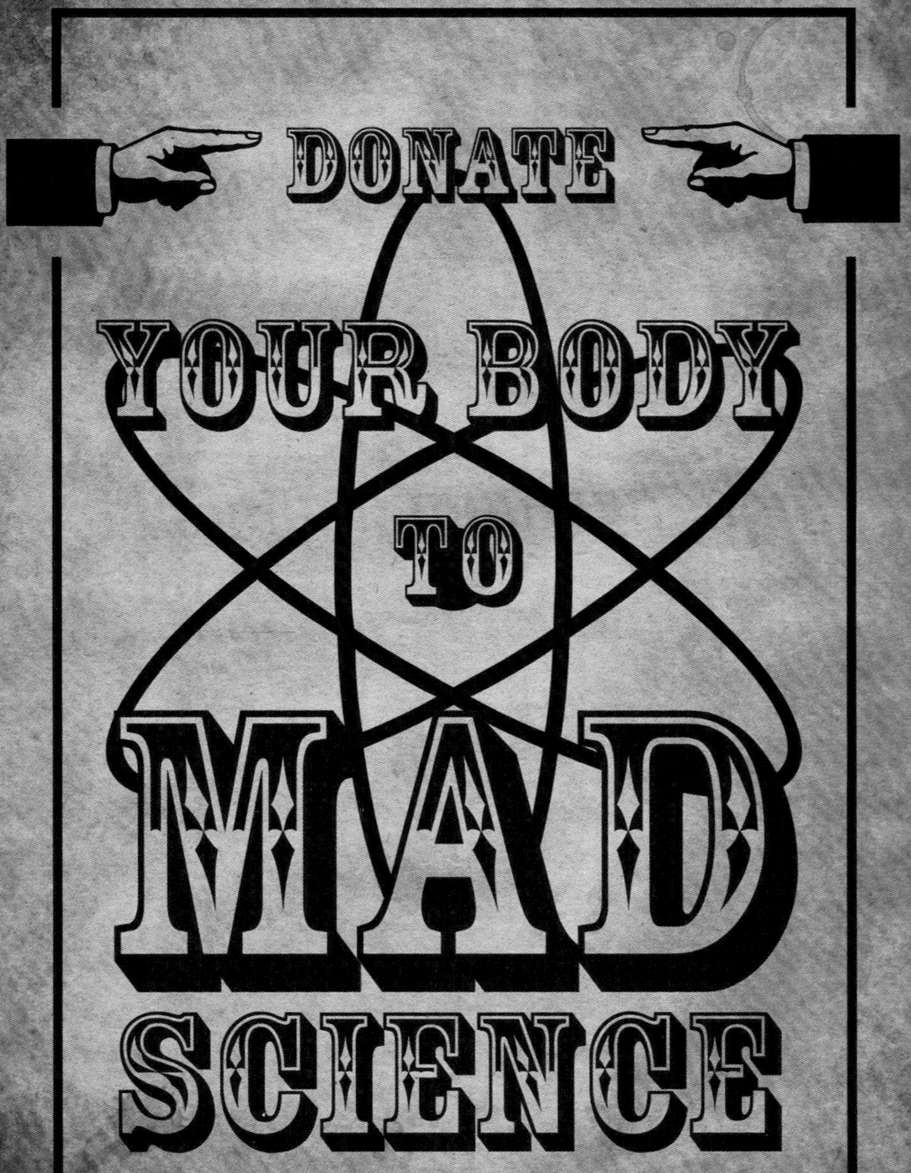
DONATE
YOUR BODY
TO
MAD
SCIENCE

OCCAM'S LASER

THE SIMPLEST EXPLANATION USUALLY DIES

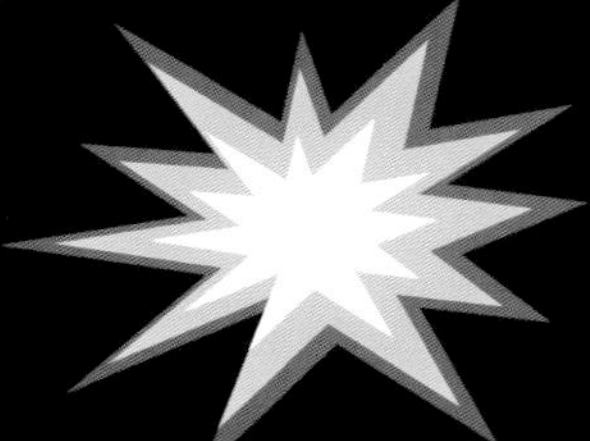

IN A SPACE DUEL AGAINST THE MOST AWESOME

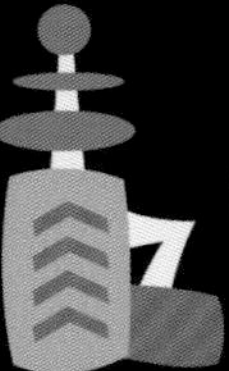

ONE

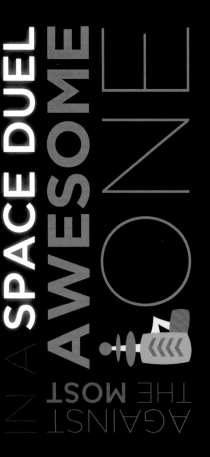

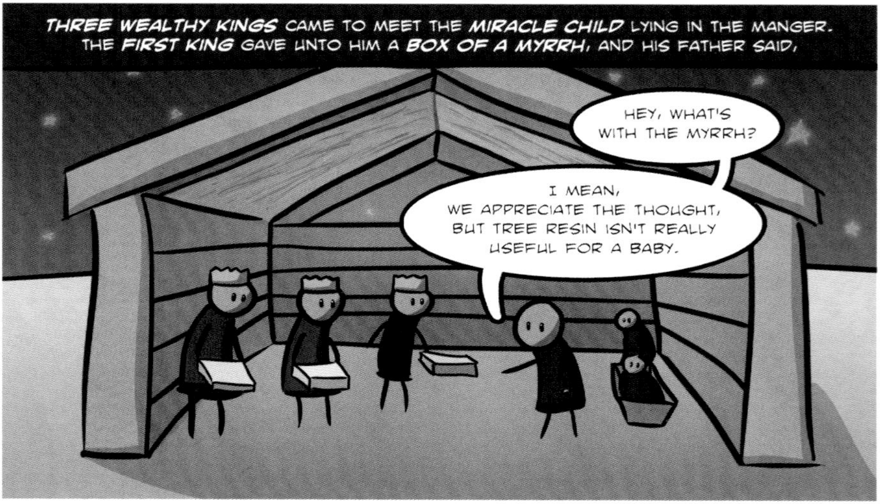
THREE WEALTHY KINGS CAME TO MEET THE MIRACLE CHILD LYING IN THE MANGER. THE FIRST KING GAVE UNTO HIM A BOX OF A MYRRH, AND HIS FATHER SAID,
HEY, WHAT'S WITH THE MYRRH?
I MEAN, WE APPRECIATE THE THOUGHT, BUT TREE RESIN ISN'T REALLY USEFUL FOR A BABY.

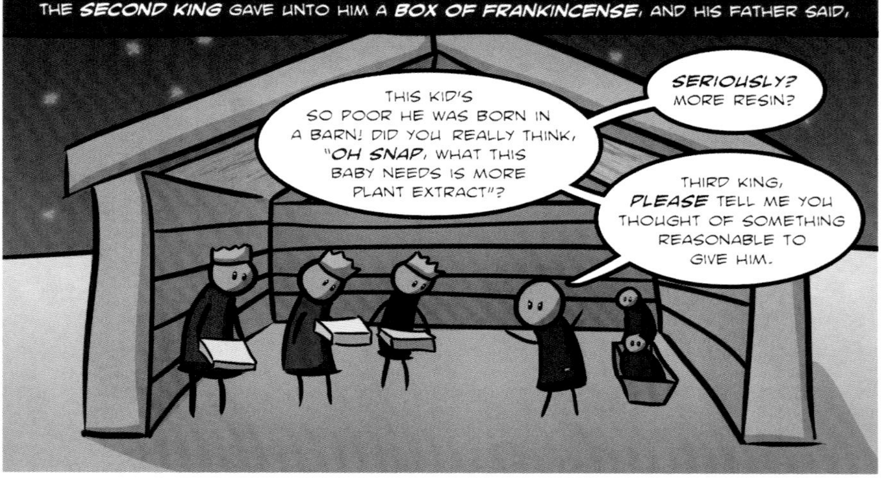
THE SECOND KING GAVE UNTO HIM A BOX OF FRANKINCENSE, AND HIS FATHER SAID,
SERIOUSLY? MORE RESIN?
THIS KID'S SO POOR HE WAS BORN IN A BARN! DID YOU REALLY THINK, "OH SNAP, WHAT THIS BABY NEEDS IS MORE PLANT EXTRACT"?
THIRD KING, PLEASE TELL ME YOU THOUGHT OF SOMETHING REASONABLE TO GIVE HIM.

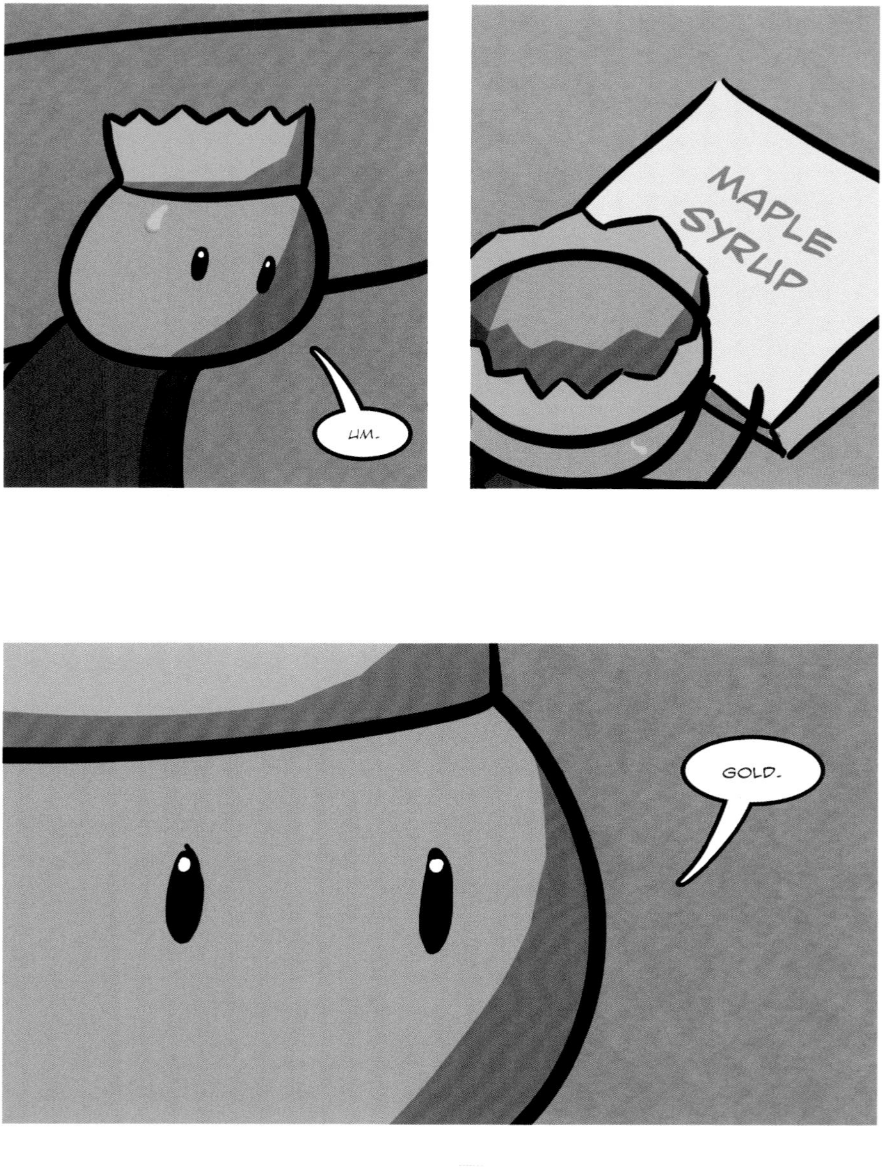
HM.
MAPLE SYRUP
GOLD.

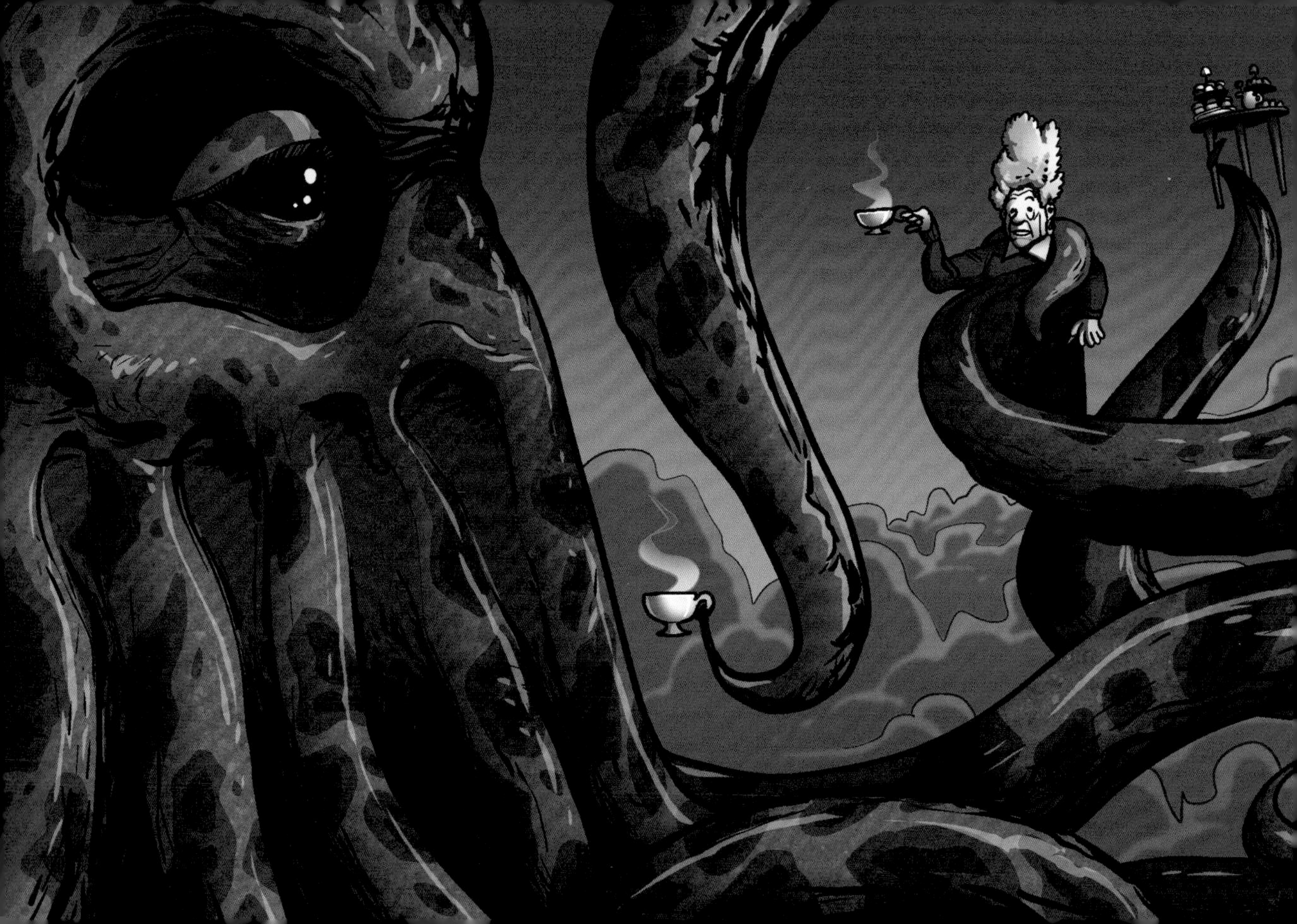

GO ON A CHEESE-ONLY DIET. * BE THE MOUNTAIN GURU OF AN ANTHILL. * PLAY "WINK MURDER" WITH MEDUSA. * BUILD BATTLE ARMOR FOR ANACONDAS. * TIME-TRAVEL TO THE PRESENT. * WEAR A MEAT DRESS TO THE ZOO TO VISIT THE LIONS AND TIGERS AND BEARS, OH MY! * TACO BELL DAY ON THE INTERNATIONAL SPACE STATION. * MAKE FUN OF THE SCARS ON THAT BIG GUY SITTING AT THE END OF THE BAR.

BAD IDEA #517: INVITE CTHULHU TO YOUR HOUSE FOR TEA.

NUCLEAR REACTIONS FOR DUMMIES. * "HUG A GREAT WHITE SHARK" DAY. * FIRE A FIELD HOCKEY BALL TOWARD YOUR OWN FACE AT A THOUSAND MILLION BILLION MILES PER HOUR. * EXPECT YOUR DOG TO DIGEST THE CONTENTS OF YOUR COMPOST BIN THE SAME WAY WORMS DO. * FOUND AN ACADEMIC SOCIETY FOR RESEARCHING RARE TWO-LEGGED CATS. * BREED AN ARMY OF HYPER-INTELLIGENT ATTACK WALRUSES.

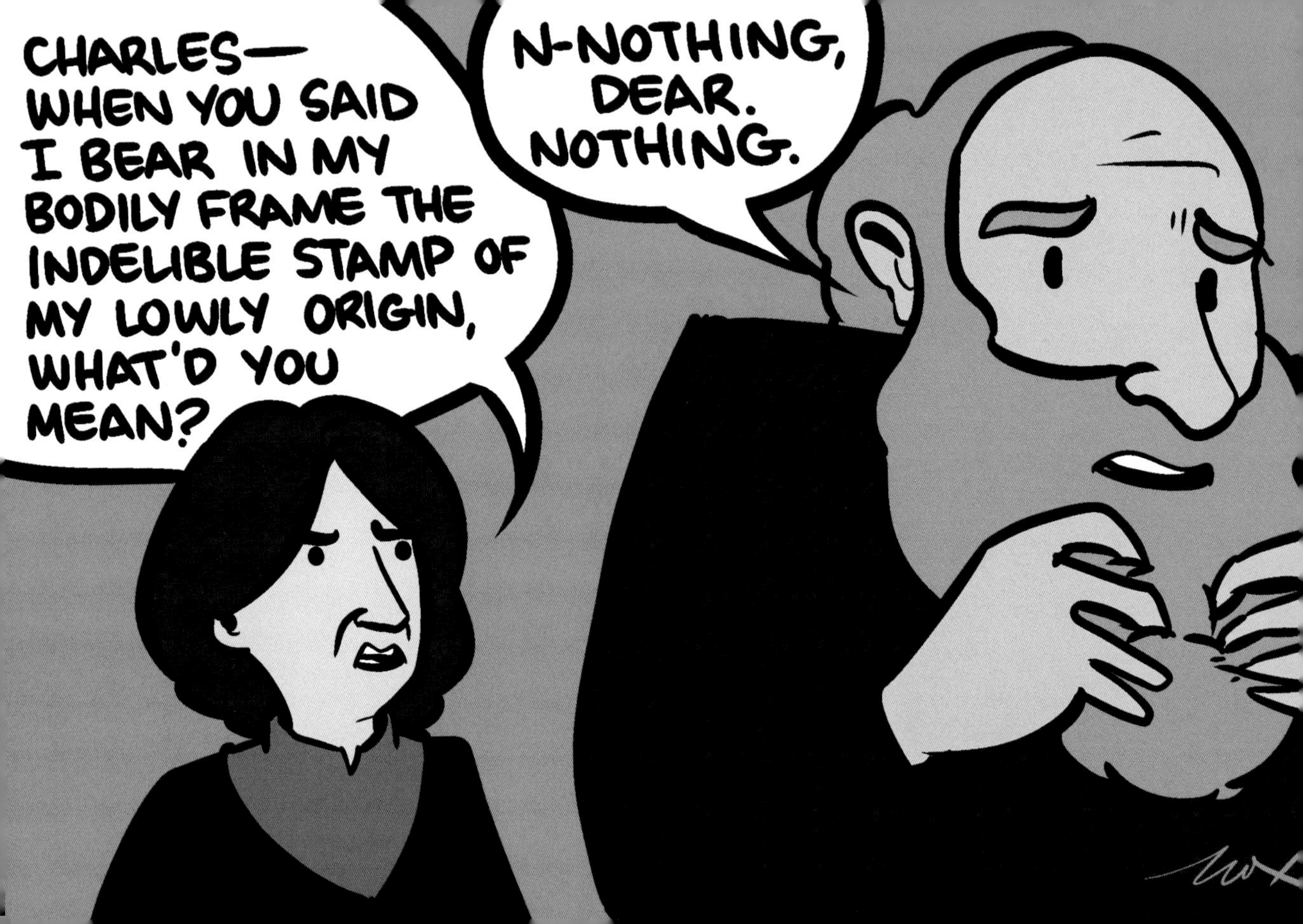
CHARLES— WHEN YOU SAID I BEAR IN MY BODILY FRAME THE INDELIBLE STAMP OF MY LOWLY ORIGIN, WHAT'D YOU MEAN?
N-NOTHING, DEAR. NOTHING.

LIVE-TWEET YOUR #FIRST #DRIVE. * CONVINCE YOUR FRIEND THAT HAZMAT SUITS ARE FOR SISSIES. * PUT YOUR LIFE SAVINGS INTO BITCOIN. * HISS WHEN A PRIEST SPRINKLES YOU WITH HOLY WATER. * GET IN A LAND WAR IN RUSSIA. * CROSS-BREED DOLPHINS WITH SNAPDRAGONS. * DANDELION CHAIN BUNGEE JUMPING. * DISCOVER AN ALIEN SPECIES THAT EATS POOP AND POOPS FOOD. INVITE THEM TO EARTH.

BAD IDEA #690:
FONDLE YOUR BEARD TO FILL CONVERSATIONAL SILENCE.

GO BEAR-HUNTING ARMED WITH ONLY YOUR RAZOR-SHARP WIT. * HIDE A DISGUISED ATOMIC BOMB IN THE FBI HEADQUARTERS DURING AN EASTER EGG HUNT. * CLIMB EVEREST IN ONLY A THONG AND A FANCY PINK FEATHER BOA. * EAT YOUR TEXTBOOKS AND LEARN BY OSMOSIS. * INVITE A SCREAMING SKULL TO YOUR APARTMENT'S MIXER. * RELEASE WOLVERINES ONTO THE COURSE TO MAKE THE GAME MORE EXCITING.

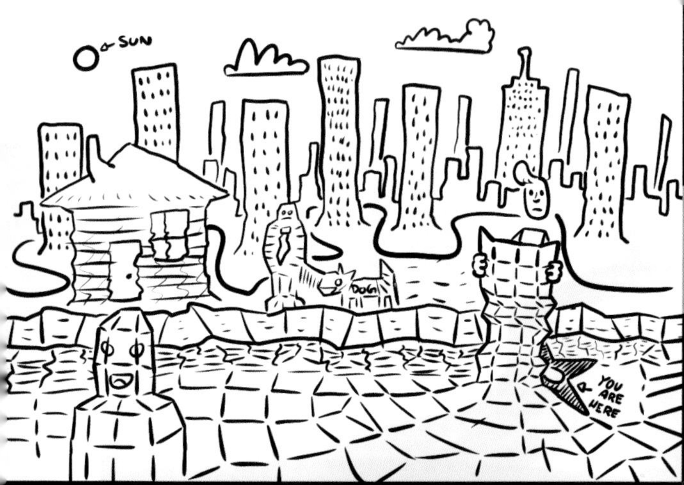
SUN
DOG
YOU ARE HERE

MAKE OUT WITH A COBRA. * CLUB CANADIANS WITH BABY SEALS TO PROTEST CLUBBING BABY SEALS. * HAVE A DELIGHTFUL CONVERSATION WITH THE T-REX THAT JUST BIT YOUR ARMS OFF. * DANCE IN THE SKY WHEN YOU CAN'T FLY * PLAY CATCH-THE-ASTEROID.

BAD IDEA #725: REPLY TO THAT POOR NIGERIAN PRINCE WHO'S DOWN ON HIS LUCK.

PLAY DODGEBALL WITH WRENCHES. * MARK, INSULT AND FORGET THE OXFORD COMMA. * WEAR A VEST OF RAW MEAT SEASONED WITH CATNIP TO THE ZOO AND JUMP INTO THE LION ENCLOSURE. * ATTEMPT TO TAKE MACROPHOTOGRAPHY OF A HIPPO'S BUTT.

WEREWOLF ASTRONAUTS. * PLAY "CHICKEN" WITH A BEAR THAT JUST CAME OUT OF HIBERNATION. * SUNBATHE ON MERCURY. * DE-ICE A PLANE WITH WATER. * REPLACE YOUR BLOOD WITH CORN STARCH AND FOOD COLORING. * ELECTRIC KAZOO.

BAD IDEA #706: 1:1-SCALED CITY MAPS.

EXPLAIN THE REAL MEANING OF A "POLAR BOND" TO A POLAR BEAR. * BEES. * THREE-LEGGED RACE RABID RACOON WRANGLING. * XBOX ROCK BAND NIGHT AT THE OLD FOLKS HOME. * LET A GRIZZLY BEAR PUT ON YOUR HAT FOR YOU.

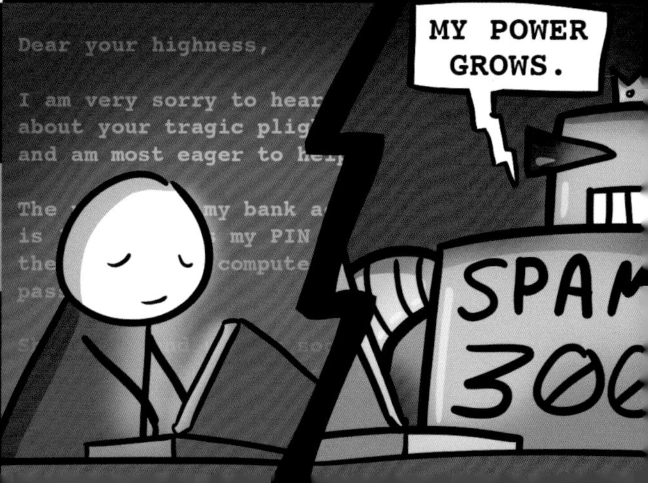
Dear your highness,
I am very sorry to hear
about your tragic
and am most eager to
my bank
my PIN
MY POWER GROWS.
SPAM

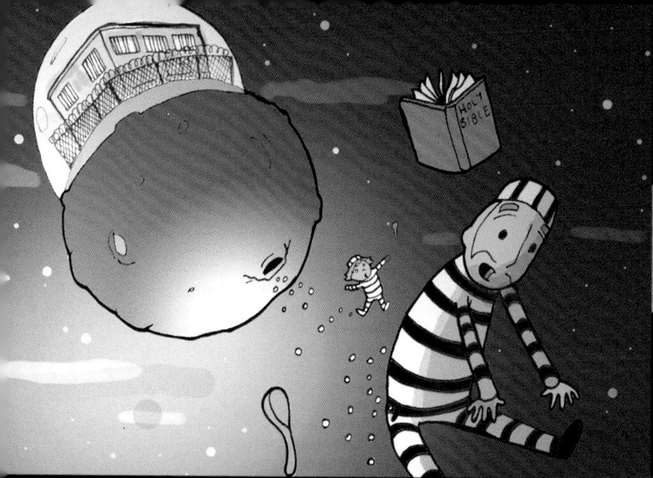
HOLY BIBLE

SET FIRE TO THE RAIN. * BECOME THE WORLD'S FIRST SPOKEN WORD MIME. * HOKEY-POKEY DANCE CIRCLE WITH A 21-GUN SALUTE. * BUILD A SCHOOL FOR ANTS TO LEARN BREAKDANCE FIGHTING. * KEEP RANCORS UNDER CITY GRATES.

BAD IDEA #780: CANADIAN MOUNTED MOOSE POLICE.

PARTY ALL NIGHT, SLEEP ALL DAY. AT YOUR DESK. OUTSIDE YOUR BOSS'S OFFICE. * SPAM GODZILLA WITH LOLCAT MEMES. THEN GIVE HIM A BUCKET OF STEROIDS. * LIVE ON THE EDGE. OF A KNIFE. * SPACESHIP DEMOLITION DERBY. * IMMORTALITY.

DO SHOTS OF PURE ALCOHOL. * CANCEL FIREFLY. * WEAR YOUR GUITAR'S G-STRING AS A THONG. AND GO A SIZE TOO TIGHT. * CHALLENGE AN ELEPHANT TO A HIGH JUMP COMPETITION. * PLAY HIDE AND SEEK WITH AN ANGEL STATUE THAT'S COVERING ITS EYES.

BAD IDEA #756: TUNNEL OUT OF SPACE-JAIL.

PI-SIDED DICE. * LIVE LIFE EXPECTING THE AUTHOR OF THIS BOOK TO TRAVEL FORWARD THROUGH TIME, FIND OUT HOW YOU DIE AND THEN COME BACK TO WARN YOU. * HOMEOPATHIC BIRTH CONTROL. * START A TICKLE WAR WITH YOUR PET OCTOPUS.

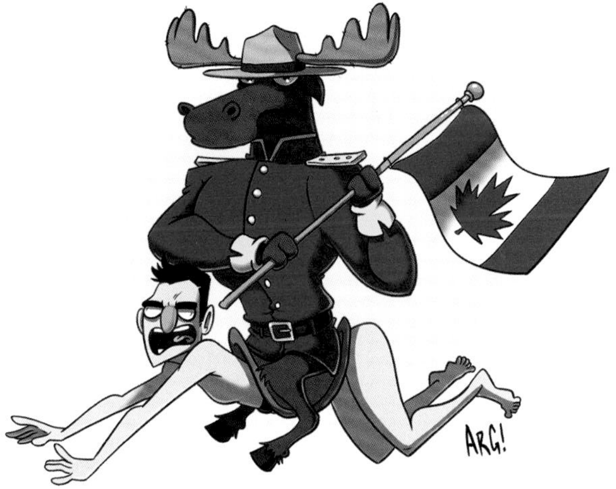
ARG!

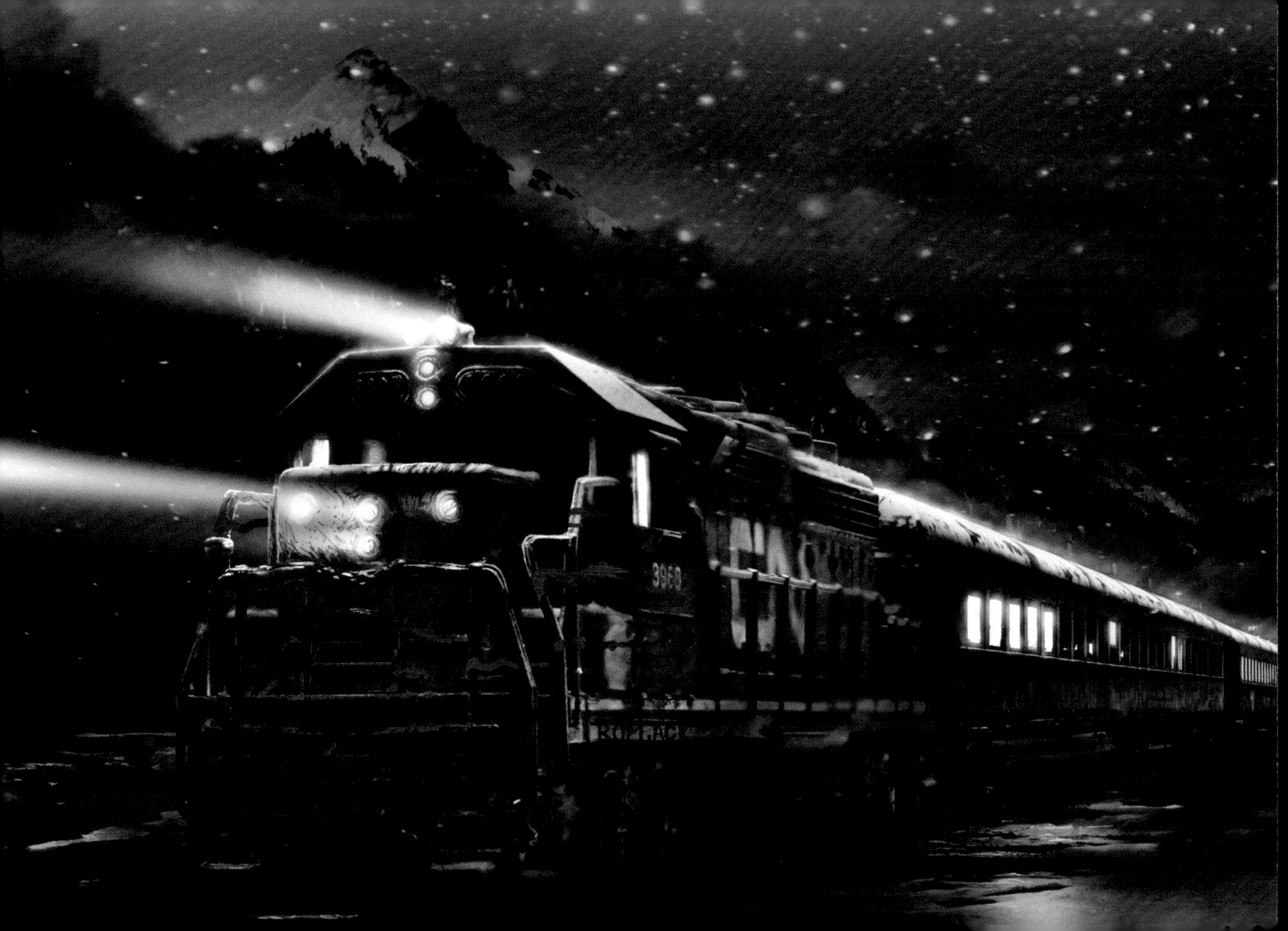

SET A TIME MACHINE TO 10 SECONDS IN THE PAST FOR TESTING AND GET TRAPPED IN AN INFINITE CYCLE OF POWERING IT ON. * HELP! HELP! I'M NOT A BAD IDEA! I JUST GOT TRAPPED INSIDE THIS BOOK! * BUMPER CARS FOR PREGNANT MOTHERS. * UMBRELLA UMBRELLAS. YOU KNOW, SO YOUR UMBRELLA DOESN'T GET WET IN THE RAIN! * GET INTO A POETRY BATTLE WITH SOMEONE FROM LIMERICK, IRELAND.

BAD IDEA #800:
TRY TO STOP A SPEEDING TRAIN IN YOUR SUPERHERO COSTUME.

LITERALLY DO ANY HYPERBOLE AT ALL, EVER, GEEZE. * LET STUDENTS APPLY FOR GRADUATION THROUGH TRIAL BY COMBAT. * YELL "HEY, LOOK OVER THERE" AT SOMEONE IN A NECK BRACE. * GANK THE MAGE LAST. * FULL BODY MASSAGES FROM ELEPHANTS. * START A TIME-TRAVELING CIRCUS OF TARDIGRADES. * AIDS-THEMED ROLLER COASTER. * DENY A CAT ATTENTION WHEN THEY WANT IT, NO MATTER THE CIRCUMSTANCES

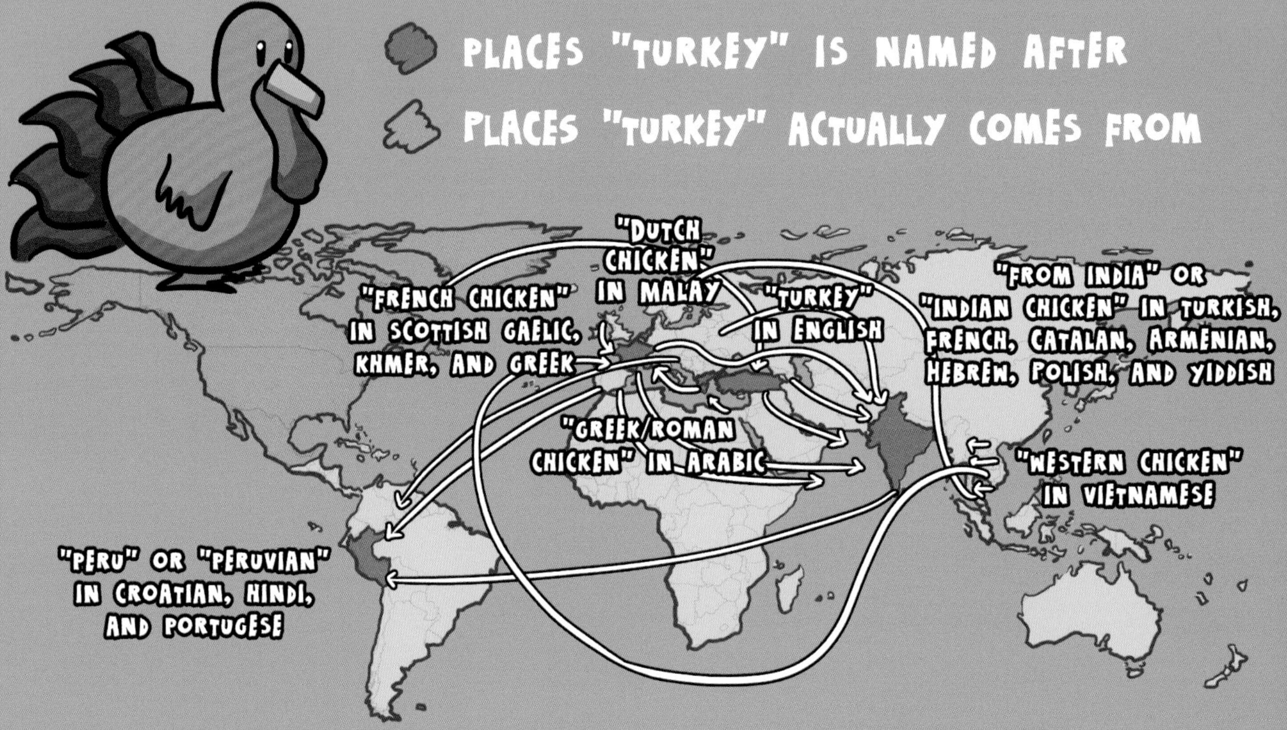
PLACES "TURKEY" IS NAMED AFTER
PLACES "TURKEY" ACTUALLY COMES FROM
"DUTCH CHICKEN" IN MALAY
"FRENCH CHICKEN" IN SCOTTISH GAELIC, KHMER, AND GREEK
"TURKEY" IN ENGLISH
"FROM INDIA" OR "INDIAN CHICKEN" IN TURKISH, FRENCH, CATALAN, ARMENIAN, HEBREW, POLISH, AND YIDDISH
"GREEK/ROMAN CHICKEN" IN ARABIC
"WESTERN CHICKEN" IN VIETNAMESE
"PERU" OR "PERUVIAN" IN CROATIAN, HINDI, AND PORTUGESE

I REALLY HOPE OTHER PLANETS AREN'T THIS STUPID.

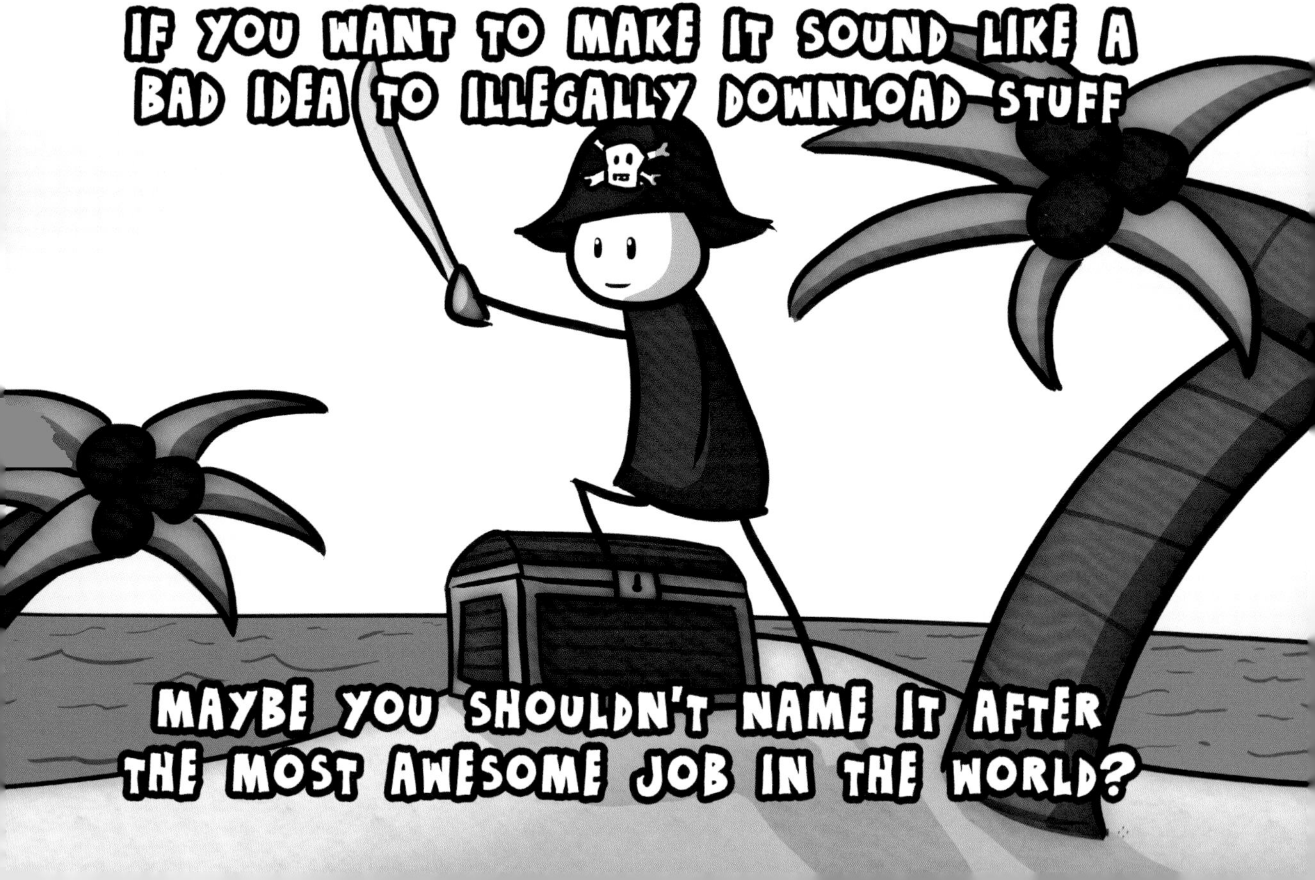
IF YOU WANT TO MAKE IT SOUND LIKE A BAD IDEA TO ILLEGALLY DOWNLOAD STUFF
MAYBE YOU SHOULDN'T NAME IT AFTER THE MOST AWESOME JOB IN THE WORLD?

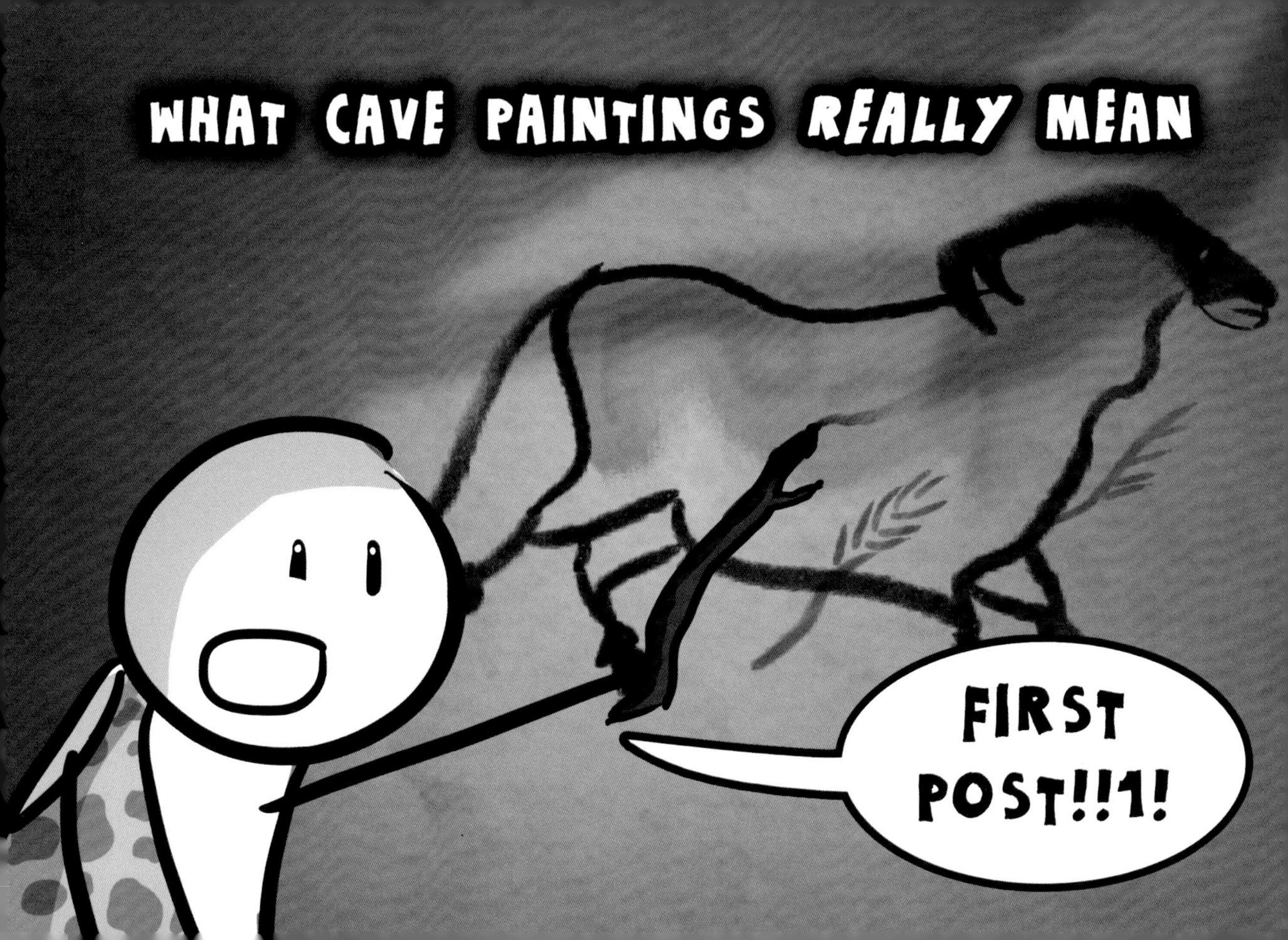
WHAT CAVE PAINTINGS REALLY MEAN
FIRST POST!!1!

KLEIN BOTTLE, N.

WHAT HAPPENS
WHEN A
MATHEMATICIAN
DISAPPEARS
UP HIS OWN
ASSHOLE.

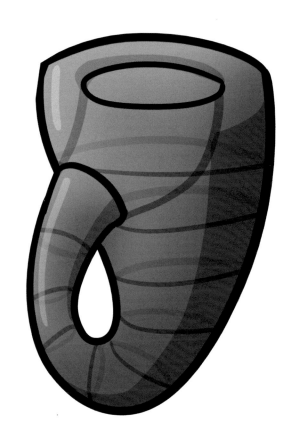

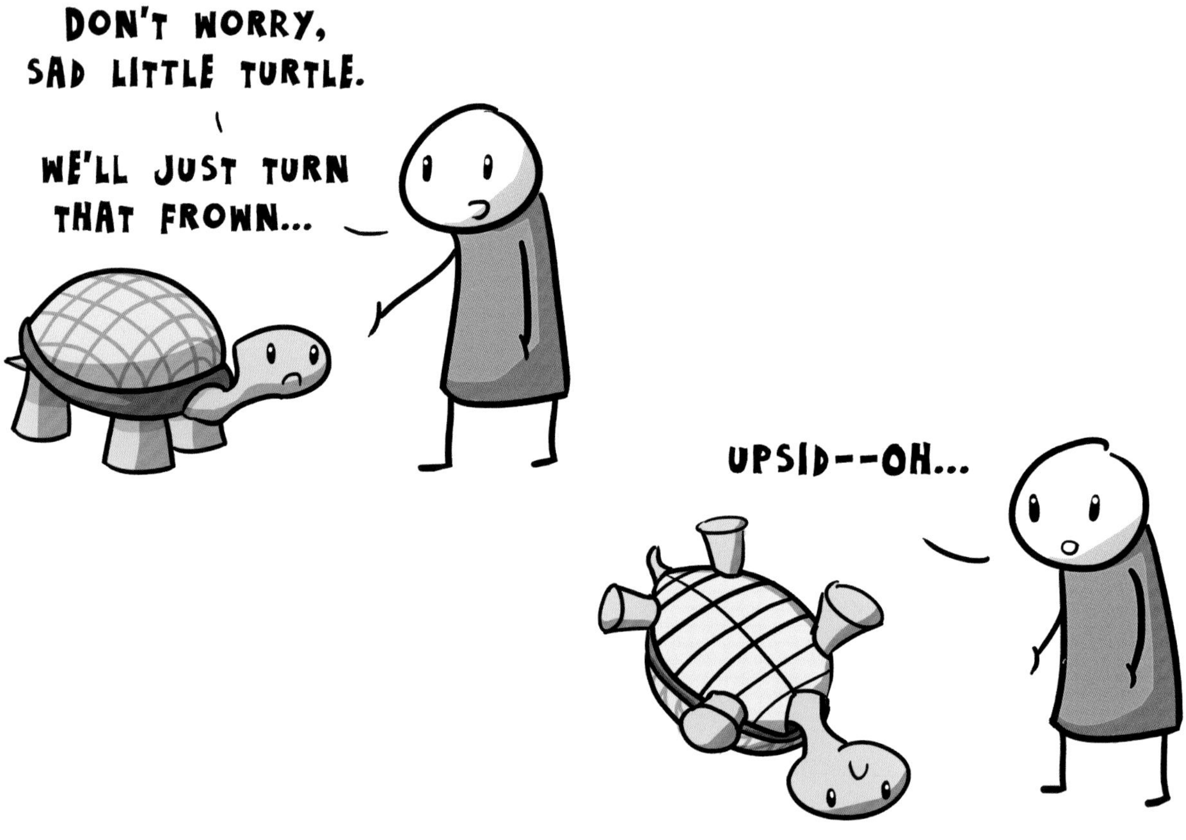
DON'T WORRY,
SAD LITTLE TURTLE.
WE'LL JUST TURN
THAT FROWN...
UPSID--OH...

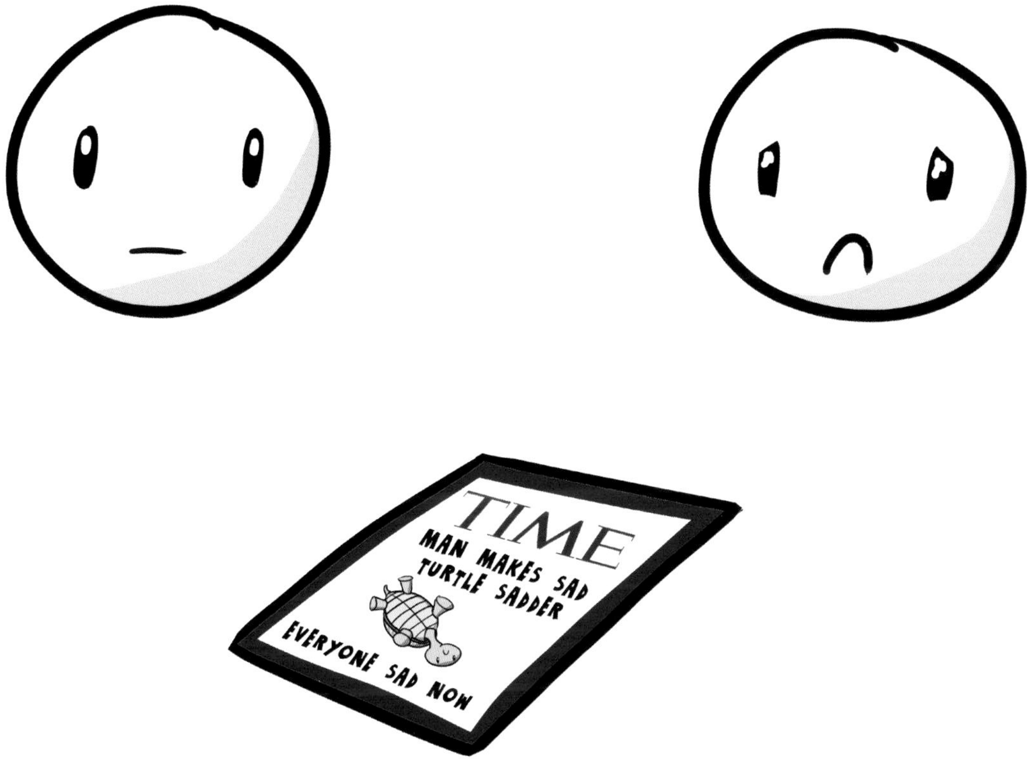
TIME
MAN MAKES SAD TURTLE SADDER
EVERYONE SAD NOW

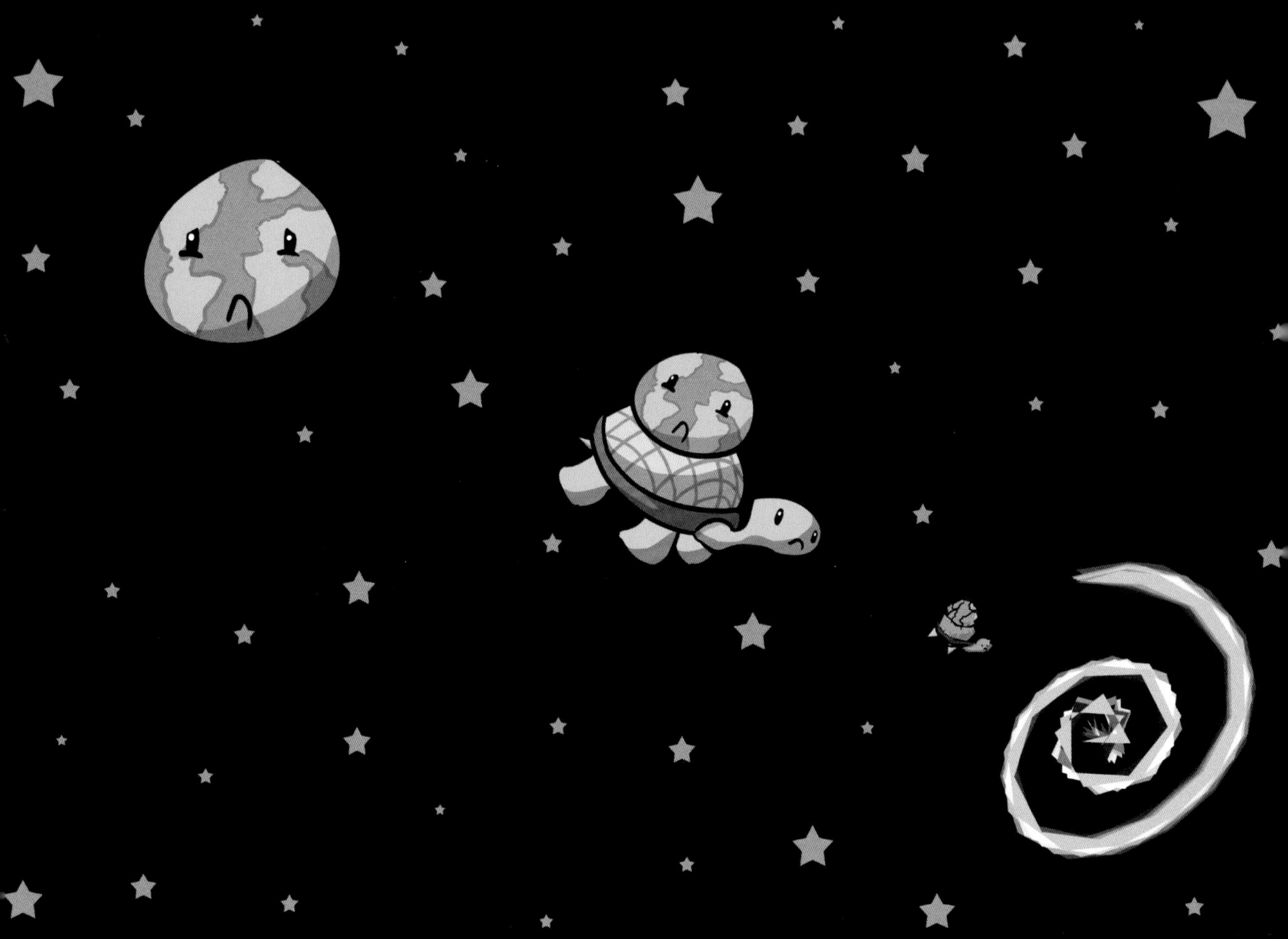

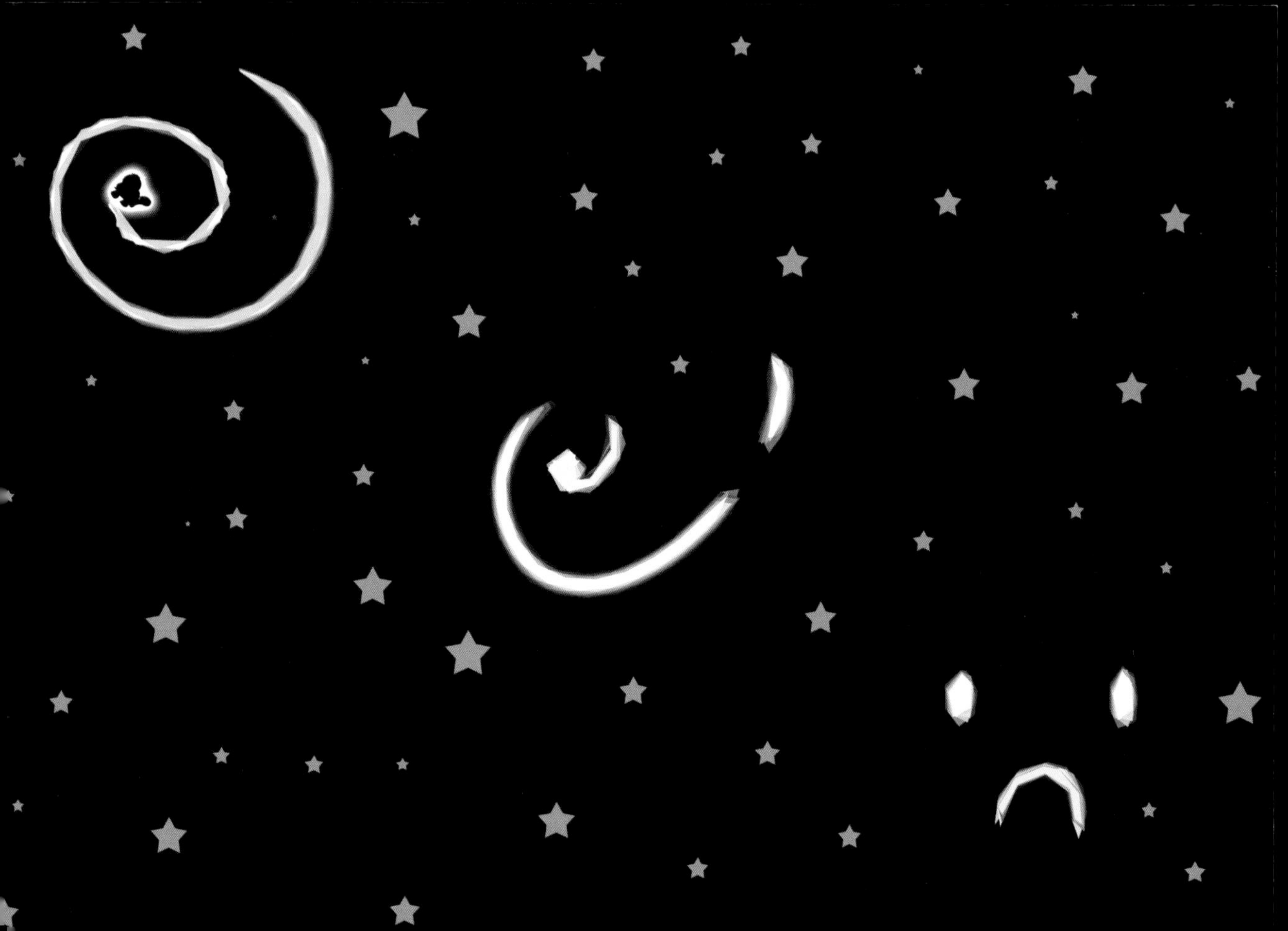

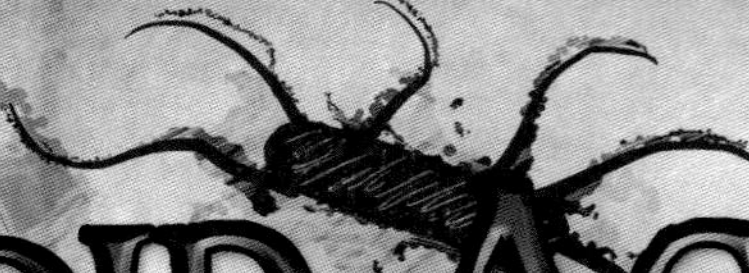

TYPHOID AGE

AN HISTORICALLY ACCURATE MEDIEVAL FANTASY RPG

Featuring amazing quests like:

Wash Your Fucking Hands

Find Water Without Poop In It

Maybe You Shouldn't Take Medical
Advice From 1000-Year-Old Greeks

Blood in Your Stool

And fearsome enemies such as:

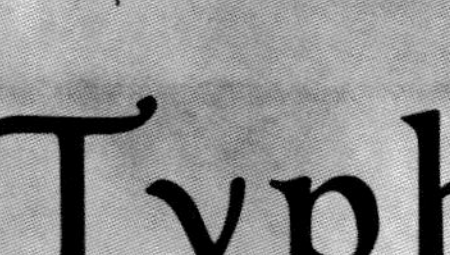

The Cholera

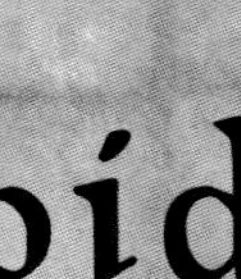

Dysentery

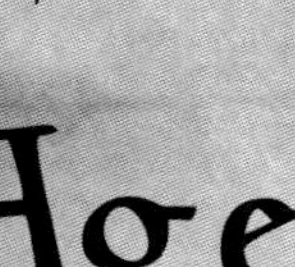

Count Scrofula

Typhoid Age

*may you live long enough
to bury your children*

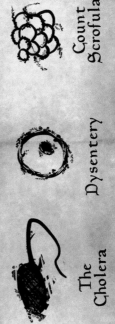

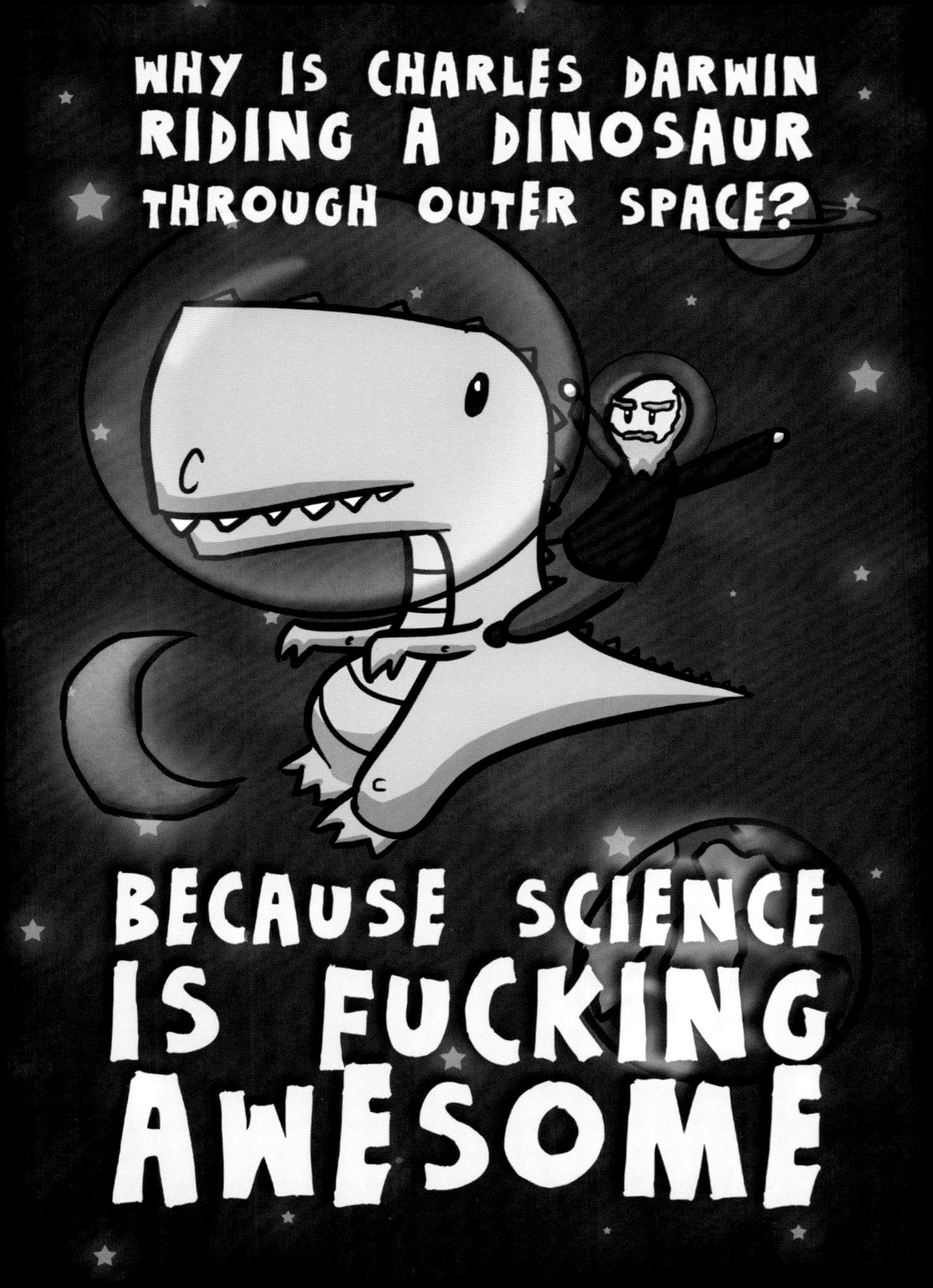
WHY IS CHARLES DARWIN RIDING A DINOSAUR THROUGH OUTER SPACE?
BECAUSE SCIENCE IS FUCKING AWESOME

THIS HALLOWE'EN,
DRESS UP AS YOUR
OWN EVIL TWIN.

WEAR A
TOP HAT.

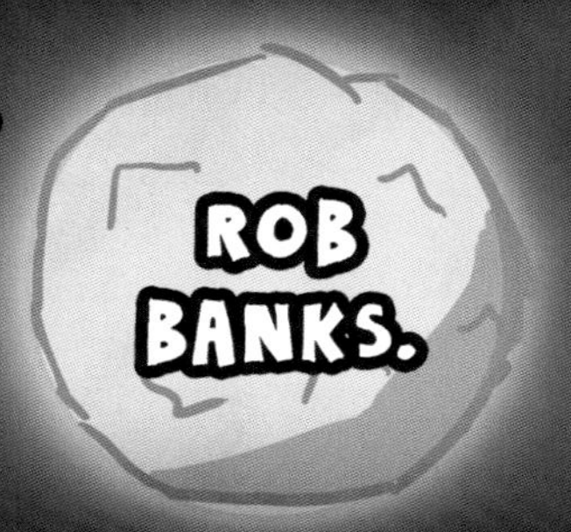
ROB
BANKS.

STEAL
CANDY.

DO EVERY STUPID,
SELFISH THING YOU'VE
EVER WANTED TO.

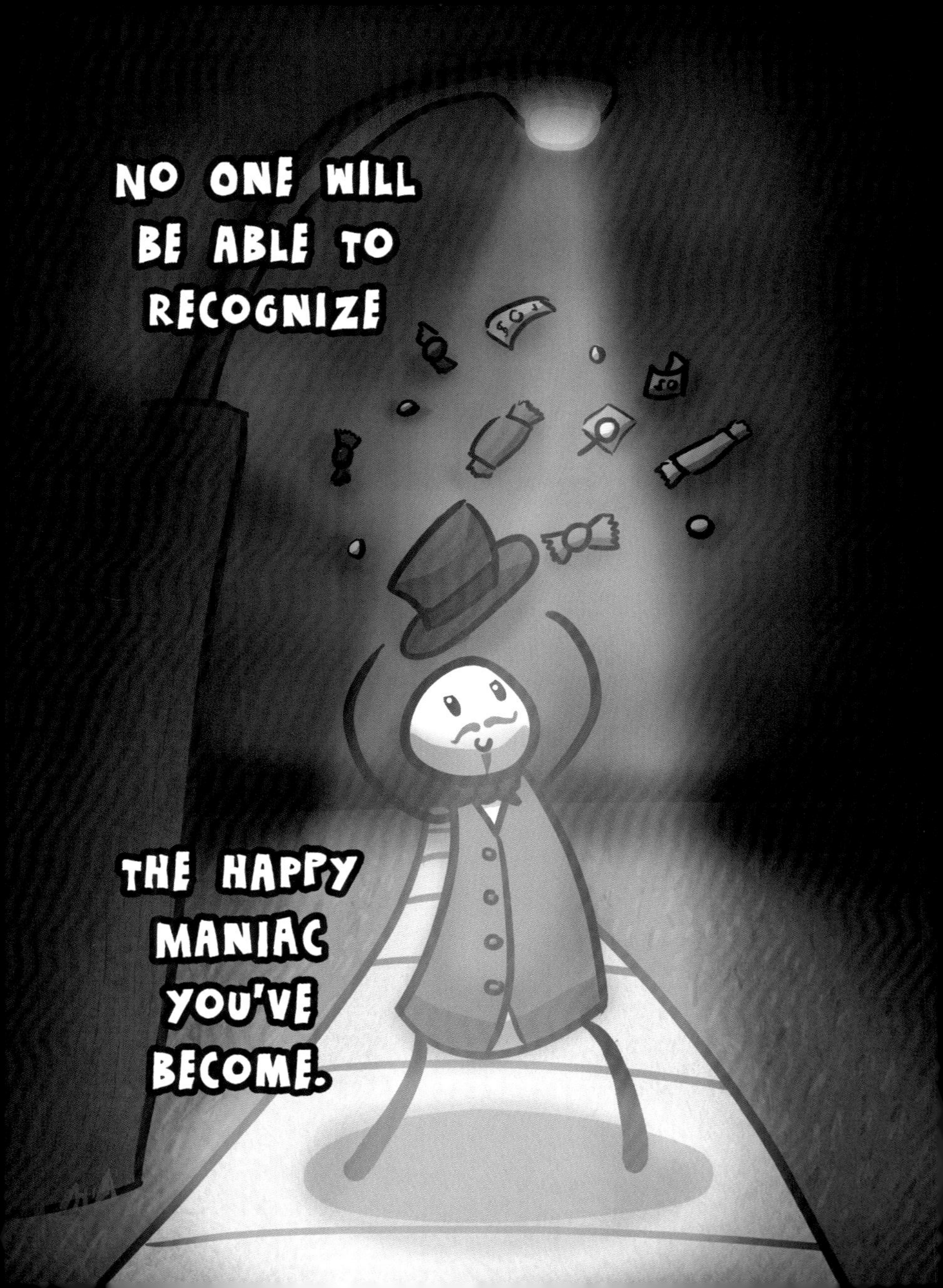
NO ONE WILL
BE ABLE TO
RECOGNIZE
THE HAPPY
MANIAC
YOU'VE
BECOME.

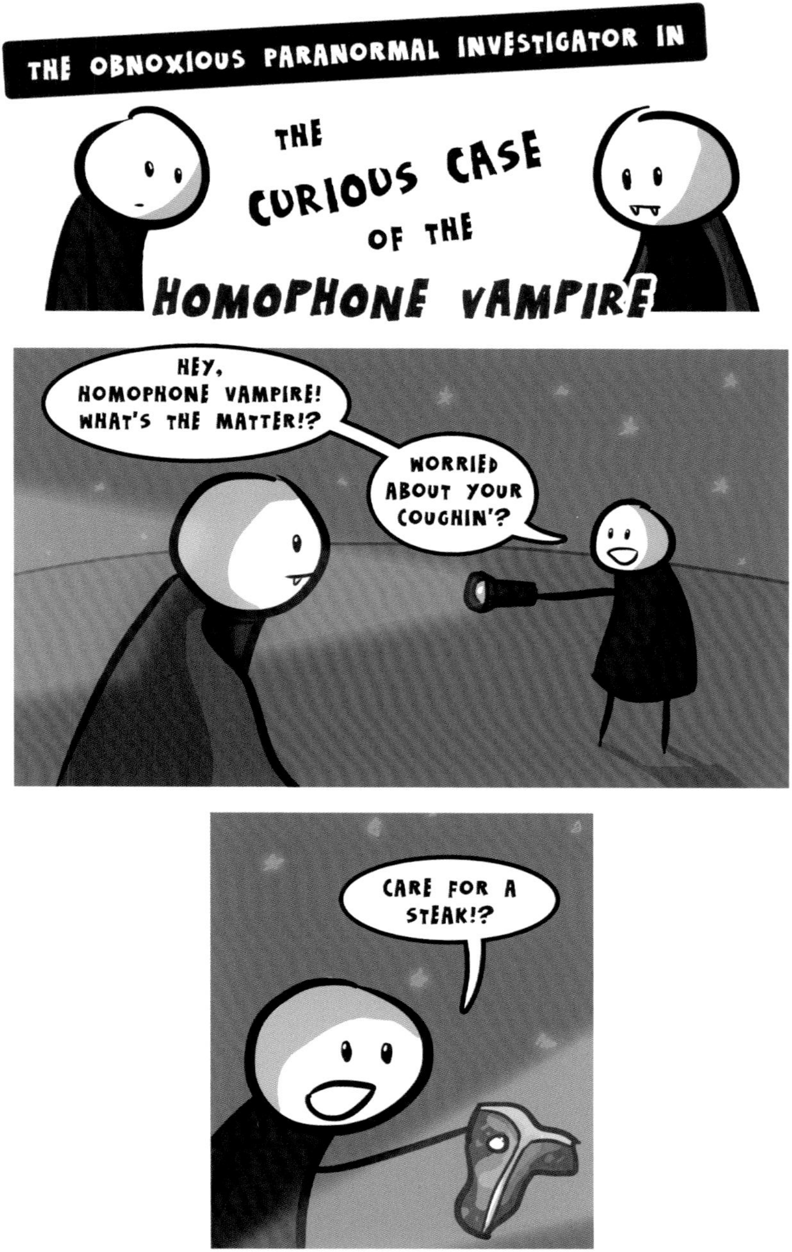
THE OBNOXIOUS PARANORMAL INVESTIGATOR IN
THE CURIOUS CASE OF THE HOMOPHONE VAMPIRE
HEY, HOMOPHONE VAMPIRE! WHAT'S THE MATTER!?
WORRIED ABOUT YOUR COUGHIN'?
CARE FOR A STEAK!?

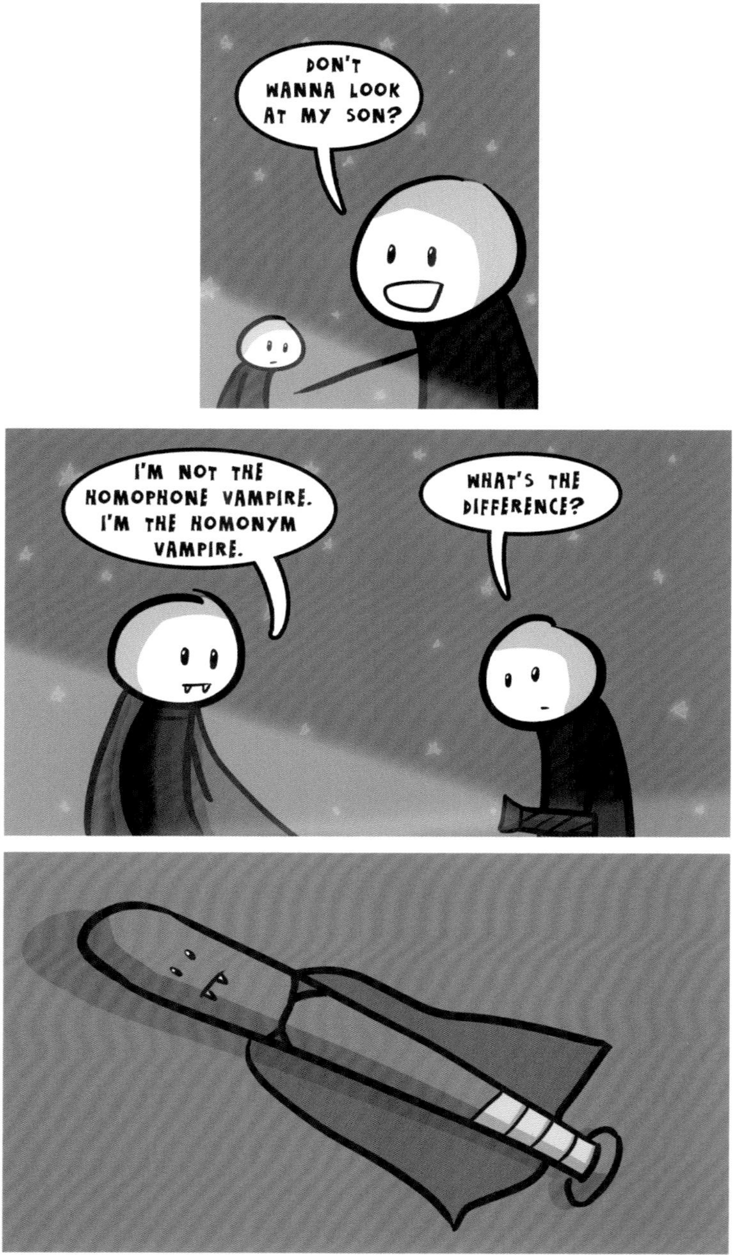
DON'T WANNA LOOK AT MY SON?
I'M NOT THE HOMOPHONE VAMPIRE. I'M THE HOMONYM VAMPIRE.
WHAT'S THE DIFFERENCE?

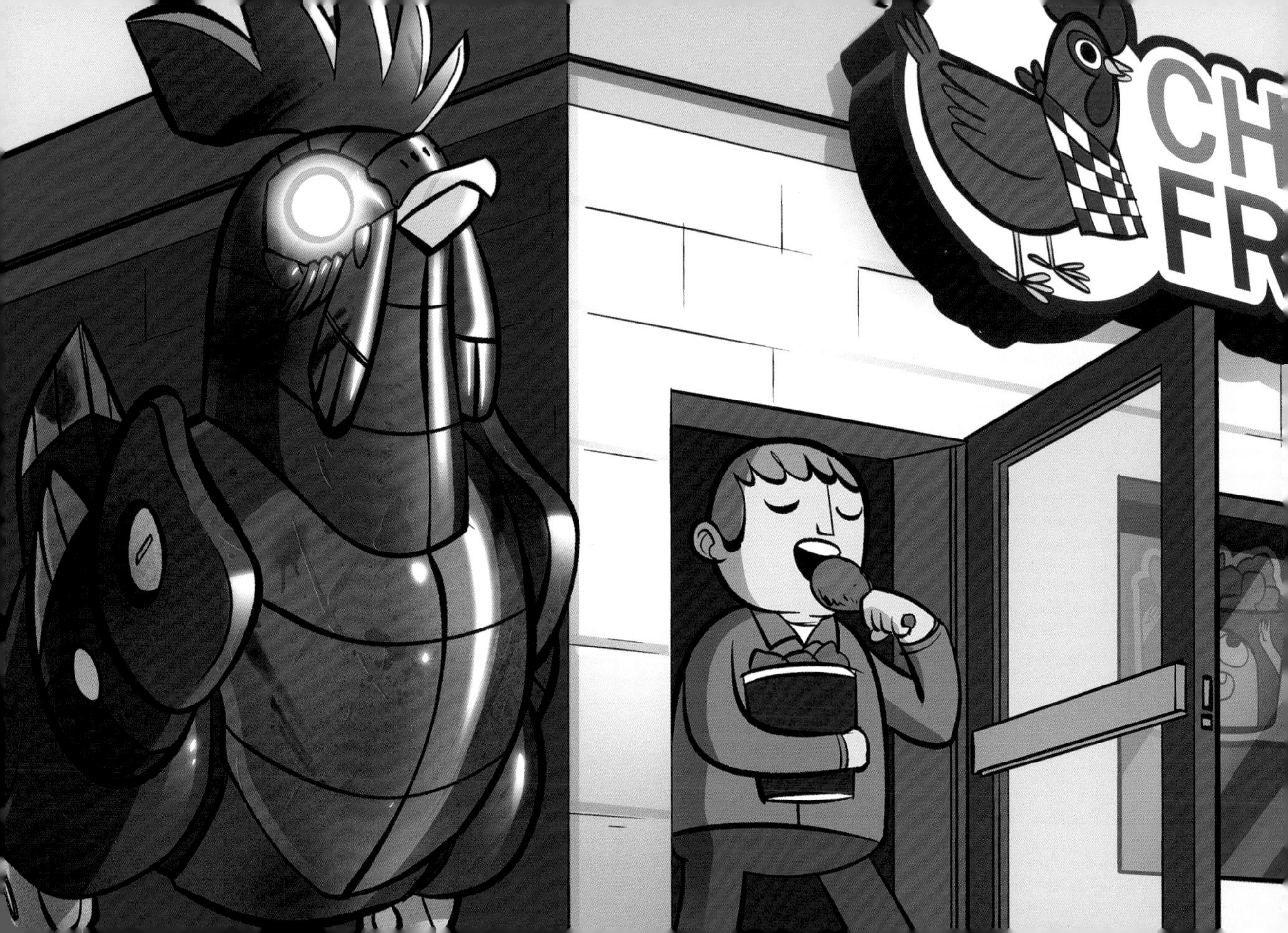
CH
FR

HIRE A NARCOLEPTIC HIGH SCHOOL SHOP TEACHER. * BLINDFOLDED BULLFIGHTING. * PORCUPINE ALARM CLOCK. * TRY TO BE FUNNY TO GET OUT OF A SPEEDING TICKET. * DESCRIBE AN IMPRESSION YOUR GIRLFRIEND DID OF YOUR MOTHER, TO YOUR MOTHER. * DIVIDE BY ZERO... FOREVER. * MISS YOUR DEADLINES. * MOVIE THEATERS THAT SHOW THE ORIGINAL MOVIE NEXT TO ITS REMAKE. * TAR GARGLING.

BAD IDEA #912: EAT CHICKEN IN FRONT OF MEGACHICKEN WHEN HE'S JUST RETURNED FROM THE KENTUCKY FRIED WARS.

TEACH YOUR PET RAVEN TO SAY "ONOMATOPOEIA." * TELL HAN SOLO THE ODDS. * PROPOSE WITH THE RING OF POWER. * REINVENT THE WHEEL. * SHOOT ARROWS IN THE AIR AND TRY TO CATCH THEM WITH YOUR MOUTH. * DATE YOUR PATIENTS AS A DOCTOR. * DATE YOUR PATIENTS AS A VET. * DO ALL OF THE ASSIGNED HOMEWORK IN DISOBEDIENCE 101. * GIVE OUT TAX RECEIPTS FOR SPERM DONATIONS

T-REX HAS BEEN SENT TO THE MOON!
THIS IS THE GREATEST IDEA EVER!
BUT WITH NO WAY OF GETTING HOME!
Hah hah hah WHO CARES??
OH ALSO DROMICEIOMIMUS AND UTAHRAPTOR AND A TINY WOMAN AND A LOG CABIN AND A BLUE CAR HAVE BEEN SENT TO THE MOON TOO.
Hey, welcome to the moon, Dromiceiomimus!
Thanks! I'm glad we're in a dome with white walls, which explains the white all around us and, also, the lack of spacesuits!
Yes, it's all quite convenient
You're not concerned at all that we can't get back to Earth? Like, ever?
Of course not! This is rad!!
Dude, unlike ALL OTHER KNOWN LIFE IN THE UNIVERSE, we're going to DIE on THE MOON. That's amazing! Kids will remember our names! And our bodies, too, since they're not gonna decay ON THE MOON. Best death ever!
I HAVE been struggling to be remembered in life. Maybe I SHOULD focus on death!
A FEW DAYS LATER, THE AIR STARTS RUNNING OUT:
gasp
soooooooo
gasp
gasp
raaaaaaaaaaaad

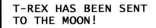

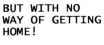

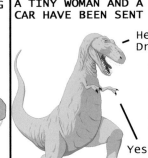

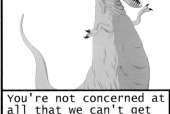

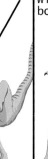

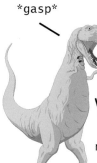

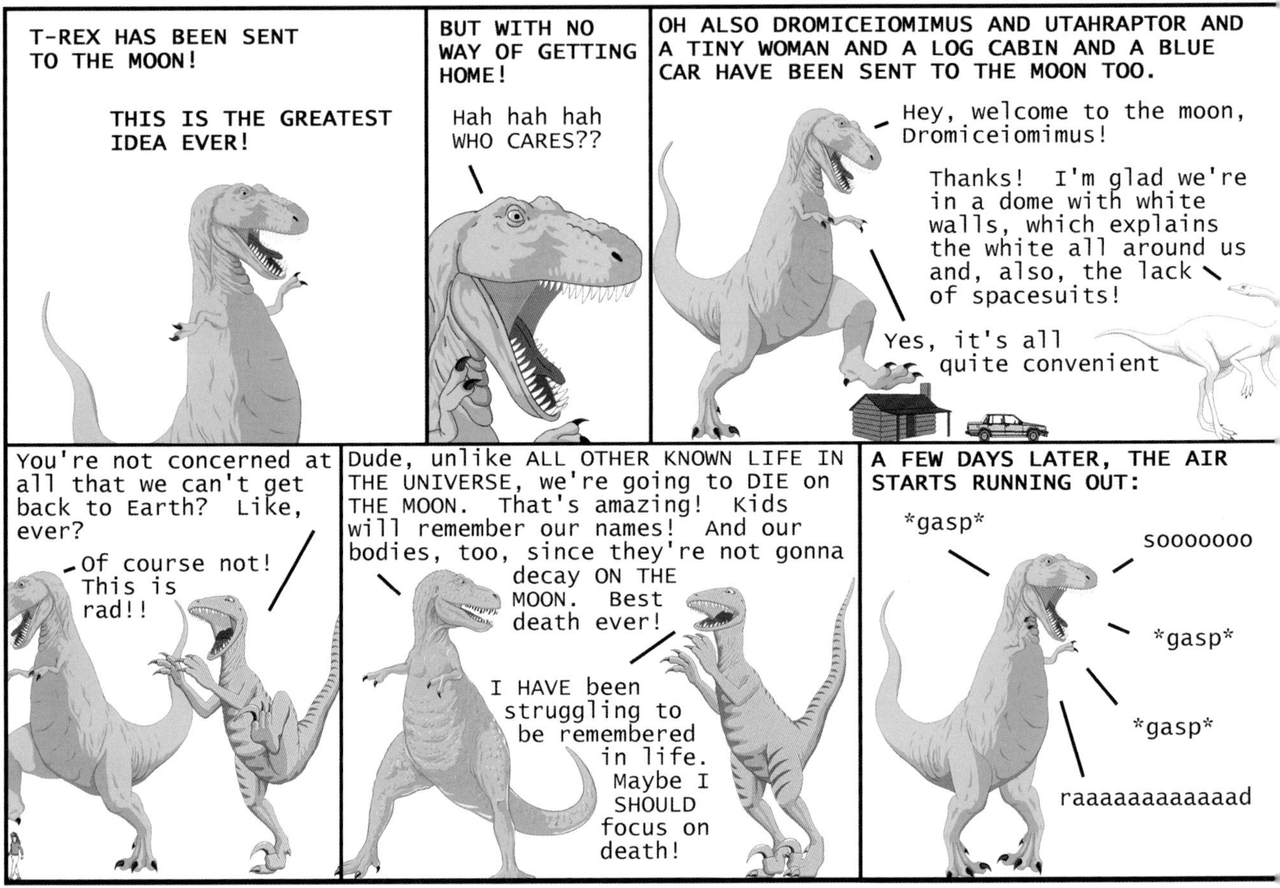

LET KING MIDAS GIVE YOU THE OL' REACH-AROUND. * INCORPORATE PROPS IN THE EULOGY YOU'RE WRITING. * START ANY SENTENCE WITH "I'M NOT RACIST BUT..." * CUT OFF YOUR NOSE TO SPITE YOUR FACE. * CUT OFF THE REST OF YOUR HEAD TO SPITE YOUR BODY. * EVOLVE INTO A TERRIFYING MIASMATIC AVATAR OF DESTRUCTION TO AVOID YOUR TURN DOING THE DISHES. * THE TITANIC REENACTMENT SOCIETY.

BAD IDEA #1032: APRIL FOOLS! SEND SOMEONE TO THE MOON WITH LOADS OF SUPPLIES BUT NO WAY OF GETTING HOME.

CHALLENGE DEATH TO A GAME OF HUNGRY HUNGRY HIPPOS. THAT JERK PLAYS, LIKE, ALL THE TIME. * RELEASE YOUR LAB-GROWN GUN-TOTING CYBORG "GLOCK-TOPUS" INTO THE WILD. * PAY YOUR TAXES BY THE BARTER SYSTEM. * INCLUDE "WAS THE FIRST SPERM" ON YOUR RESUME. * START A SIGHTSEEING TOUR CALLED "OH THE ANIMALS YOU'LL SEE SQUISHED INTO THE SIDE OF THE ROAD!" * HEMOPHILIAC MOSH-PIT

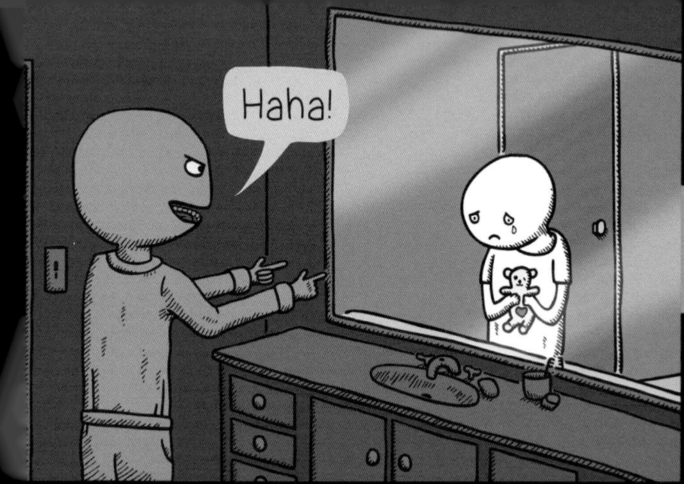

Haha!

BUILD A TIME MACHINE TO TEACH DODOS KRAV MAGA. * WRITE YOUR WEDDING VOWS AS A BUZZFEED LIST. * TRY OUT THAT NEW "ALL DEEP FRIED" (A.K.A. "FAIR FOOD") DIET. * HOT SAUCE HOT TUB. * MOLASSES-COATED SHARK RACES.

BAD IDEA #1107: RAISE YOUR NEMESIS FROM THE DEAD TO GLOAT.

ENCOURAGE THE CROWD TO START A WAVE AT A SWIM MEET. * GWAR MITZVAH! * PUNCH A NARWHAL IN A BILL COSBY SWEATER. * CONTRIBUTE TO A "BAD IDEA" PROJECT WHEN YOU DO NOT HAVE A BAD IDEA. * BATTLE DOLPHINS.

GO ON IMGUR FOR A "QUICK BREAK." * GO ON REDDIT FOR A "QUICK BREAK." * BRING A JAR OF PEANUT BUTTER TO THE DOG PARK WITH NO INTENTION OF SHARING. * DISOBEY MORTIKON, KING OF FEAR. * GASOLINE PUMP WATER FIGHT.

BAD IDEA #1120: PLAY CHICKEN WITH A SUPER-MASSIVE BLACK HOLE.

LEAVE YOUR CHILDREN "A LIFETIME FULL OF REGRET" IN YOUR WILL. * TAUNTAUN SPACE HEATER. * BATHTUB CIRCUS APPARATUSES. * STARFLEET RED WEDDING. * PUT AN ICE CREAM FRIDGE NEXT TO YOUR BED. * CROSS THE STREAMS. * ANGER A WOMBAT.

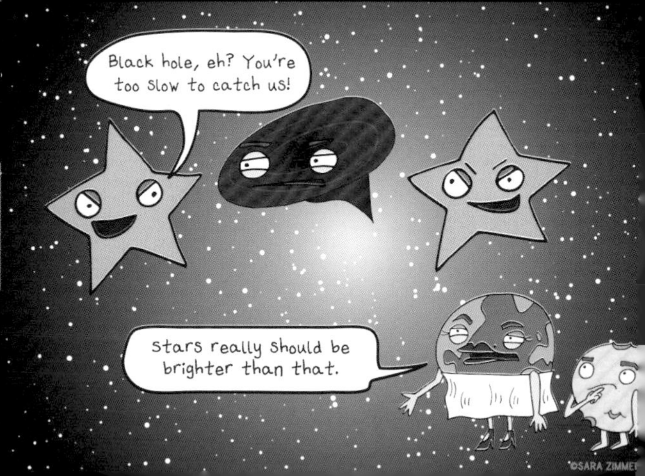

Black hole, eh? You're too slow to catch us!
Stars really should be brighter than that.
©SARA ZIMMER

PLAY HIDE-AND-SEEK WITH SUPERMAN. * CHANGE YOUR FIRST NAME TO "FIRST NAME." * SHOW THE POLICE OFFICER THAT YOUR PEPPER SPRAY IS NOT EXPIRED BY TESTING IT ON HIM. * CUDDLE PARTY WITH BOA CONSTRICTORS. * SENTIENT FARTS.

BAD IDEA #1175: TELL YOUR CHILDREN THAT SPIDERS TASTE LIKE CHOCOLATE.

MESS WITH A GREEK GOD. * MAKE A BIRTHDAY CAKE WITH YELLOW CAKE (U308). * CLIMB INTO A BEAR ENCLOSURE AT THE ZOO WHILE WEARING A BEARD OF BEES. * HAVE AN EMBROIDERY PARTY WITH YOUR CAT AND A T-REX. * HANG A PINATA NEXT TO A BEE HIVE.

LIVE COMMENTARY FOR FUNERALS. * PLAY FETCH WITH A VELOCIRAPTOR. * CUT HABANERO PEPPERS BEFORE GETTING TO THIRD BASE WITH YOUR GIRLFRIEND. * HARDCORE HAND-HELD LICKABLE LASERS. * WATERMELON SAFETY HELMETS.

BAD IDEA #1191: OPEN THE ELDRITCH BOOK WITH THE COVER MADE OF HUMAN SKIN.

ROB FORT KNOX WITH A BANANA. * PUBLISH A LIST OF WORST-SELLING BOOKS. * TRY TO PICK UP WOMEN USING LESSONS LEARNED FROM PLAYING COMPUTER PORN GAMES. * SWITCH ALL PATIENT RECORDS IN THE HOSPITAL. * DIREWASPS.

UMMM....

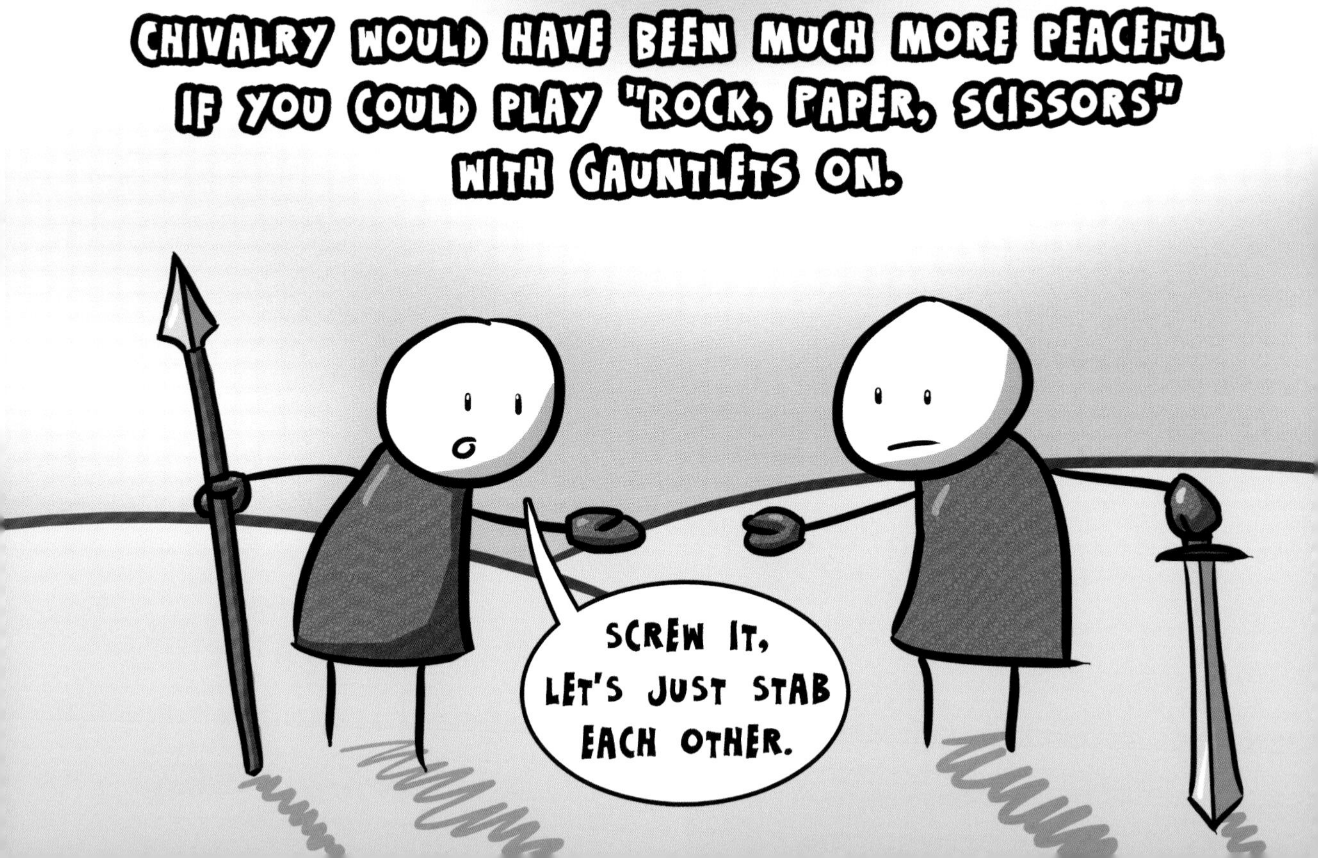
CHIVALRY WOULD HAVE BEEN MUCH MORE PEACEFUL IF YOU COULD PLAY "ROCK, PAPER, SCISSORS" WITH GAUNTLETS ON.
SCREW IT, LET'S JUST STAB EACH OTHER.

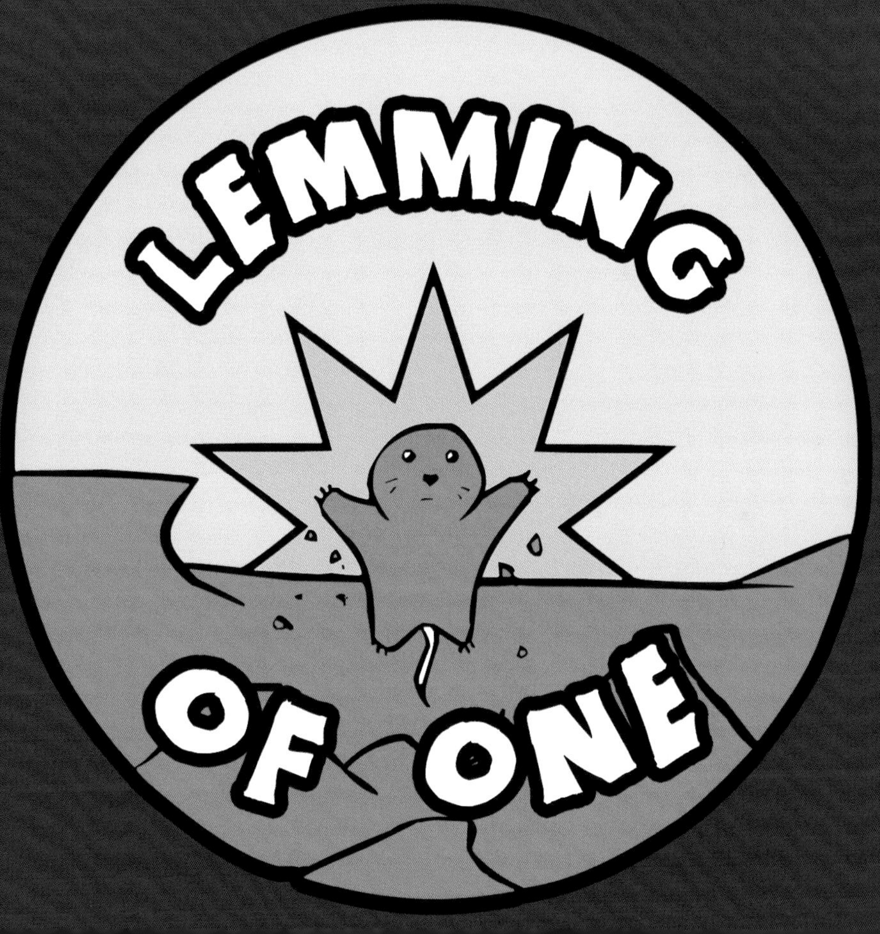
LEMMING
OF ONE

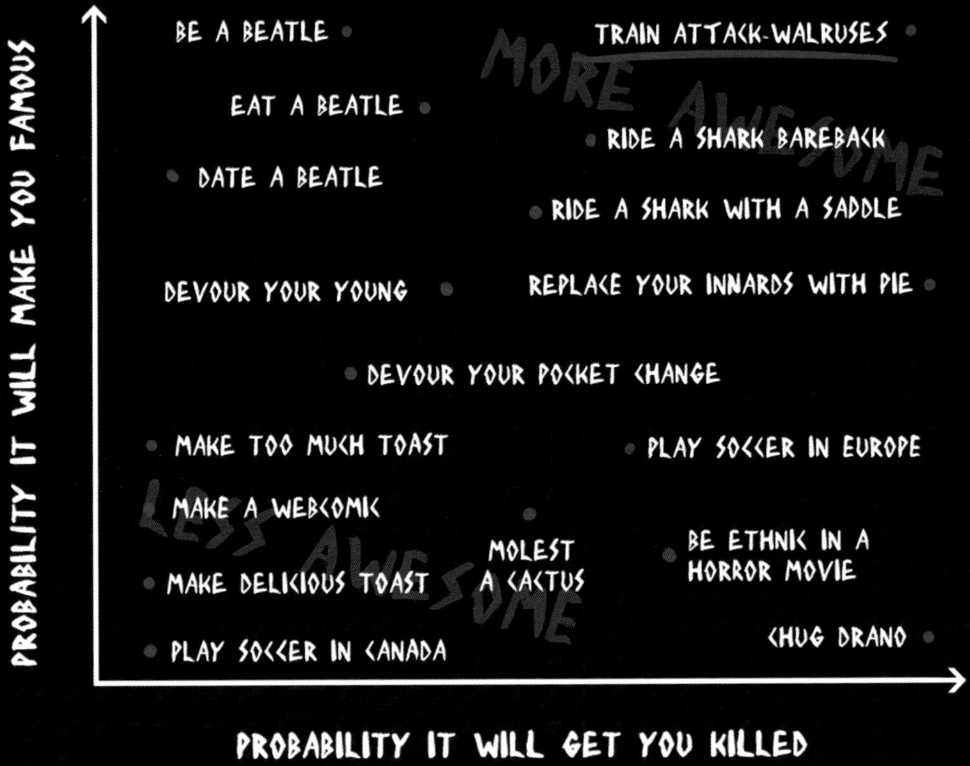
BE A BEATLE
TRAIN ATTACK-WALRUSES
MORE AWESOME
EAT A BEATLE
RIDE A SHARK BAREBACK
DATE A BEATLE
RIDE A SHARK WITH A SADDLE
DEVOUR YOUR YOUNG
REPLACE YOUR INNARDS WITH PIE
DEVOUR YOUR POCKET CHANGE
MAKE TOO MUCH TOAST
PLAY SOCCER IN EUROPE
MAKE A WEBCOMIC
LESS AWESOME
MOLEST A CACTUS
BE ETHNIC IN A HORROR MOVIE
MAKE DELICIOUS TOAST
CHUG DRANO
PLAY SOCCER IN CANADA
PROBABILITY IT WILL MAKE YOU FAMOUS
PROBABILITY IT WILL GET YOU KILLED

IF I EVER HAVE TO CHOOSE BETWEEN A FUTURE WHERE KILLER ROBOTS HUNT HUMANS OR A FUTURE WHERE BACON SUPPLIES HAVE RUN OUT...

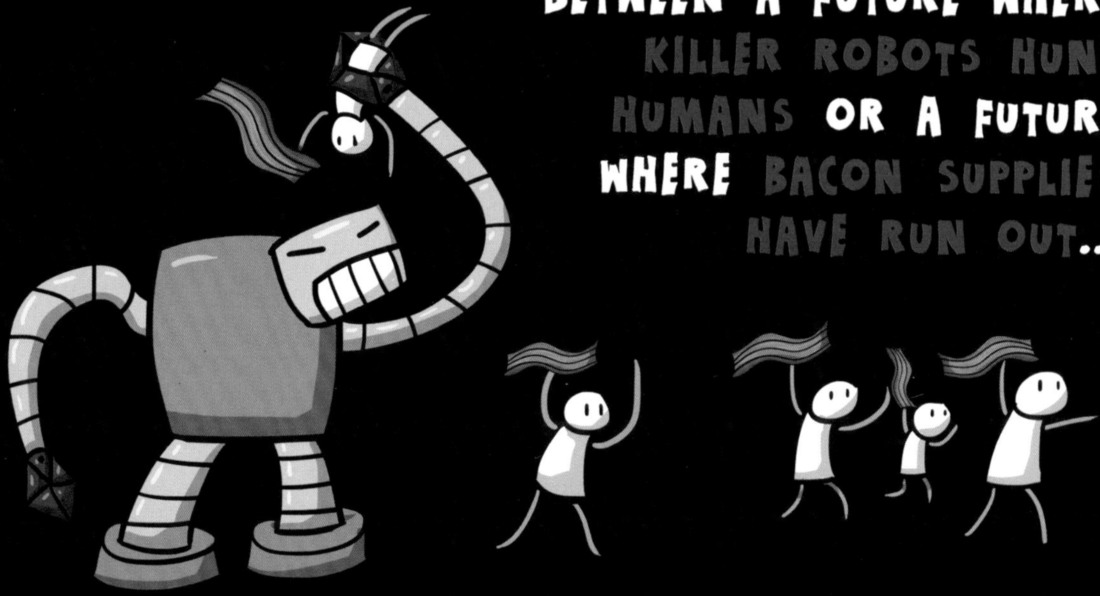

LET'S JUST SAY YOU BETTER START RUNNING.

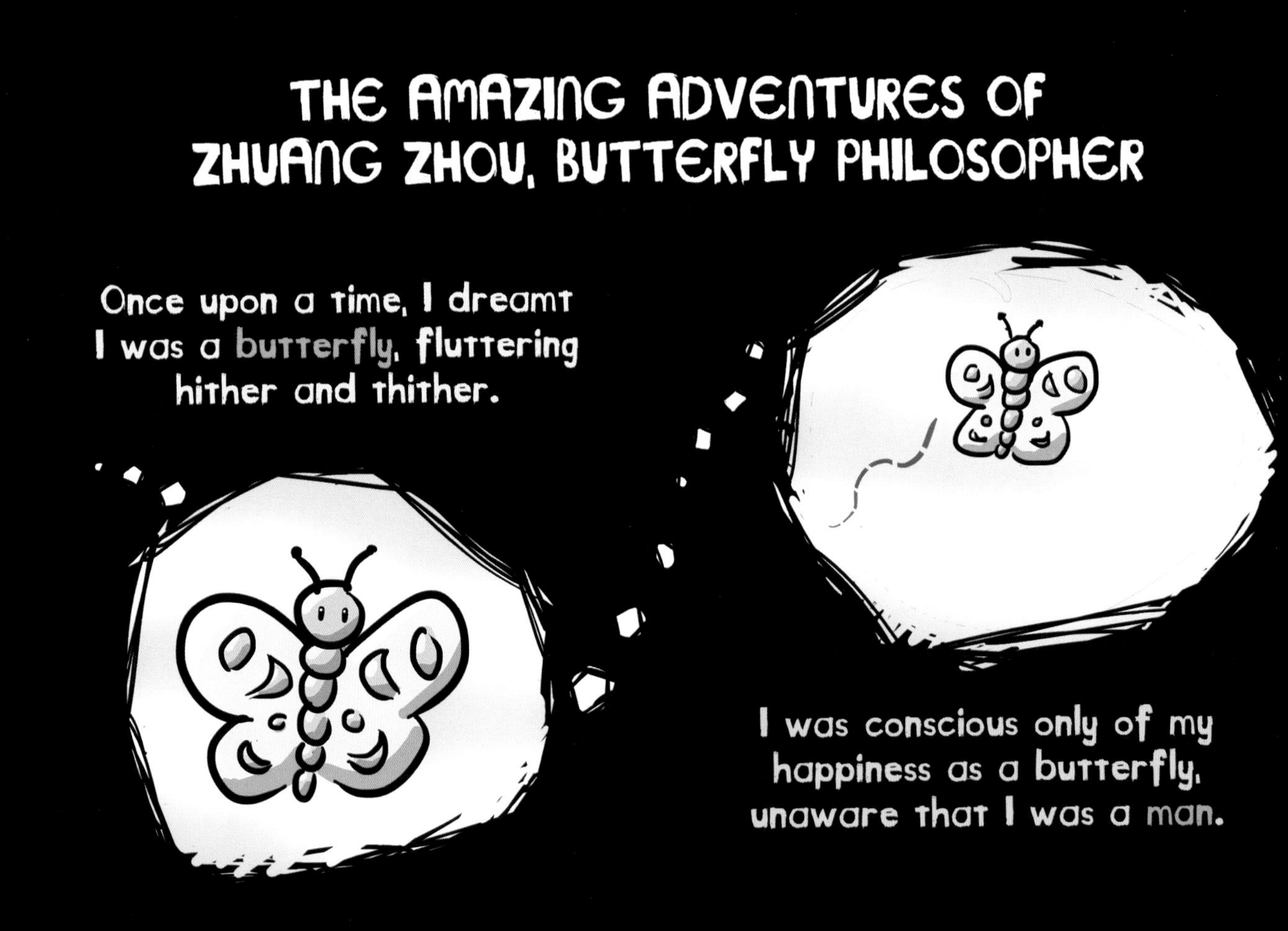
THE AMAZING ADVENTURES OF
ZHUANG ZHOU, BUTTERFLY PHILOSOPHER
Once upon a time, I dreamt I was a butterfly, fluttering hither and thither.
I was conscious only of my happiness as a butterfly, unaware that I was a man.

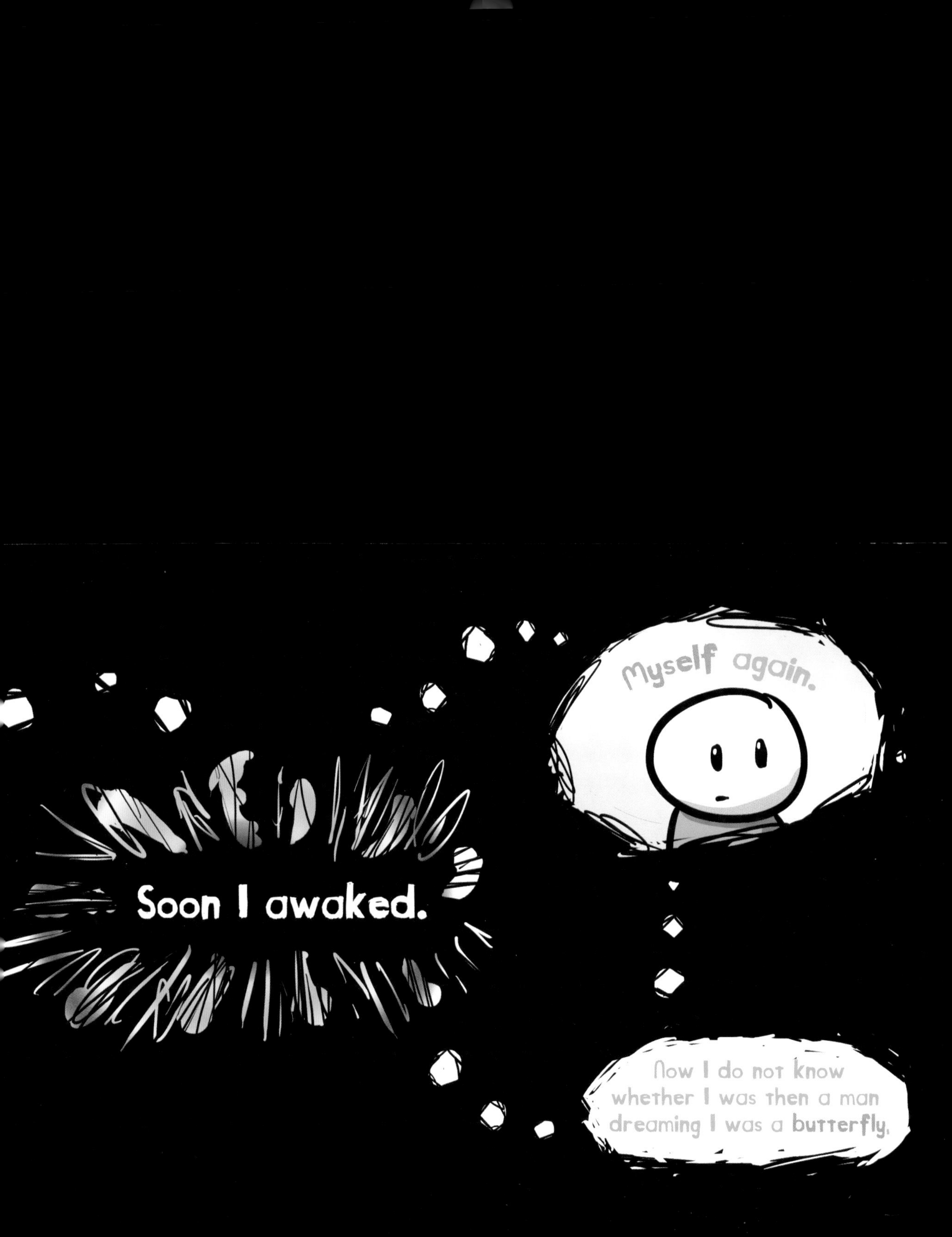
Soon I awaked.
Myself again.
Now I do not know whether I was then a man dreaming I was a butterfly,

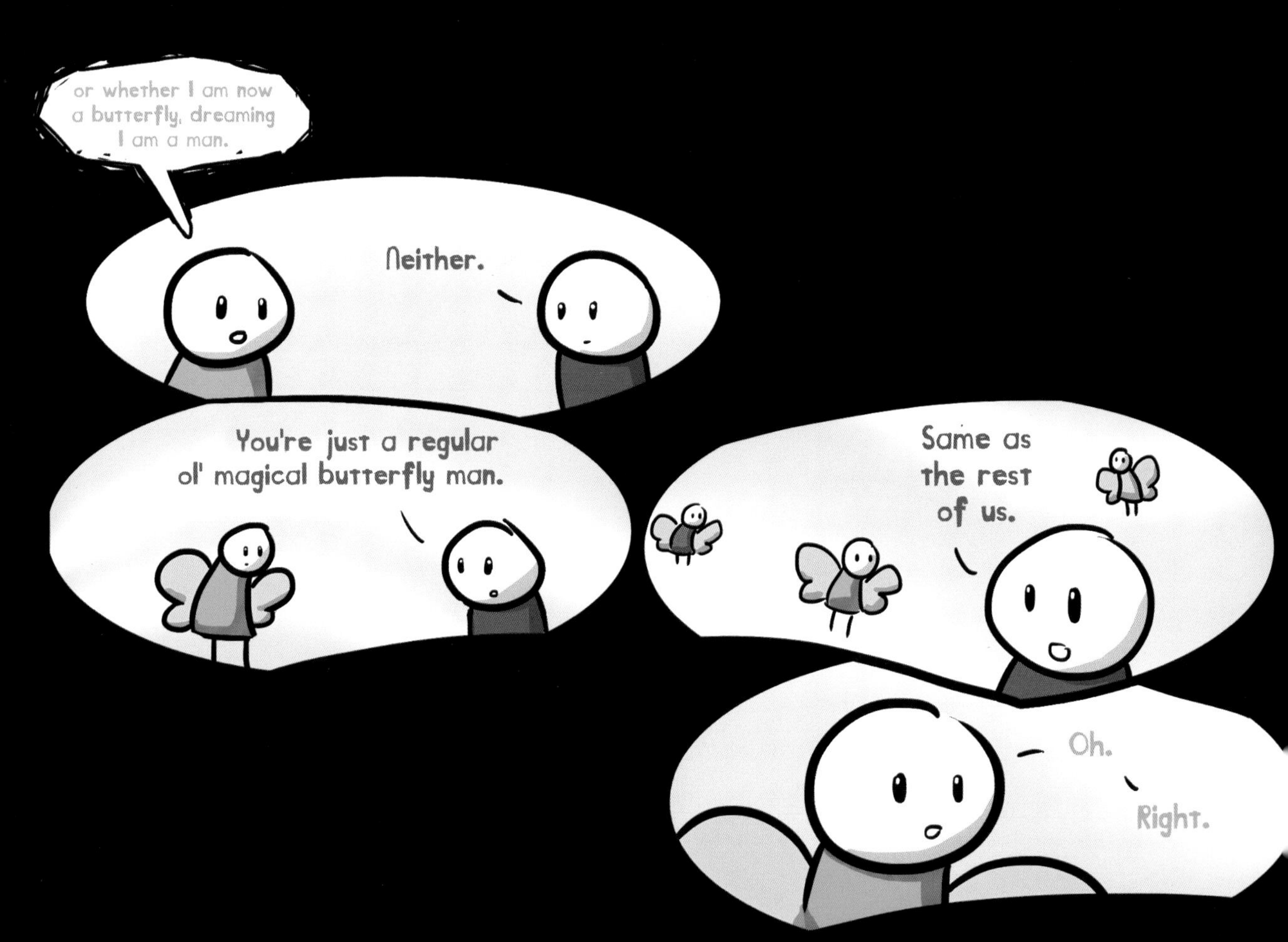
or whether I am now a butterfly, dreaming I am a man.
Neither.
You're just a regular ol' magical butterfly man.
Same as the rest of us.
Oh.
Right.

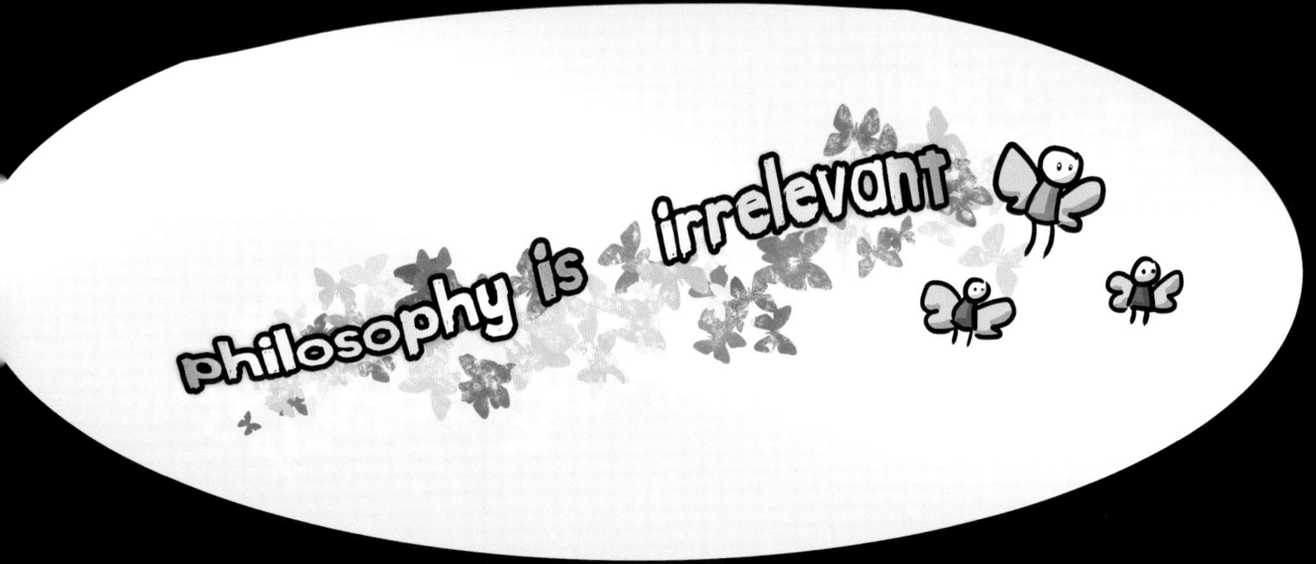
philosophy is irrelevant

THE END.

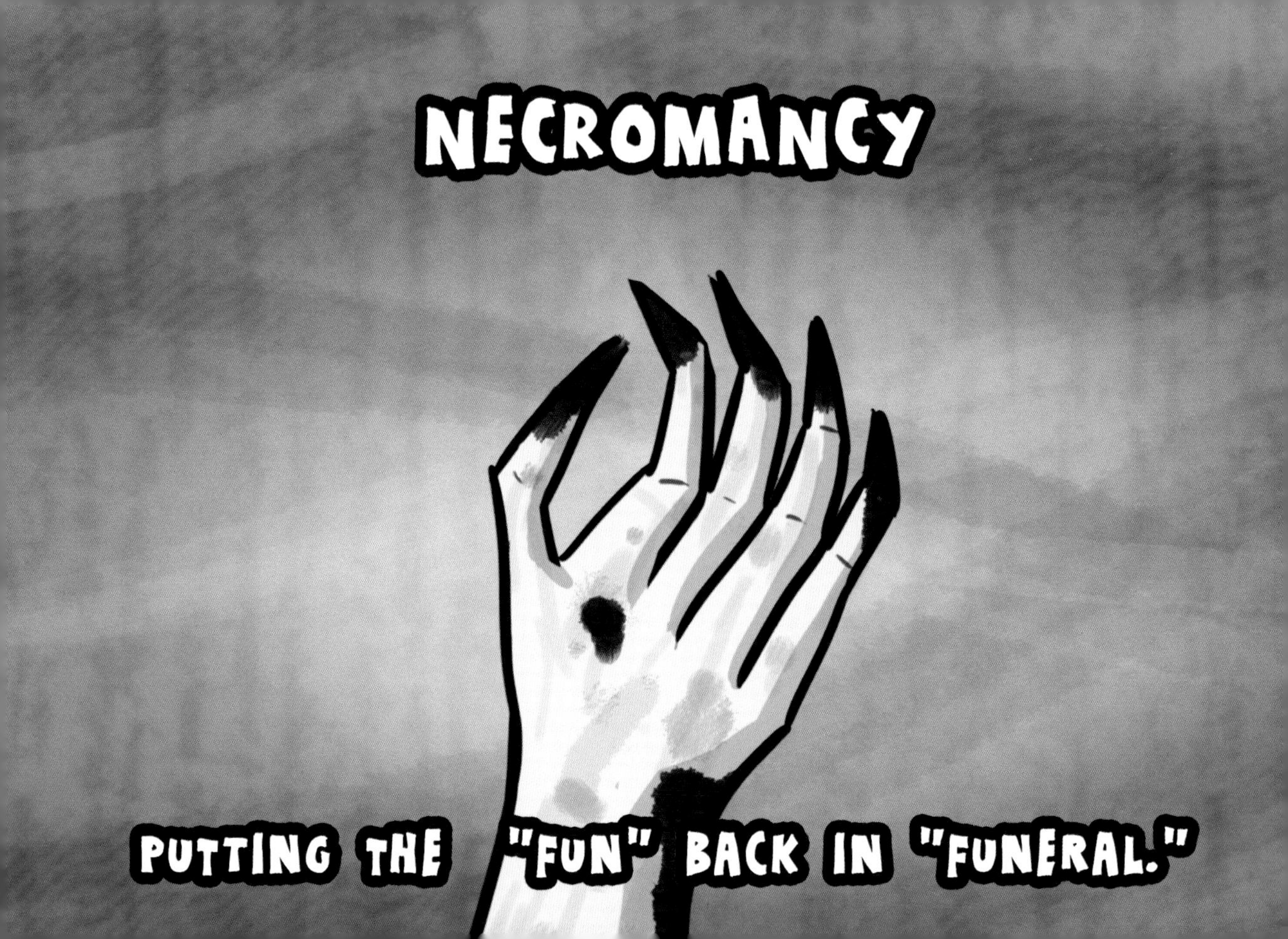
NECROMANCY
PUTTING THE "FUN" BACK IN "FUNERAL."

THE EGYPTIAN GAMING PANTHEON

ANOOBIS
GOD OF THE NEOPHYTES,

WHOSE WRATH IS
FREQUENT AND
LAUGHABLE.

HAXTHOR
ROCKET-WHORE GODDESS,

WHO CAMPS IN WAIT
FOR THE PASSING
OF THE WEAK.

AMUN-ROFL
THE GIGGLING GOD,

WHOSE LOLZ ARE
AS ABUNDANT AS
THE STARS.

GAY PRIDE

TEAMWORK TURTLE SAYS:

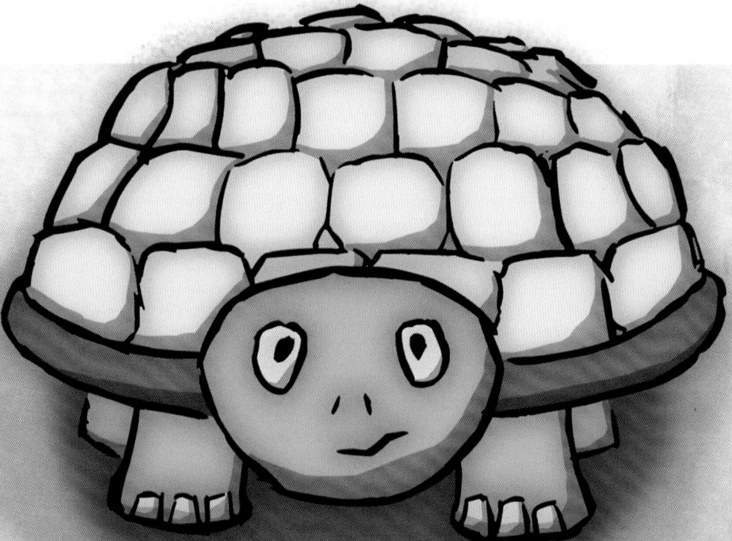

THERE'S NO "CONDESCENDING PRICK" IN "TEAM"

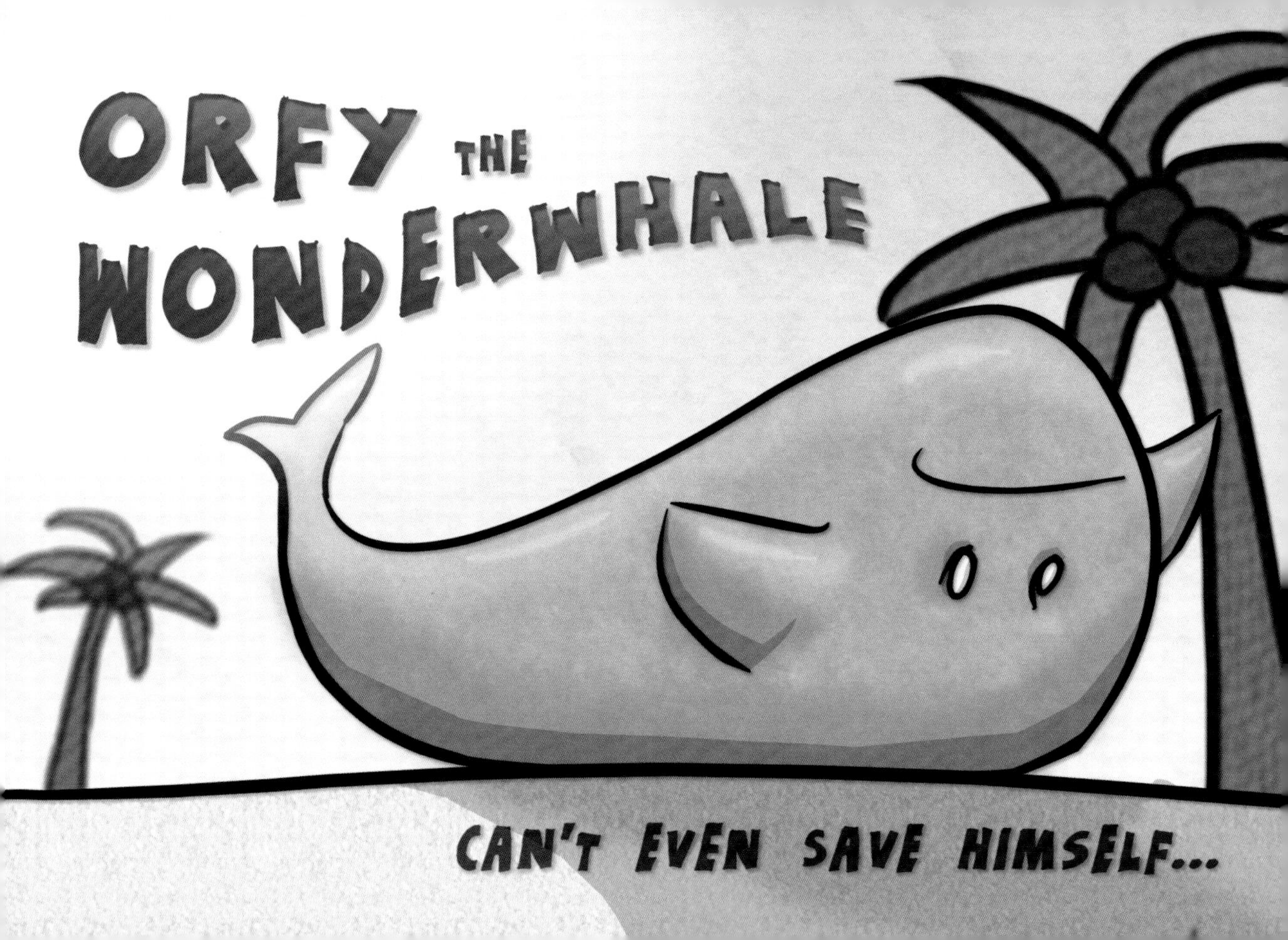
ORFY THE
WONDERWHALE
CAN'T EVEN SAVE HIMSELF...

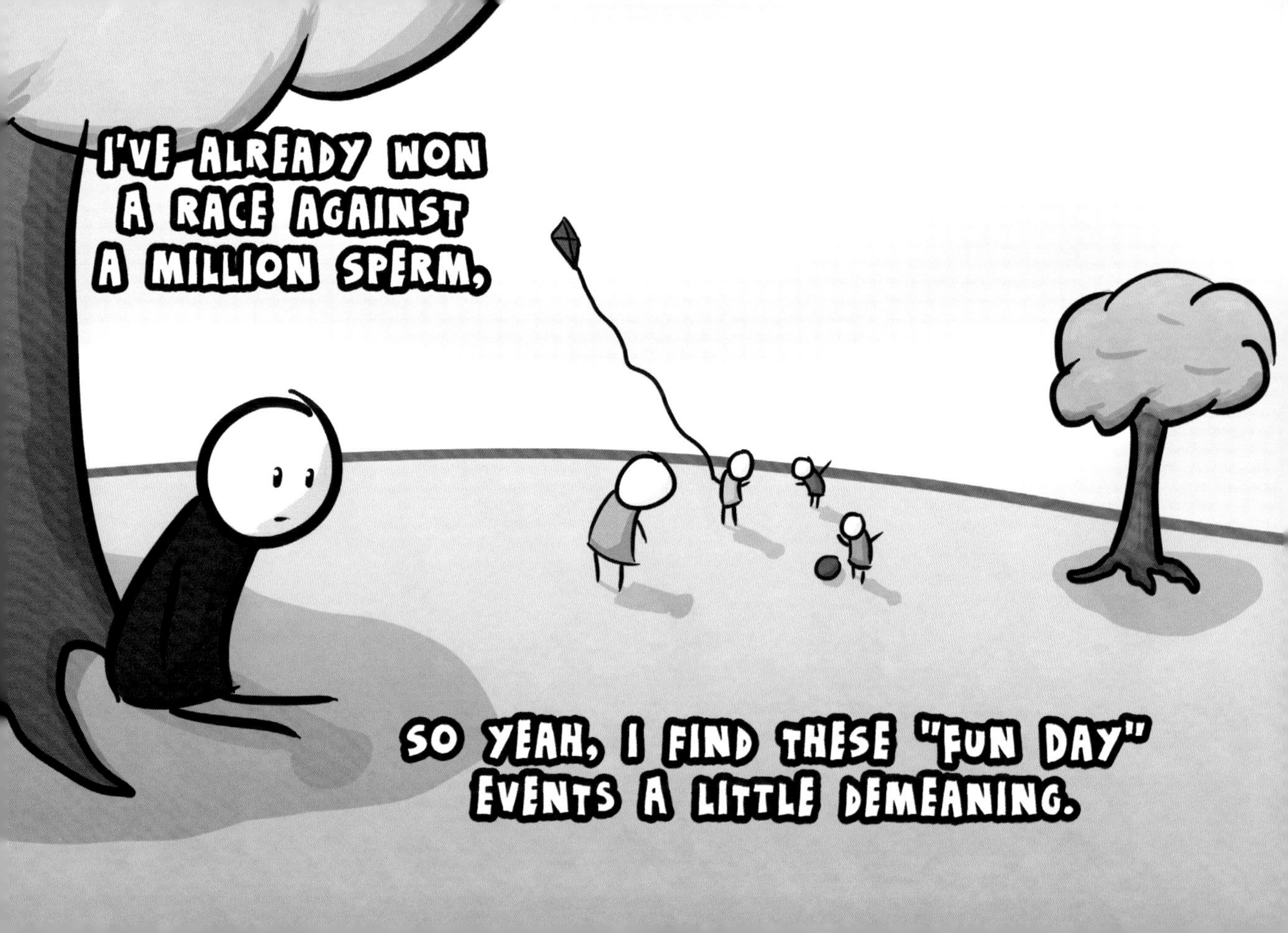
I'VE ALREADY WON A RACE AGAINST A MILLION SPERM,
SO YEAH, I FIND THESE "FUN DAY" EVENTS A LITTLE DEMEANING.

INTERMISSION

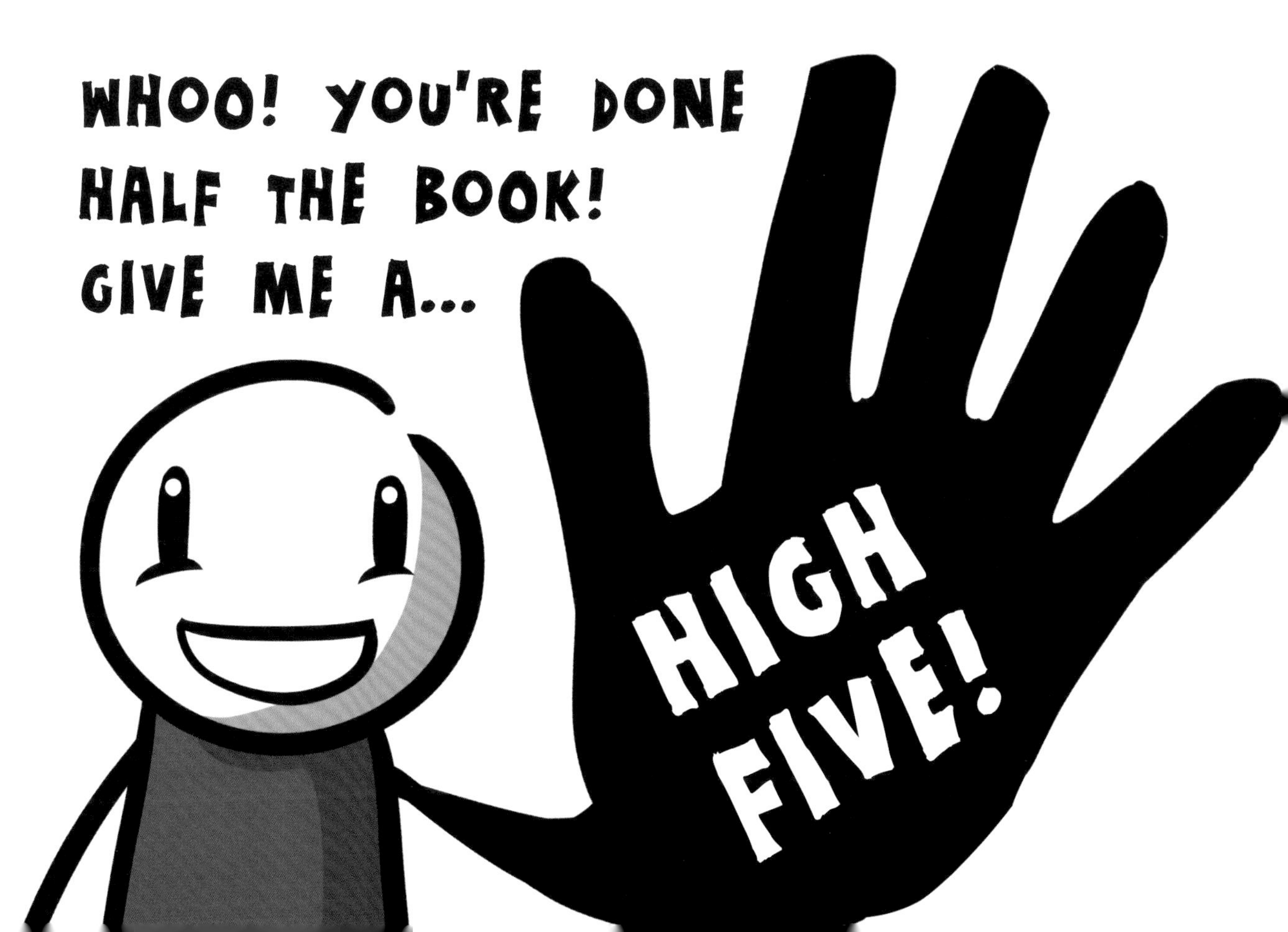
WHOO! YOU'RE DONE HALF THE BOOK! GIVE ME A...
HIGH FIVE!

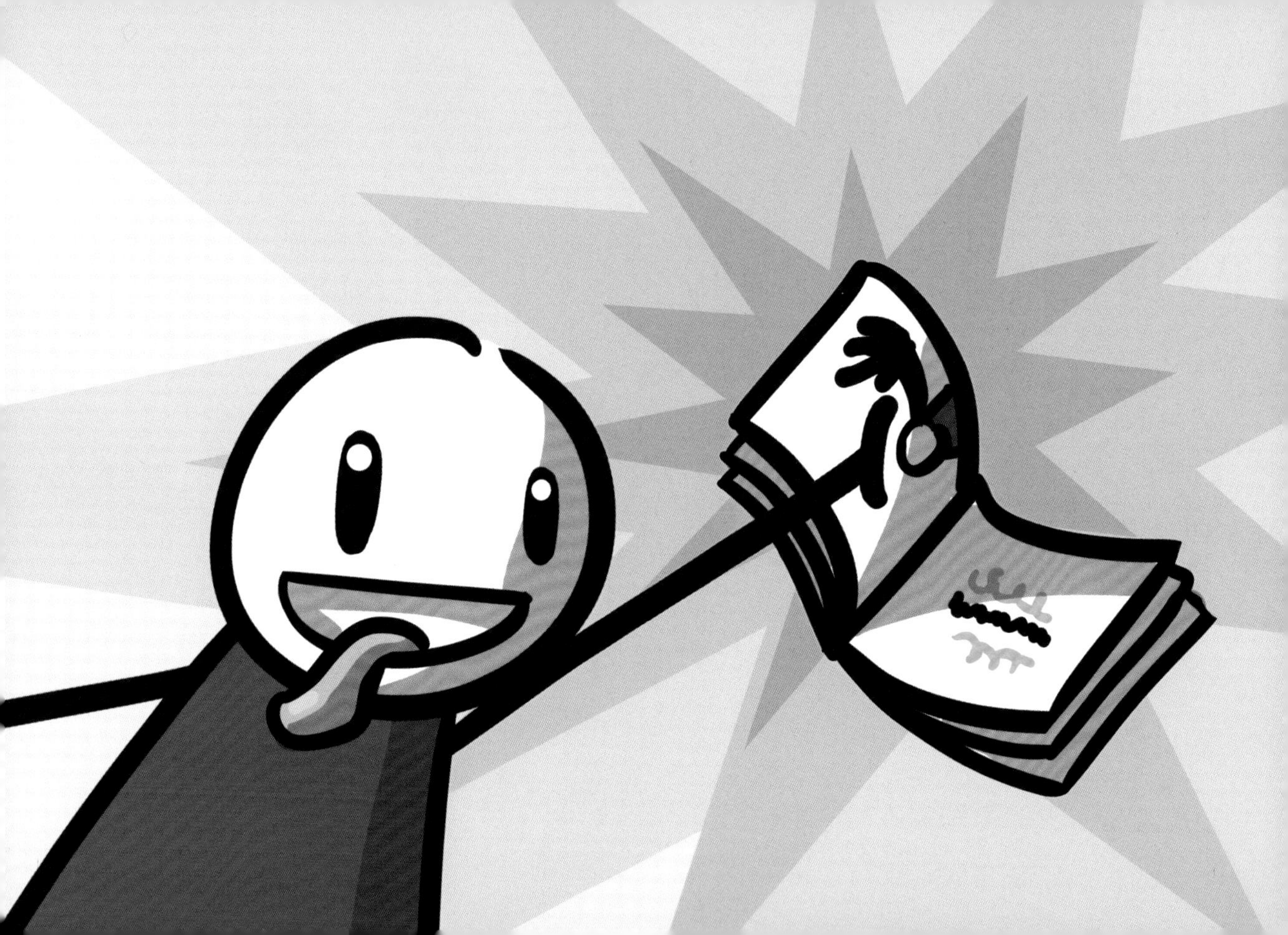

TRY TO SELL DRUGS TO YOUR PAROLE OFFICER. * PICK YOUR TEETH WITH A HARPOON GUN. * GO ON A GAMBLING SPREE WITH YOUR STUDENT LOAN. * COCKROACH FIGHTS. * DECLARE WAR ON THE PLANET OF THE KNIFE PEOPLE. * PICK A FIGHT WITH A VENDING MACHINE. * BELIEVE EVERYTHING YOU SEE ON SHARK WEEK. * TRY TO MAKE A PRISON SHIV OUT OF BEDSHEETS AND AN ESCAPE ROPE OUT OF A SCREWDRIVER.

BAD IDEA #1201:
HIGH-FIVE A BOOK BECAUSE AN IMAGINARY MAN TOLD YOU TO.

ENCASE A MIME IN A BOX OF AIRTIGHT GLASS. * ATLANTIS AIRLINES. * SNAKES ON A PLANE 2: PLANES ON A SNAKE. * SKIP THE INSTRUCTIONS. * TAKE A BATH WITH YOUR TOASTER. * SWAP YOUR LUNGS OUT WITH WHOOPEE CUSHIONS. * DRUNKEN HOUSE RENOVATIONS. * SNORT ANTHRAX. * SLIDE-TACKLE SOMEONE ON GRAVEL. * REPLACE THE "BREAK IN CASE OF EMERGENCY" GLASS WITH SOMETHING BULLETPROOF.

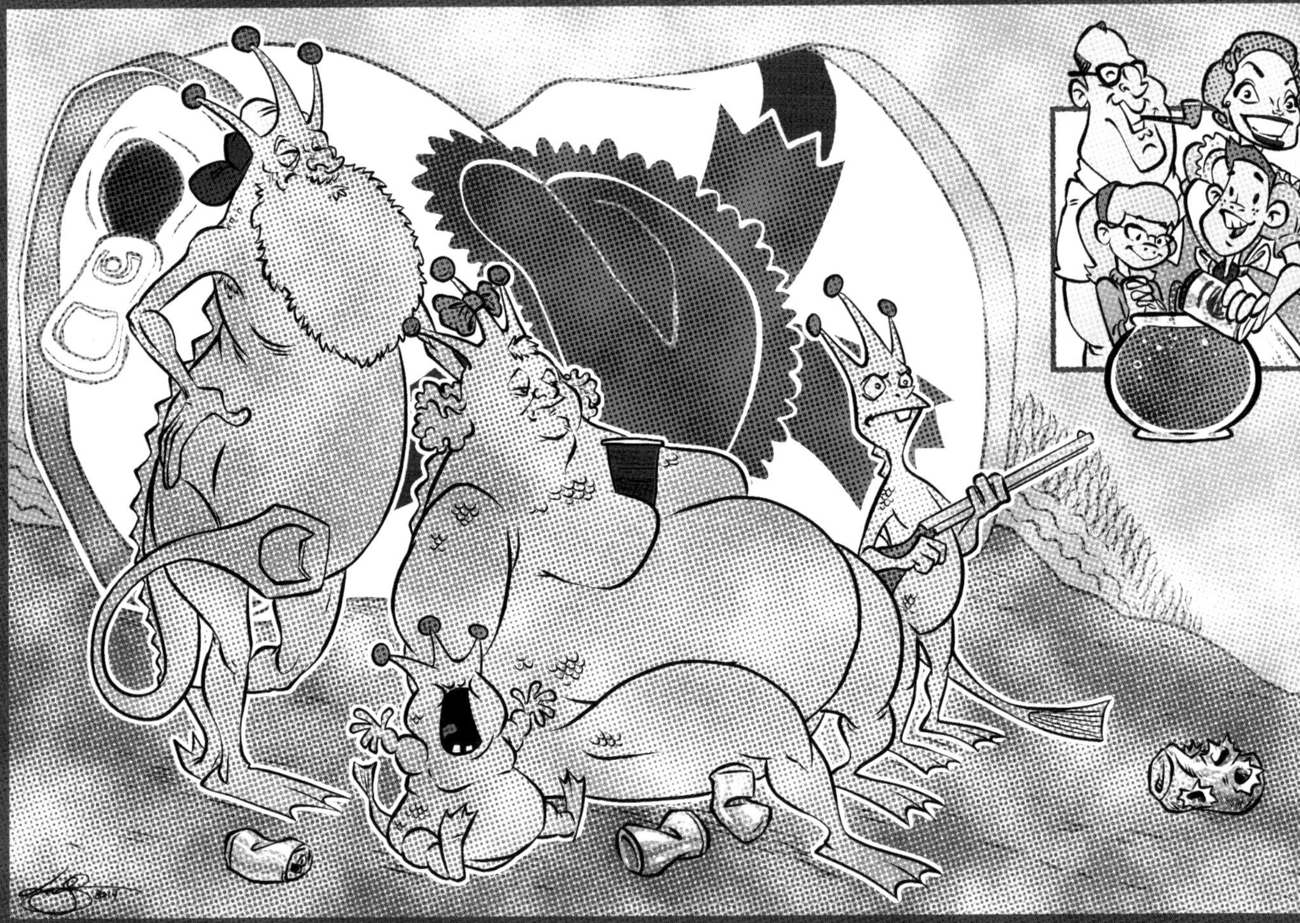

TAKE BIG SPOON IN A PORCUPINE CUDDLE. * MAKE A SEQUEL. * WATCH A SEQUEL. * ADMIT TO A HIPSTER THAT YOU LIKED THE NORTH AMERICAN VERSION. * THROW AWAY ALL THOSE RAZOR-SHARP BOOMERANGS NOBODY WANTED. * CACTUS PANTS. * PUT HEDGEHOGS IN THE BALL PIT. * SEND YOUR BROWSER HISTORY TO THE NSA. * PREPARE YOUR FIRST DATE NIGHT MEAL FROM THE COOKBOOK OF VILE DARKNESS.

BAD IDEA #1248: RAISE A FAMILY OF SEA MONKEYS IN BEER.

TYRRANODENTISTRY. * ADVERTISE A SUPERVILLAIN CONVENTION ON TWITTER. #NOSUPERHEROESPLEASE #KEEPDEATHRAYSATHOME. * BOOK A NICE FAMILY REUNION BARBEQUE IN A TENTED CHALET ON THE SLOPES OF SUPERWOLF MOUNTAIN. * ASK THE APOTHECARY FOR A POTION OF "MISSED ERECTION" INSTEAD OF "MISDIRECTION." * HOST A "SWIM WITH THE GREAT WHITE SHARKS"-THEMED CHILDREN'S BIRTHDAY PARTY

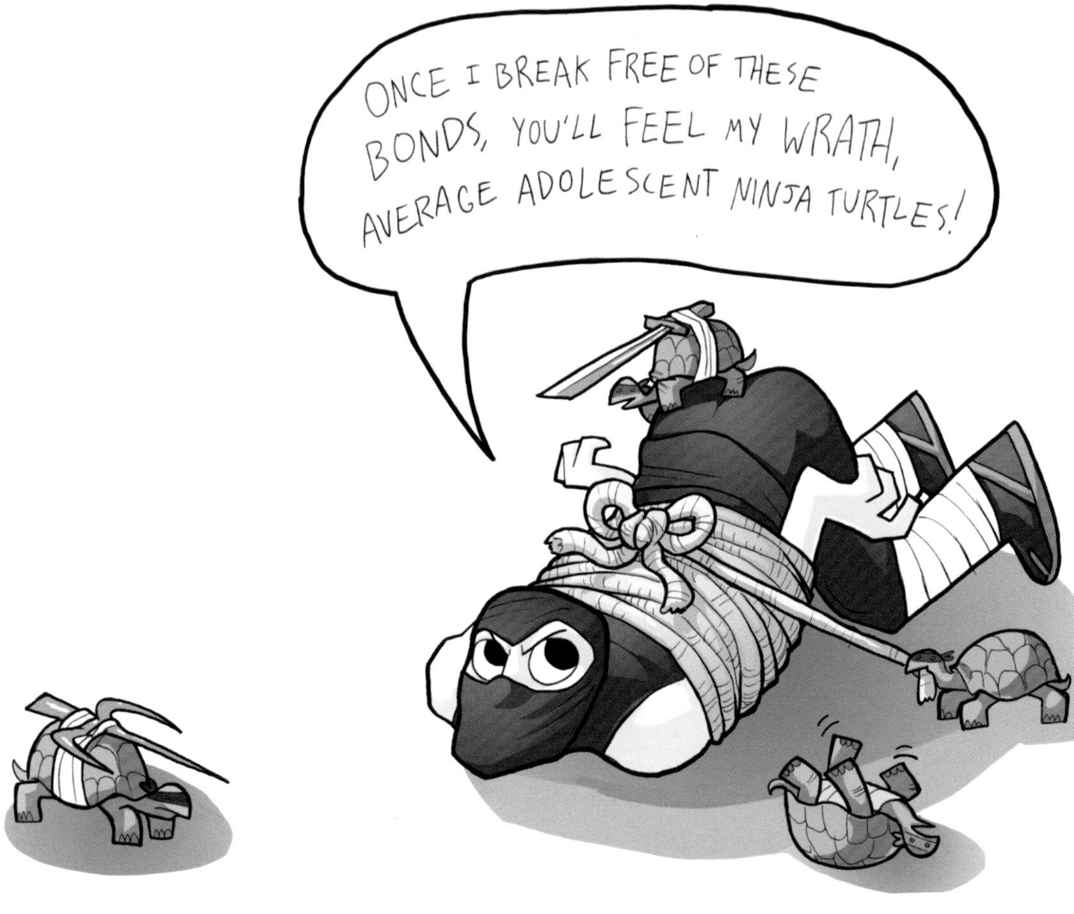
ONCE I BREAK FREE OF THESE BONDS, YOU'LL FEEL MY WRATH, AVERAGE ADOLESCENT NINJA TURTLES!

INVENT THE FIRST ONE-WAY TIME MACHINE. * BOOK THE ULTIMATE FAMILY VACATION GETAWAY IN SUNNY GUANTANAMO BAY. * TITANIC 2: THIS TIME IT'S **TITANICKER.** * GIVE STEVE BUSCEMI THE LEAD IN A FILM MADE ENTIRELY OF CLOSE-UPS. * GENETICALLY ENGINEER A LASER-SHOOTING HONEY BADGER AND SET HIM LOOSE IN A NURSING HOME. * SPEND YOUR LOTTERY WINNINGS ON LOTTERY TICKETS.

BAD IDEA #1355: USE NON-GENETICALLY MUTATED TURTLES TO BATTLE YOUR LOCAL CRIME SYNDICATE.

GIRAFFE GUILLOTINES. * BABY VS. GLACIER: THE ULTIMATE SHOWDOWN. * TELL A METHOD ACTOR TO PLAY DEAD. * CONCOCT A SERUM THAT MAKES YOU GROW TINY WHEN ENRAGED. * JELLY-WRESTLE WITH JELLYFISH. * CAGE-DIVE WITH THE SHARK INSIDE THE CAGE. * STOW AWAY UNDER THE ENGINE OF A ROCKET SHIP. * GIVE YOU UP, LET YOU DOWN, RUN AROUND AND DESERT YOU. * LET YOUR DOG WALK YOU.

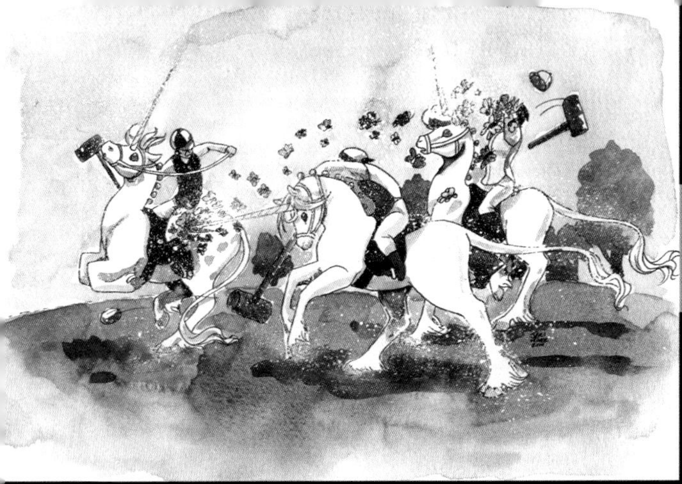

BREED A WILD POPULATION OF ZOMBIE MANATEES AND EXPECT ANYONE TO NOTICE. * SET THE SONG OF TIME TO PLAY ON REPEAT. * NUCLEAR WARHEAD BUMPER CARS. * LIVE LIFE THROUGH A SCREEN, FILTERING OUT THE BLEMISH WE ONCE CALLED BEAUTY.

BAD IDEA #1431: BRING A KNIFE TO A LASER-WHIP FIGHT.

COSPLAY AS LINK FROM ZELDA: HARPSICHORD OF TIME. * BLINDLY FOLLOW A BEAGLE. * ASK A BASEBALL TEAM WHO'S ON FIRST. * TELL YOUR DOG TO "GET THE BUNNY." UNLESS YOU REALLY WANT A DEAD BUNNY. * SKYDIVE WITHOUT A PARACHUTE.

DESIGN A VIDEO GAME WHERE CHILDREN CAPTURE WILD ANIMALS AND FORCE THEM INTO RING FIGHTS FOR MONEY. * DESIGN FELT FURNITURE PADS FOR PEG LEGS. * DESIGN A STEREOTYPING TUTOR TO HELP PEOPLE INCREASE THEIR SLURS PER MINUTE.

BAD IDEA #1419: EXTREME UNICORN POLO.

TRY TO GET AN "A" ON YOUR HEPATITIS TEST. * EAT AT A RESTAURANT CALLED MOM'S. * INSTALL A "CLAP ON" LIGHT SWITCH SYSTEM IN YOUR THEATER HALL. * BRIBE A MONGOLIAN WARLORD WITH A LIFETIME SUPPLY OF CARICATURE PORTRAITS.

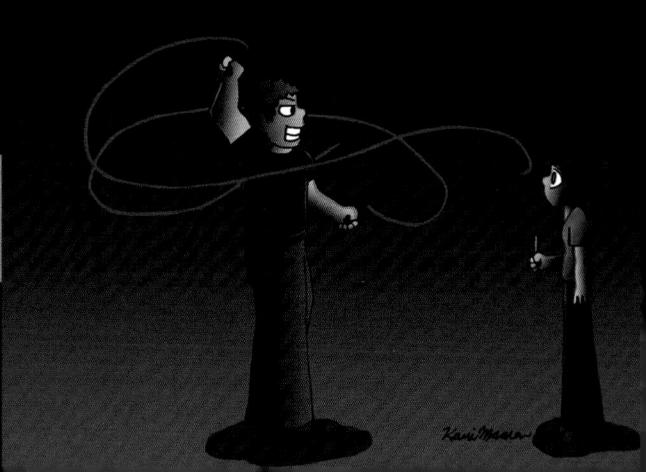

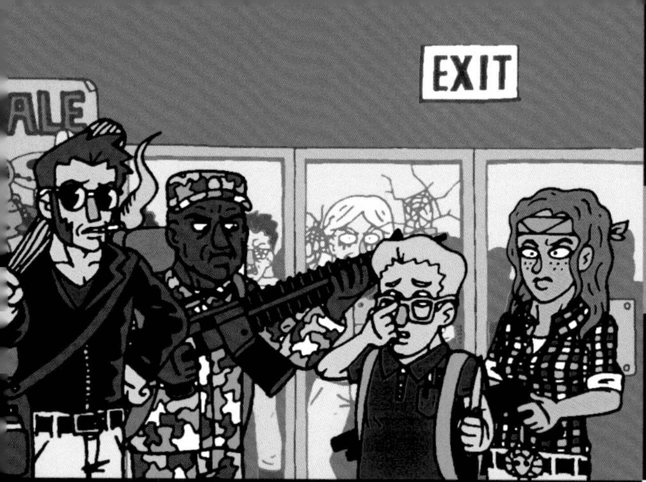
EXIT

GO PARASAILING WITH A FISHING NET. * FALL DOWN THE "UP" ESCALATOR. * ADD GANON TO LINKED IN. * TRUST A BASSET HOUND TO BE YOUR SNOOZE ALARM. * HIGH-FIVE FREDDY KRUEGER. * TORTOISE RACING. * GET CHANGED IN A PHONE BOOTH.

BAD IDEA #1488: EQUIP YOUR WORLD-DOMINATING CAT ARMY WITH LASER SIGHTS.

BET THE FARM. * FRACK. UNLESS YOU'RE A CYLON. AND THEN WE HAVE BIGGER PROBLEMS. * GET BUCK NAKED, SMEAR YOURSELF IN HONEY, AND THEN CHALLENGE A GRIZZLY BEAR FOR ITS FRESHLY CAUGHT SALMON. * GO FOR A SWIM IN QUICKSAND.

USE A LIT MATCH TO CHECK THE FUEL LEVEL IN YOUR GAS TANK. * USE A SIX-FOOT-TALL CACTUS AS A TACKLE DUMMY. * CREATE LINE OF DEHYDRATED SNACKS FOR SCUBA DIVERS. * FRAME A PAINTING FOR MURDER AND HAVE IT HANGED. * SUB-ATOMIC WEDGIES.

BAD IDEA #1461: BE THE BRAIN OF THE GROUP DURING A ZOMBIE APOCALYPSE.

VISIT WIKIPEDIA JUST BEFORE BEDTIME. * CHALLENGE A NINJA TO HIDE AND SEEK. * BUTTER TOAST ON BOTH SIDES AND THEN THROW IT IN THE AIR. * GIVE CRASH TEST DUMMIES A BREAK BY TAKING THEIR PLACE. * RIDE A BULL TO A RED CARPET EVENT.

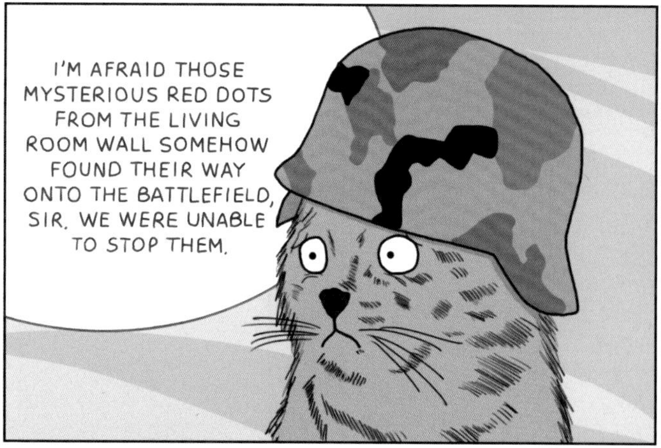
I'M AFRAID THOSE MYSTERIOUS RED DOTS FROM THE LIVING ROOM WALL SOMEHOW FOUND THEIR WAY ONTO THE BATTLEFIELD, SIR. WE WERE UNABLE TO STOP THEM.

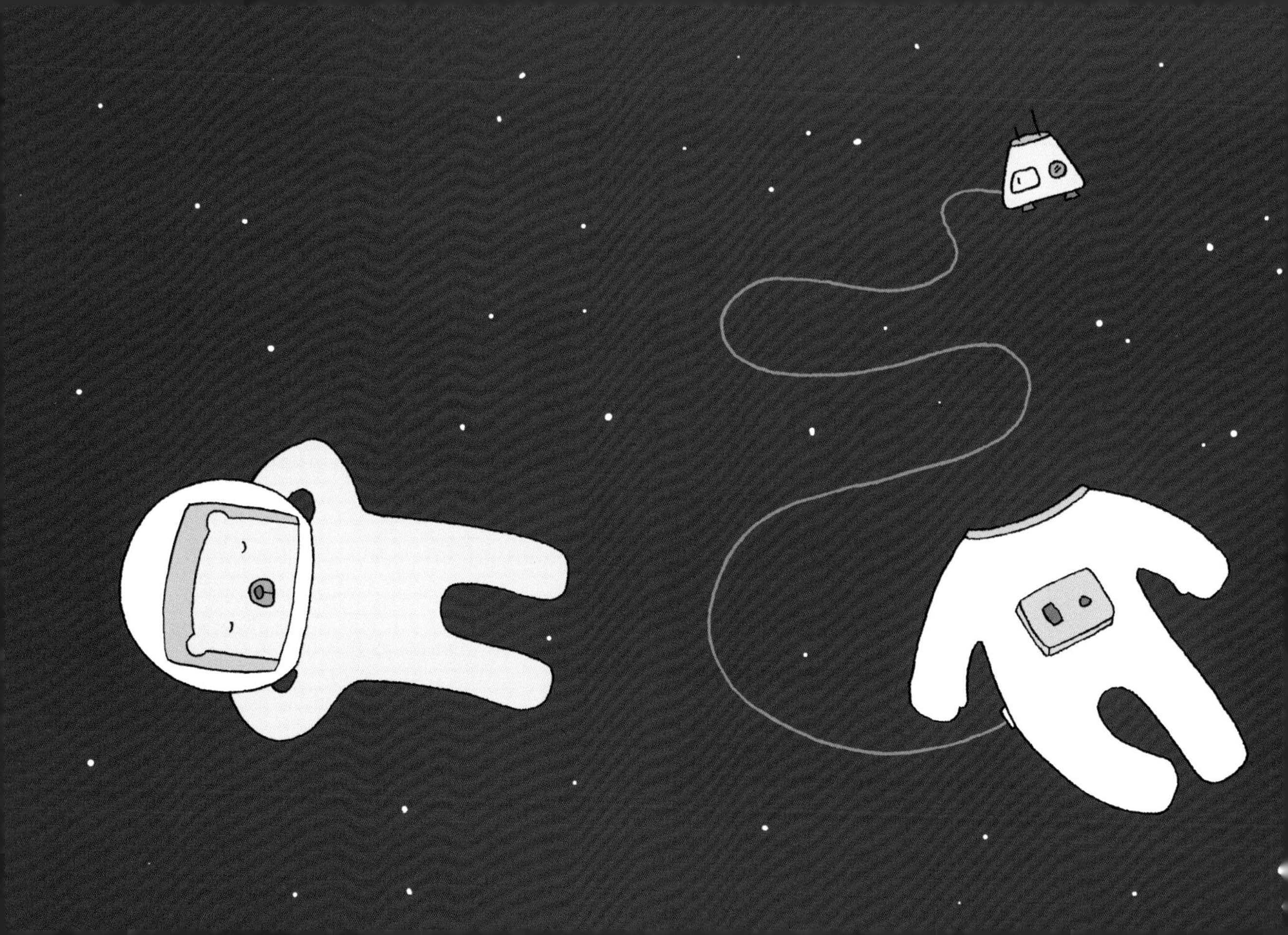

CHALLENGE PUMMELBOT 3000 TO A BOXING MATCH. * DESIGN AN EMOTICON FOR POWER WORD: KILL. * TRY TO BECOME THE POPE BY EATING HIM AND ABSORBING HIS POWERS. * MARKET COOKBOOKS AS HORROR STORIES FOR VEGETABLES. * ACCEPT A FRUIT DRINK LADLED FROM A METAL TUB WHILE VISITING A LARGE RELIGIOUS COMMUNE. * PLAY "I SPY" TO KILL TIME ON YOUR 100-YEAR SPACE VOYAGE.

BAD IDEA #1571:
SKINNY-DIP IN OUTER SPACE.

GIVE OUT NON-BIODEGRADABLE PLASTIC BAGS AT EVERY SUPERMARKET IN NORTH AMERICA. * USE THE CHEESE GRATER ON YOUR FOOT CALLUSES BEFORE MAKE-YOUR-OWN-PIZZA NIGHT. * KEEP UP WITH MODERN TECHNOLOGIES BY ATTEMPTING A WIRELESS BUNGEE JUMP. * LET YOUR FINANCIAL ADVISOR USE TAROT TO DETERMINE YOUR MORTGAGE RATE. * ASK THE GREAT VINCENT VAN GOGH TO LEND YOU AN EAR

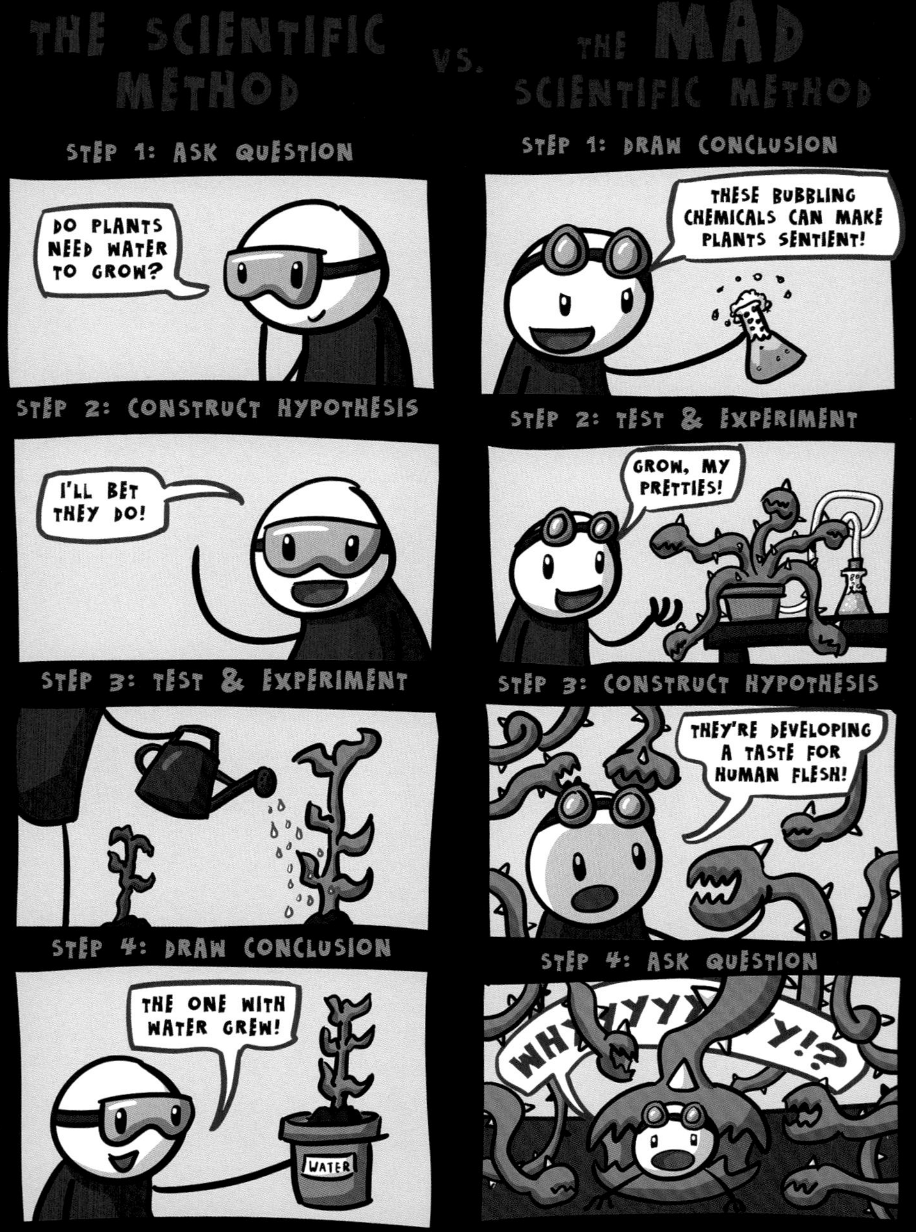
THE SCIENTIFIC METHOD
VS.
THE MAD SCIENTIFIC METHOD
STEP 1: ASK QUESTION
DO PLANTS NEED WATER TO GROW?
STEP 2: CONSTRUCT HYPOTHESIS
I'LL BET THEY DO!
STEP 3: TEST & EXPERIMENT
STEP 4: DRAW CONCLUSION
THE ONE WITH WATER GREW!
WATER
STEP 1: DRAW CONCLUSION
THESE BUBBLING CHEMICALS CAN MAKE PLANTS SENTIENT!
STEP 2: TEST & EXPERIMENT
GROW, MY PRETTIES!
STEP 3: CONSTRUCT HYPOTHESIS
THEY'RE DEVELOPING A TASTE FOR HUMAN FLESH!
STEP 4: ASK QUESTION
WHYYYYYYY?!

A DEFENSE OF TEDDY BEARS

THE WORLD DOESN'T GET ANY LESS SCARY AS WE GROW UP, BUT SOMEHOW WE'RE ASKED TO SHED THE ICONS OF OUR CHILDHOOD SO WE CAN BECOME BIG PEOPLE.

TO HELL WITH THAT.

THERE'S SOME IMPOSSIBLE PROPERTY IN THEIR STUFFING WHICH SOAKS UP ALL OF OUR ANGER AND FEAR AND UNCERTAINTY.

WE TRY TO REPLACE THEM WITH OTHER PEOPLE, BUT OTHER PEOPLE ARE FILLED WITH THE SAME SELFISH GOO AS WE ARE, WITH NO ROOM LEFT TO STORE SOMEONE ELSE'S INSECURITY, EVEN FOR A LITTLE WHILE.

WHATEVER ATTIC HE'S BEEN SITTING IN FOR HOWEVER LONG, HE'LL LOVE YOU JUST AS MUCH AS THE DAY YOU LEFT HIM THERE. HE'LL ACCEPT YOUR ABUSE AND YOUR TEARS AND YOUR SELFISH LOVE, LIKE HE ALWAYS HAS.

HE'LL REMIND YOU HOW TO BE BRAVE.

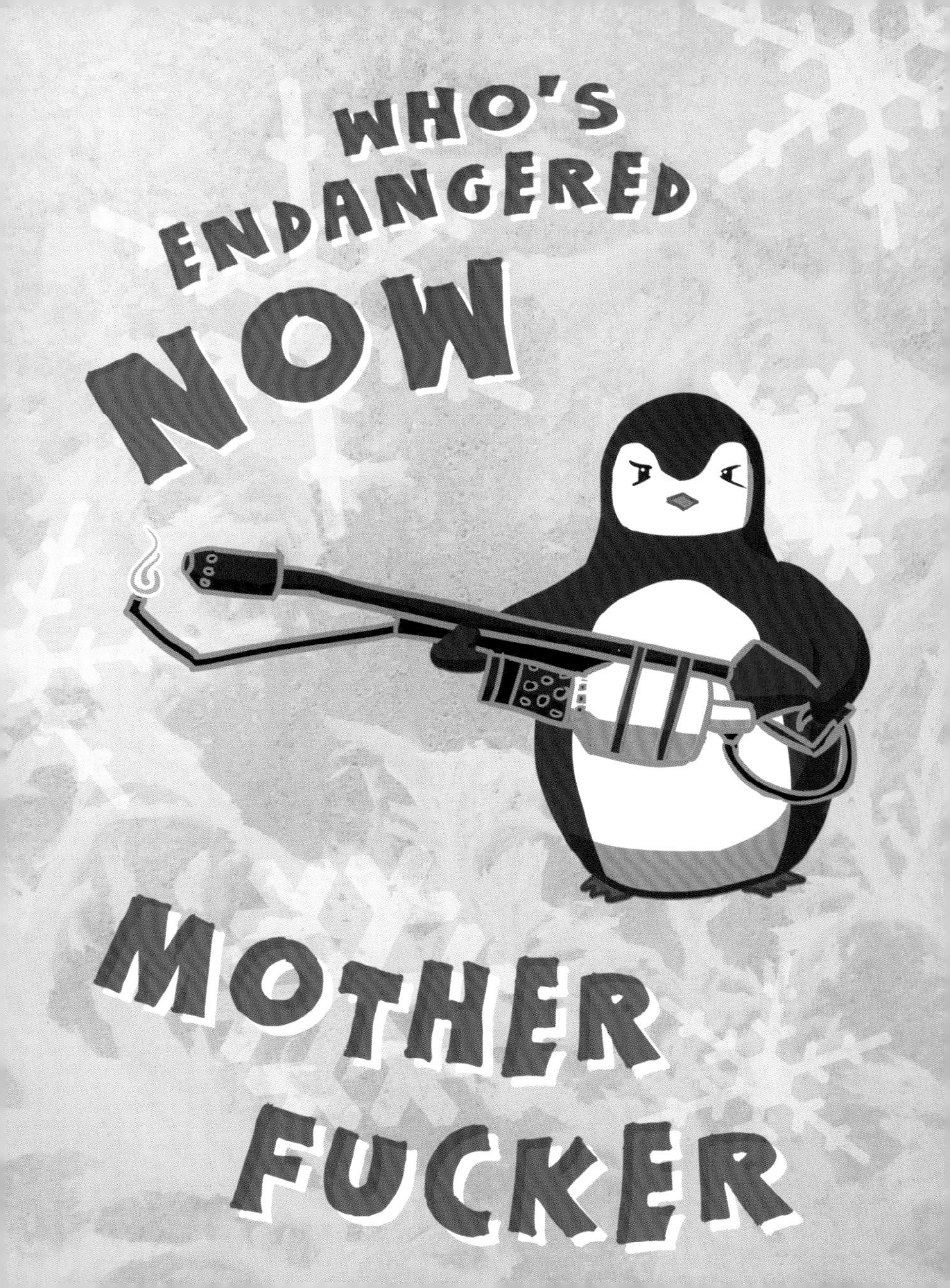
WHO'S
ENDANGERED
NOW
MOTHER
FUCKER

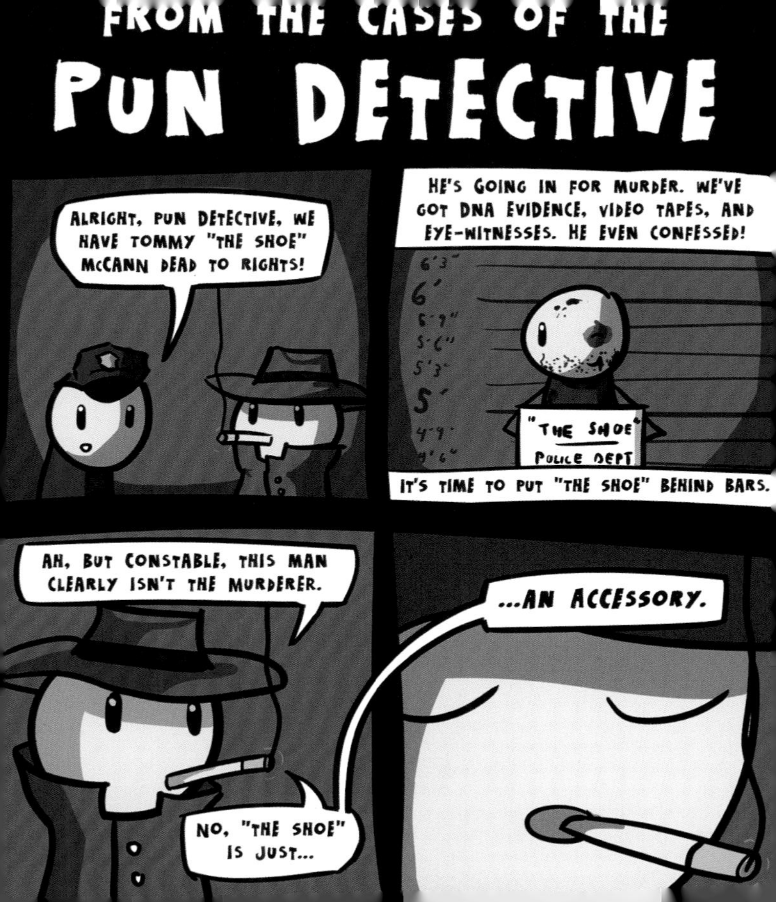
FROM THE CASES OF THE
PUN DETECTIVE
ALRIGHT, PUN DETECTIVE, WE HAVE TOMMY "THE SHOE" McCANN DEAD TO RIGHTS!
HE'S GOING IN FOR MURDER. WE'VE GOT DNA EVIDENCE, VIDEO TAPES, AND EYE-WITNESSES. HE EVEN CONFESSED!
"THE SHOE"
POLICE DEPT
IT'S TIME TO PUT "THE SHOE" BEHIND BARS.
AH, BUT CONSTABLE, THIS MAN CLEARLY ISN'T THE MURDERER.
NO, "THE SHOE" IS JUST...
...AN ACCESSORY.

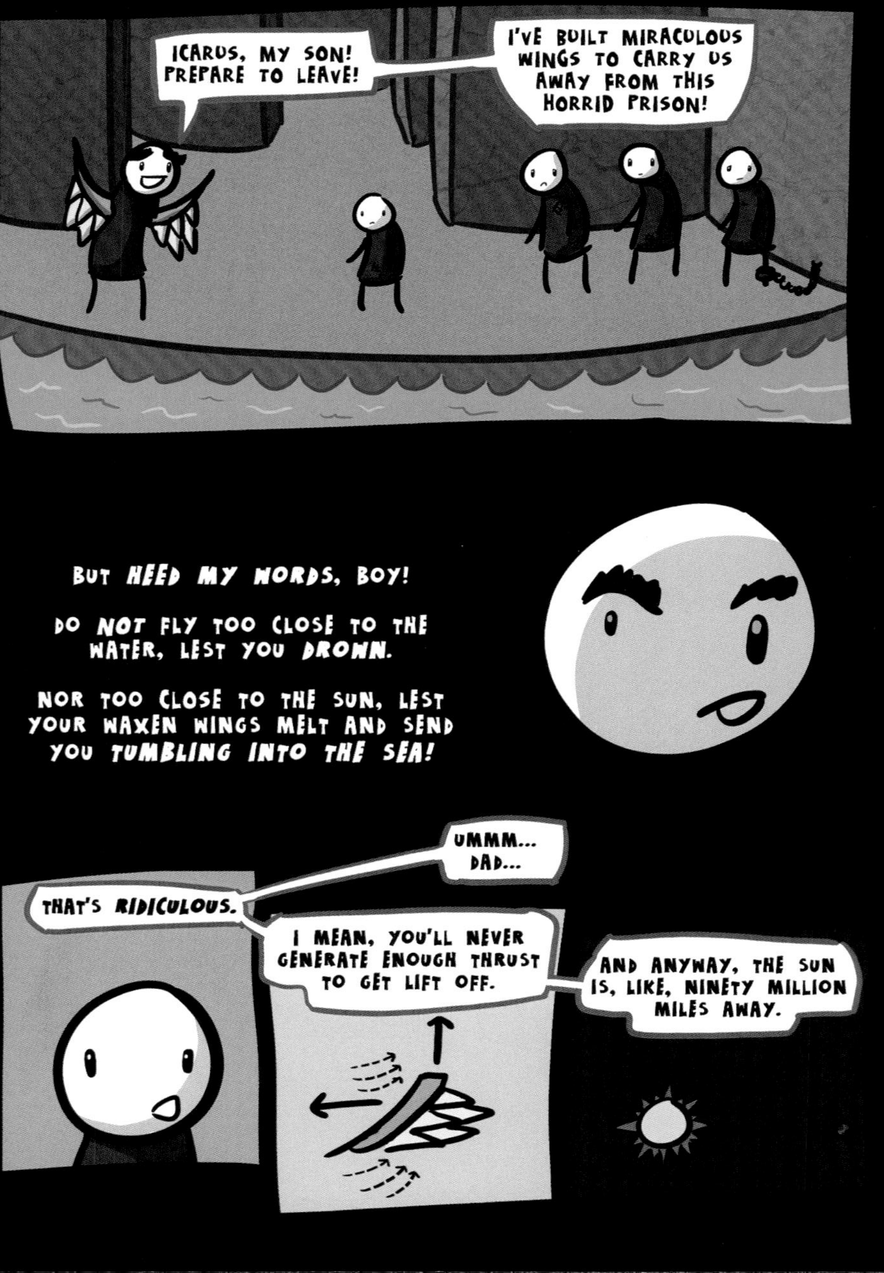

ICARUS, MY SON! PREPARE TO LEAVE!
I'VE BUILT MIRACULOUS WINGS TO CARRY US AWAY FROM THIS HORRID PRISON!
BUT HEED MY WORDS, BOY!
DO NOT FLY TOO CLOSE TO THE WATER, LEST YOU DROWN.
NOR TOO CLOSE TO THE SUN, LEST YOUR WAXEN WINGS MELT AND SEND YOU TUMBLING INTO THE SEA!
UMMM... DAD...
THAT'S RIDICULOUS.
I MEAN, YOU'LL NEVER GENERATE ENOUGH THRUST TO GET LIFT OFF.
AND ANYWAY, THE SUN IS, LIKE, NINETY MILLION MILES AWAY.

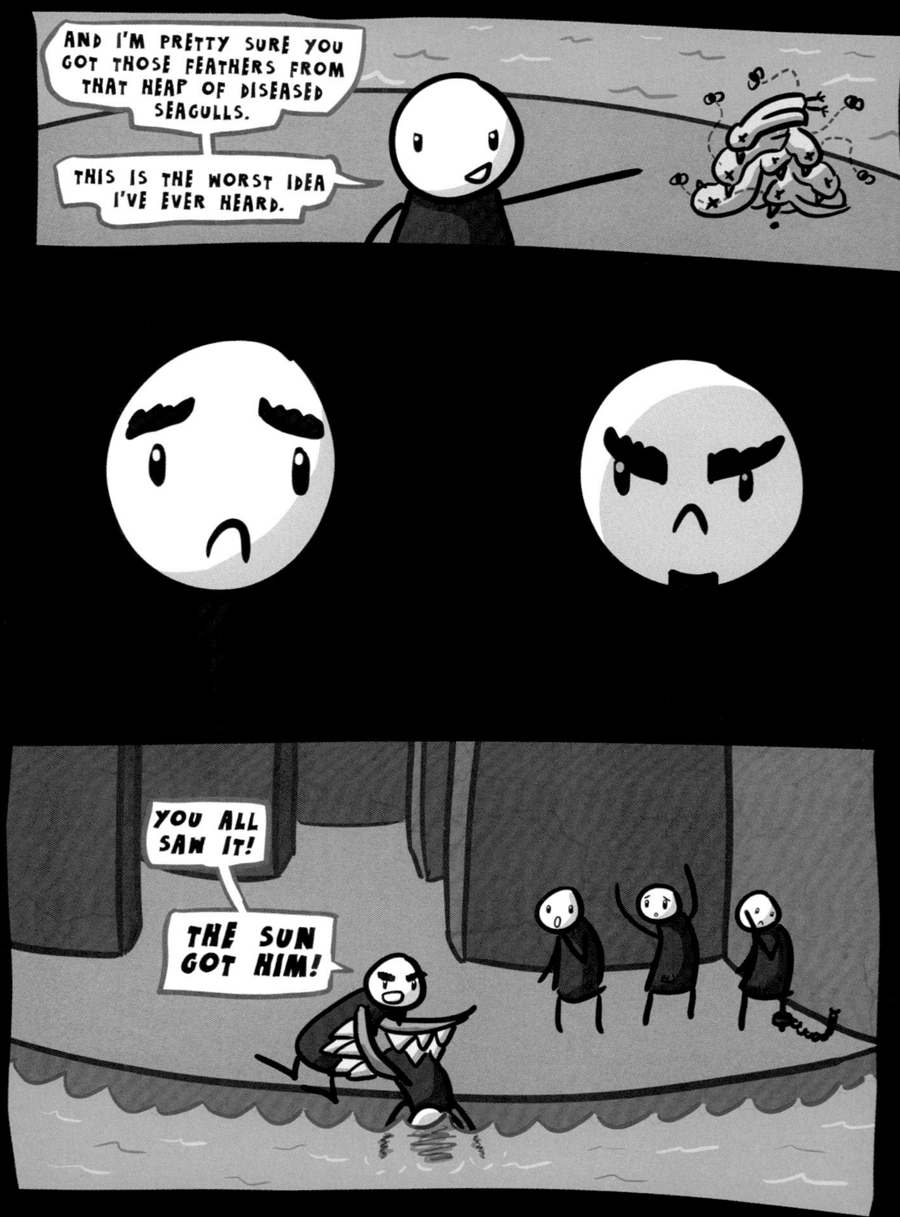
AND I'M PRETTY SURE YOU GOT THOSE FEATHERS FROM THAT HEAP OF DISEASED SEAGULLS.
THIS IS THE WORST IDEA I'VE EVER HEARD.
YOU ALL SAW IT!
THE SUN GOT HIM!

I FIGURE THAT IF CATHOLICS CAN EAT THE BODY OF CHRIST WITHOUT BEING CANNIBALS,

THEN I CAN EAT BACON AND STILL BE VEGETARIAN. AFTER ALL, JESUS AND BACON AREN'T SO MUCH MEAT AS THEY ARE MIRACLES.

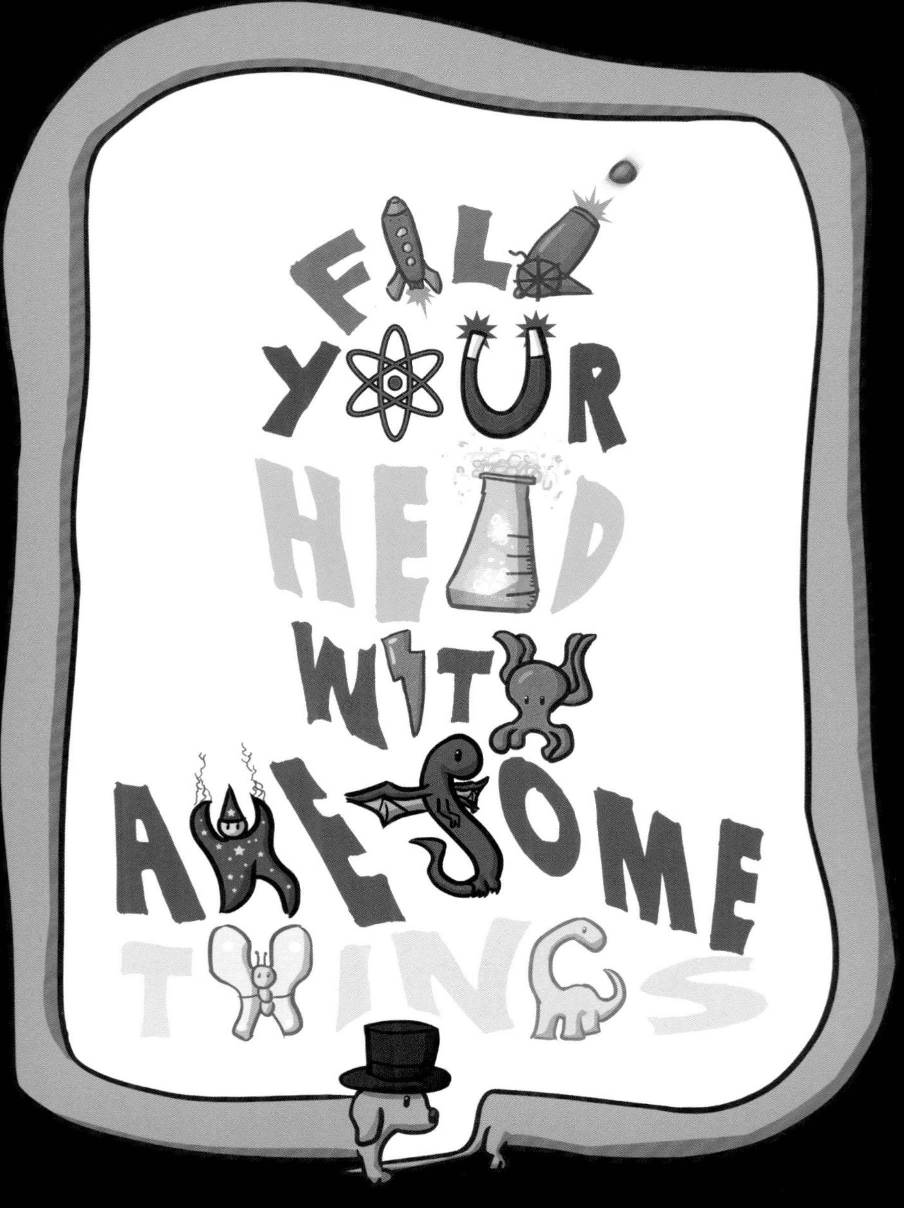
FILL YOUR HEAD WITH AWESOME THINGS

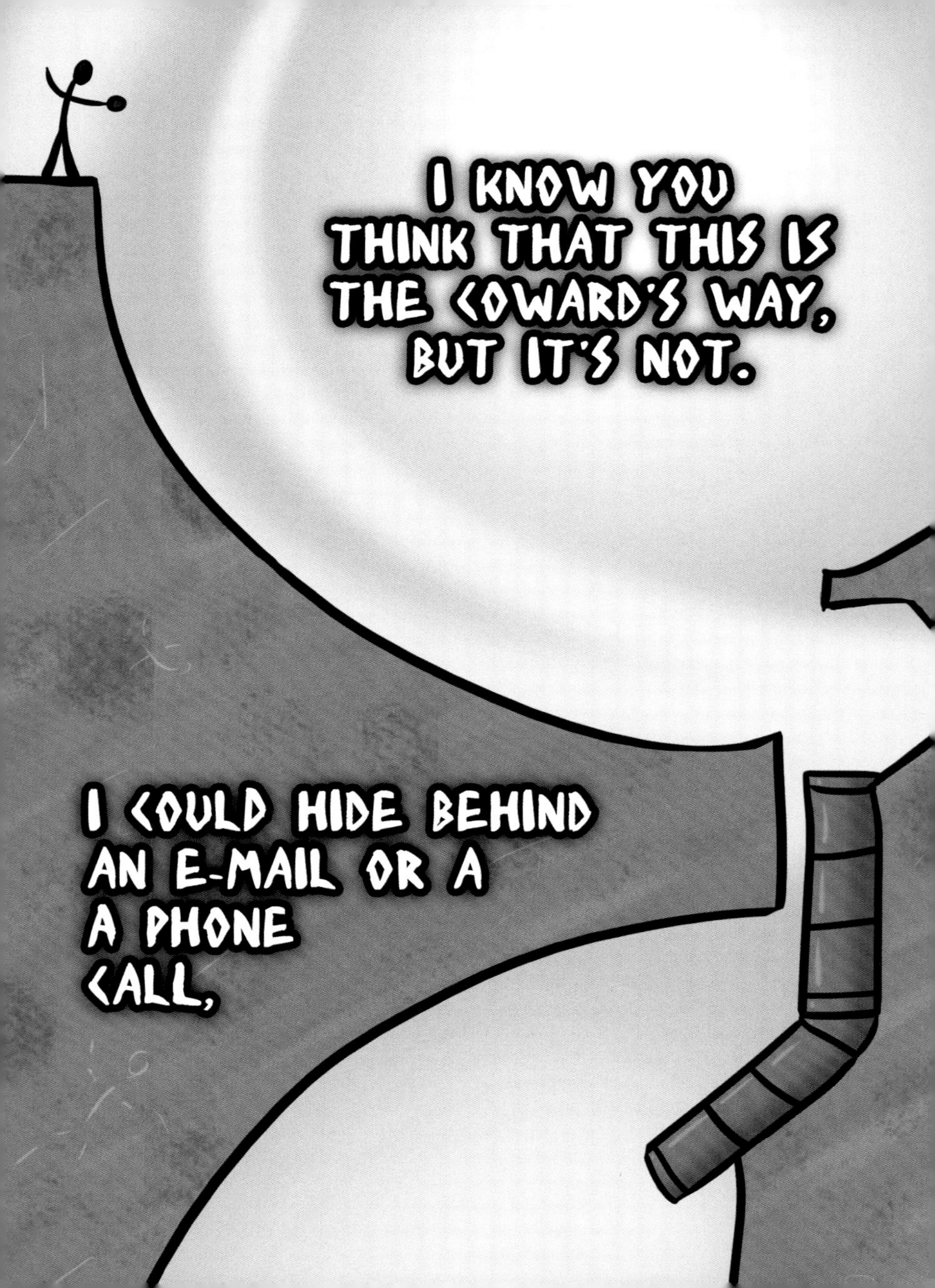
I KNOW YOU
THINK THAT THIS IS
THE COWARD'S WAY,
BUT IT'S NOT.
I COULD HIDE BEHIND
AN E-MAIL OR A
A PHONE
CALL,

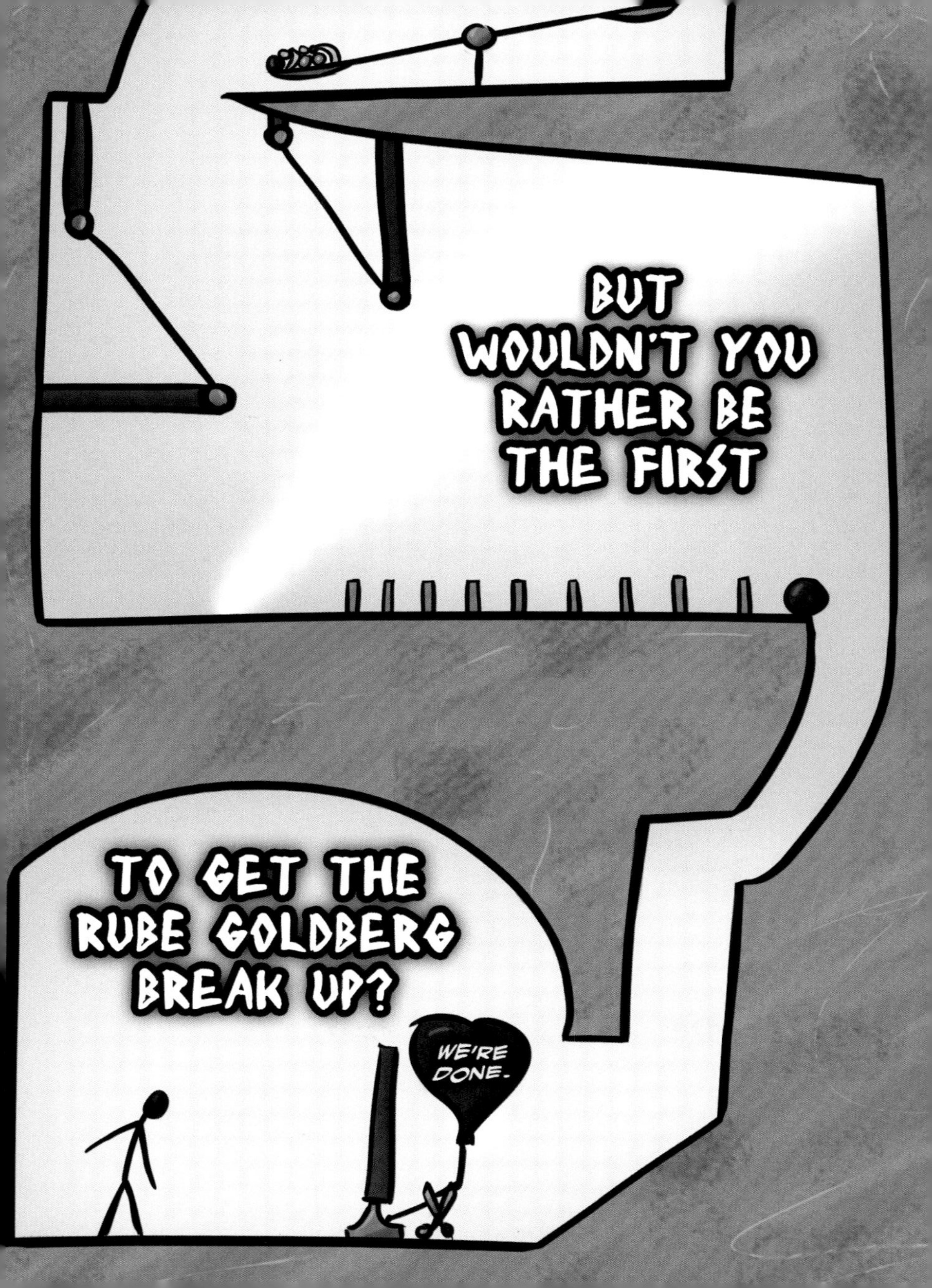
BUT WOULDN'T YOU RATHER BE THE FIRST
TO GET THE RUBE GOLDBERG BREAK UP?
WE'RE DONE.

AT THIS POINT, THERE'S NOTHING YOU COULD SAY THAT WOULD MAKE ME LOVE YOU MORE...

...WITH THE POSSIBLE EXCEPTION OF "BOUNCY BALLS."

12 LEGITIMATELY LIFE-IMPROVING LESSONS YOU CAN LEARN FROM WATCHING DOGS

1. EAT MORE STUFF THAT MAKES YOU FEEL GOOD.
2. POOP FREQUENTLY.
3. GREET EVERYTHING.
4. PICK FIGHTS WITH SHOES AND PILLOWS.
5. SMELL THINGS THAT LOOK INTERESTING.
6. BE LESS SCARED OF TELEPHONES, VACUUMS, AND STRANGERS.
7. RUN OUTSIDE AND YELL MORE.
8. FORGET WHAT YOU WERE DOING AND NAP INSTEAD.
9. TAKE CARE OF YOUR GENITALS.
10. BE NICE TO NICE PEOPLE.
11. FART WITHOUT SHAME.
12. WORRY LESS ABOUT THINGS YOU CAN'T EAT OR PLAY WITH.

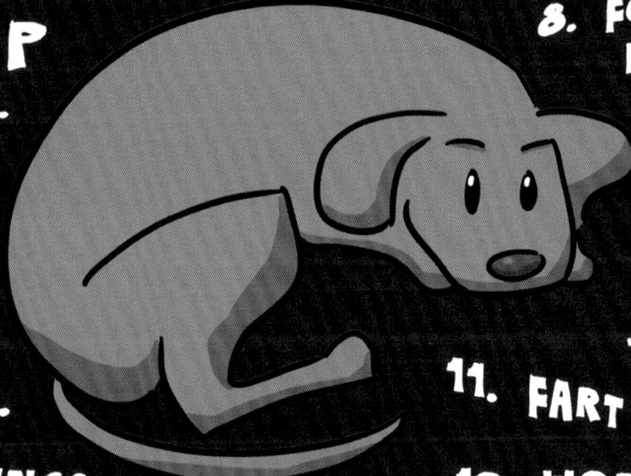

CALL ME WEAK-MINDED FOR
BELIEVING THE WORLD SITS ON
THE BACK OF A TURTLE,

AND THAT TURTLE IS SITTING
ON ANOTHER TURTLE,

AND IT'S TURTLES
ALL THE WAY DOWN,

BUT DON'T TELL ME THE
UNEXAMINED LIFE ISN'T
WORTH LIVING

AS I RIDE MY INFINITE
TURTLE FORTRESS
ACROSS THE SKY.

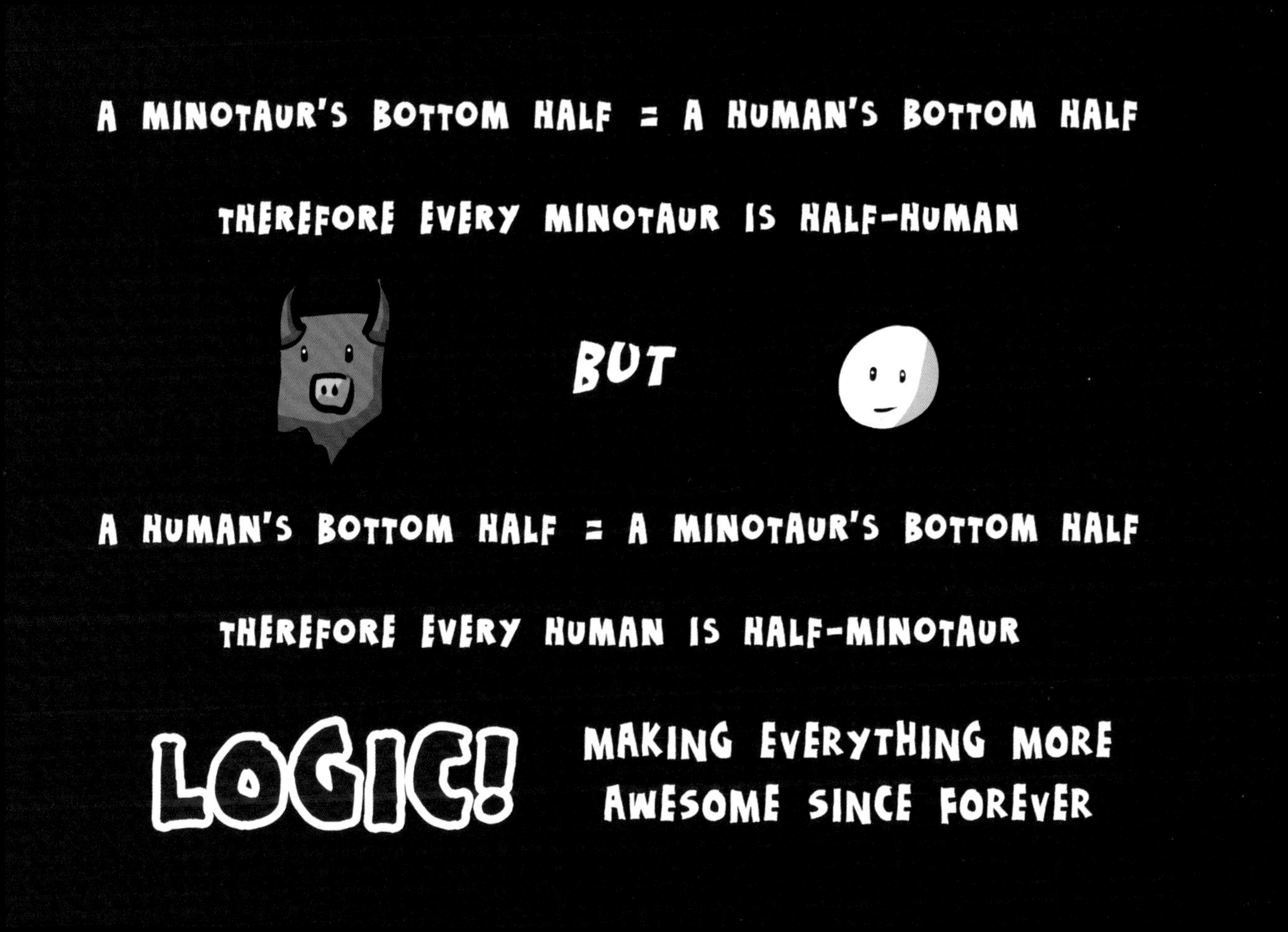
A MINOTAUR'S BOTTOM HALF = A HUMAN'S BOTTOM HALF
THEREFORE EVERY MINOTAUR IS HALF-HUMAN
BUT
A HUMAN'S BOTTOM HALF = A MINOTAUR'S BOTTOM HALF
THEREFORE EVERY HUMAN IS HALF-MINOTAUR
LOGIC!
MAKING EVERYTHING MORE AWESOME SINCE FOREVER

HOMER'S GUIDE
TO *PROPERLY* USING
THE WORD "EPIC"

THIS SANDWICH? WHY YES, IT *IS* KINDA
BIG AND TASTY. BUT HOW MANY
MYRMIDONS WOULD IT FEED? WILL ITS
SONGS ECHO FOR MILLENNIA TO COME?

PROBABLY NOT! SO, HAM ON RYE?

PRETTY SWELL, BUT NOT EPIC!

NOTICE HOW DIOMEDES LOOKS
DISTRACTED AS HE SPEARS APHRODITE?
THAT'S 'CAUSE HE'S IMAGINING
HOW HE'S ABOUT TO STAB ARES
SO HARD HE LITERALLY
RUNS HOME CRYING TO ZEUS.

CELEBRATING THAT YOU SHANKED
THE GOD OF LOVE BY
SHANKING THE GOD OF WAR?

✔ FUCKING EPIC!

IF IT DOESN'T END IN A GOD BLEEDING OR A THOUSAND DEAD
TROJANS POUNDING ON THE GATES OF HADES, DON'T SAY "EPIC."

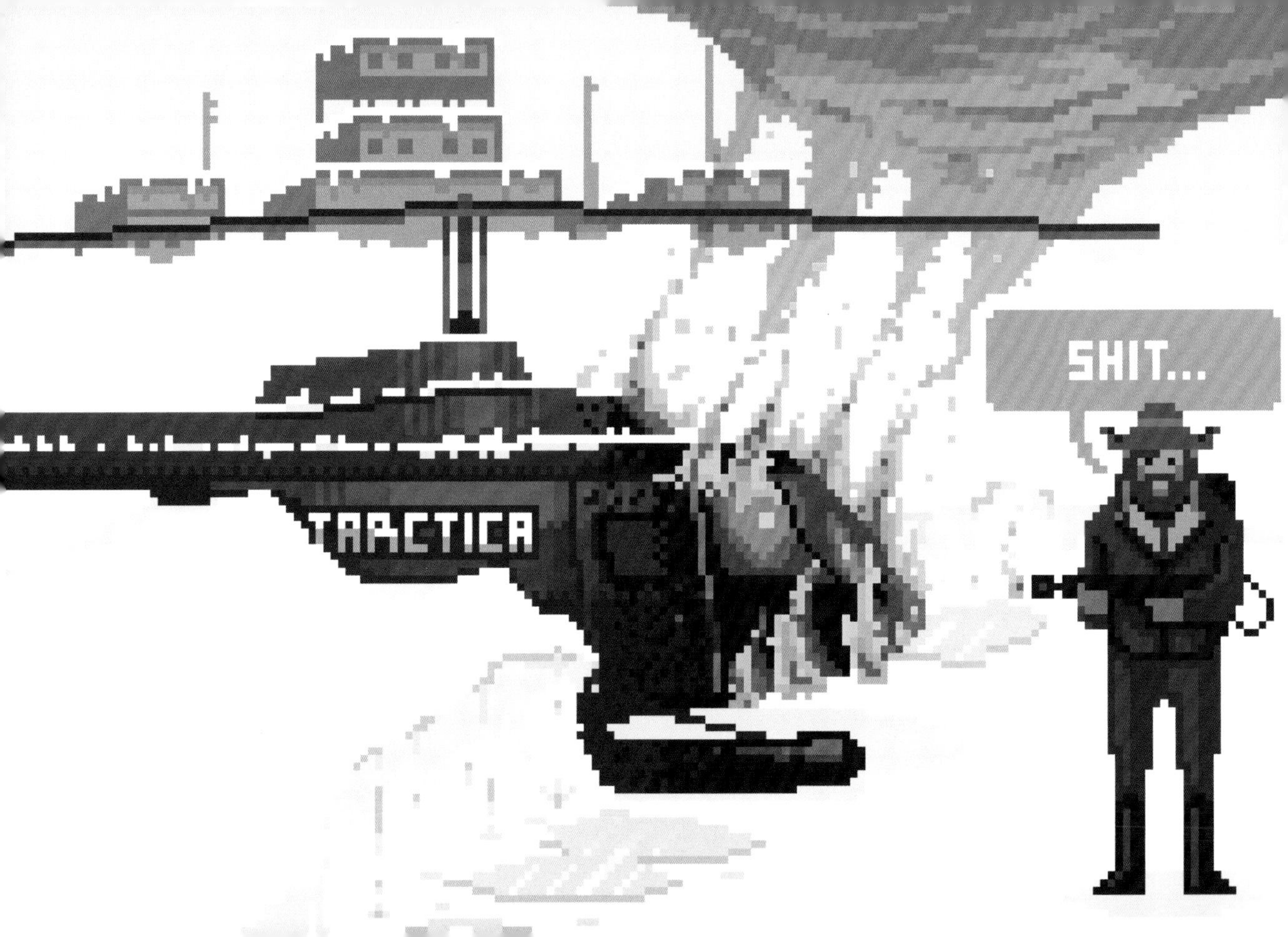

TARCTICA
SHIT...

THAT RUNS EXCLUSIVELY ON MODERN BATTERIES. * CLEAN A SEPTIC TANK WITH A TOOTHBRUSH. * DEHYDRATED WATER. * SKI DOWN A BLACK DIAMOND SLOPE DURING THE OFF-SEASON. * BRING ETHERNET CABLES TO A NETWORKING EVENT. * ATTEMPT TO BREAK INTO ALCATRAZ.

BAD IDEA #1678: FLAMETHROWER SNOWBLOWER.

DO A GROUP PROJECT WITH A DUDE NAMED "DEADWEIGHT." * SYNTHETIC SNOWBALL FIGHT. * STRESSED? BATHE IN FIRE ANTS! AFTER THAT, EVERYTHING ELSE JUST WON'T SEEM QUITE AS IMPORTANT! (YOU MIGHT ALSO BE DEAD.) * NICKELBACK'S NEWEST ALBUM: MARIACHI MAYHEM * START A DEATH METAL POLKA ABBA COVER BAND. * ENGINEER A CAR POWERED BY AN UNDYING LOVE OF OBSCURE CHEESES.

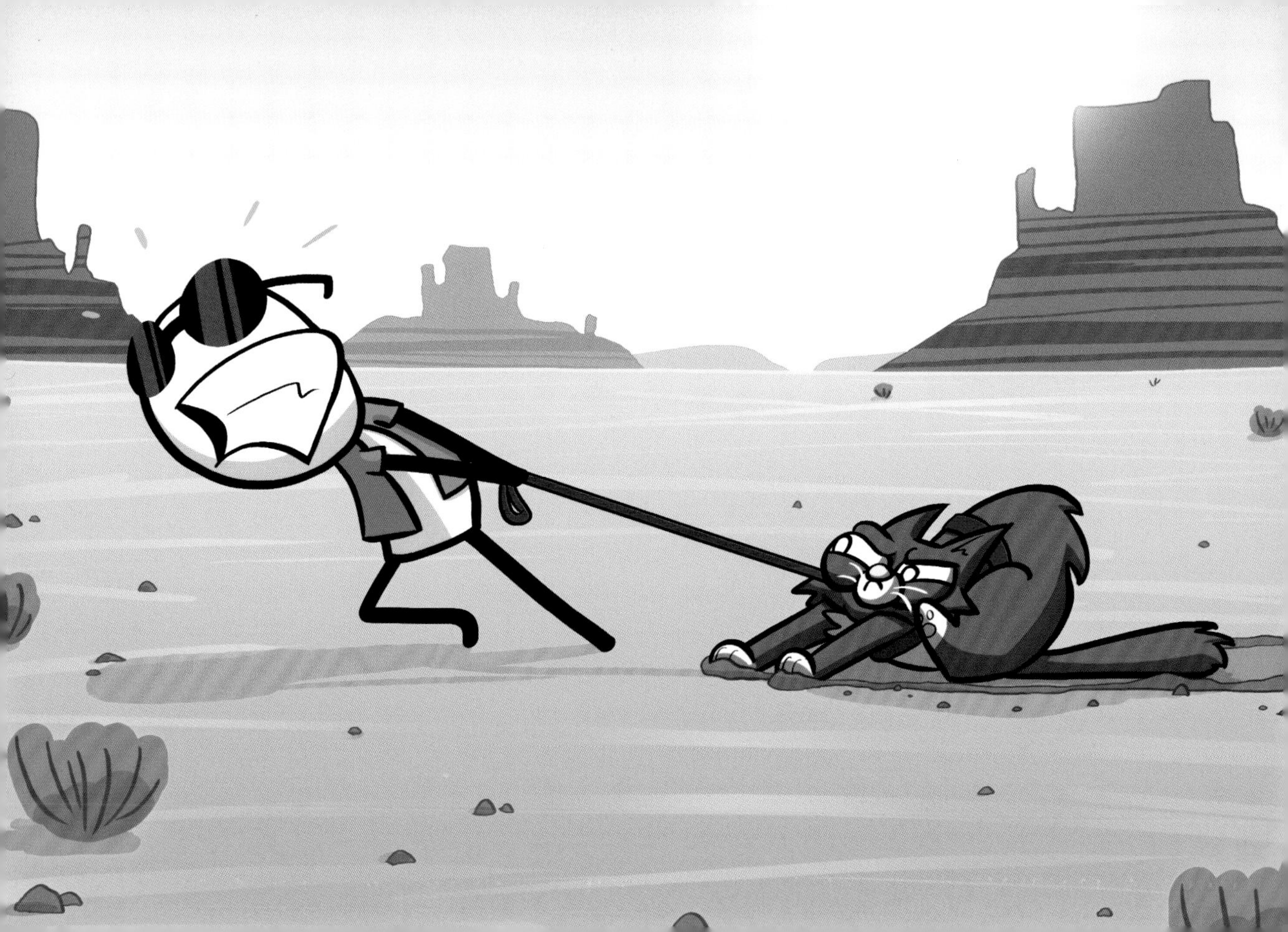

TEXT WHILE DRIVING A MECHA. * PLAY REPEAT GAMES OF SINGLE-PLAYER RUSSIAN ROULETTE. * CHALLENGE GODZILLA TO A DANCE DANCE REVOLUTION SHOWDOWN. * USE HOT SAUCE AS A LUBRICANT. * THE DAY OF THE DOPPLE-GINGER: A HORROR MOVIE WHERE EVERYONE ON EARTH SPONTANEOUSLY FORMS AN IDENTICAL GINGER TWIN WHO MISTREATS THEM THE WAY THEY'VE MISTREATED GINGERS.

BAD IDEA #1702: GUIDE CATS FOR THE BLIND.

COBRA JOUSTING. * START A "BACTERIA-ONLY" ZOO. * STAND ON THE SHOULDERS OF FROST GIANTS. * TAKE YOUR SMOKIN'-HOT DATE TO THE SHORE TO WATCH A BEACHED WHALE EXPLODE. * SCIENTIFICALLY PROVE WHICH IS MORE POWERFUL: DUCT TAPE OR THE TRUE MEANING OF FRIENDSHIP. * CONFUSE YOUR VACATION DESTINATION SWITZERLAND WITH SWAZILAND (AND PACK ONLY SKIS). * FORGE TINFOIL PLATE ARMOR.

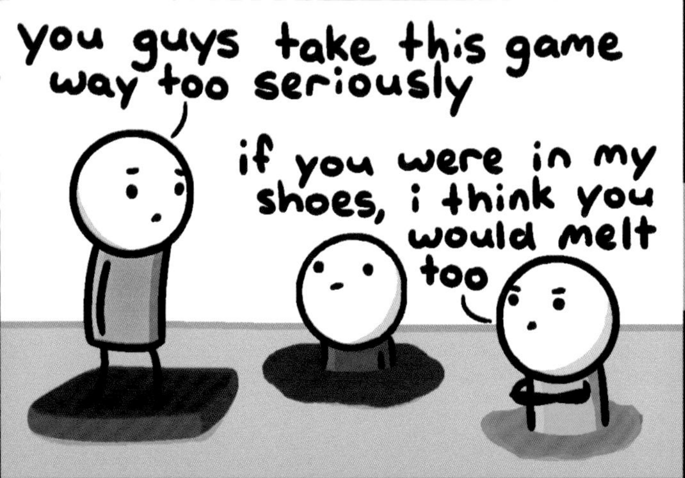
you guys take this game way too seriously
if you were in my shoes, i think you would melt too

ALL-YOU-CAN-EAT POUTINE. * PAY YOUR STUDENT LOAN BILLS IN PENNIES. * NAME A SPACE STATION "KEYBOARD" BECAUSE IT'S GOING TO HAVE A SPACE BAR. * LOOK AT THE ARK OF THE COVENANT. * GLUTEN-FREE URINAL CAKES. * STEEL WOOL SOCKS.

BAD IDEA #1825: TRY TO GET REVENGE ON THE METEOR THAT KILLED YOUR PEOPLE.

SET UP A DENTIST APPOINTMENT FOR NOVEMBER 1ST. * FART IN THE FACE OF MADNESS. * DO A BACKSTROKE IN A WISHING WELL. * FORCE A PORCUPINE AND SKUNK TO BECOME FRIENDS, NO MATTER HOW MUCH THEY RESIST. * SELF-ADMINISTERED ICE-PICK LOBOTOMY.

SEGUE DRUNK. * SEGWAY DRUNK. * LEAD OFF A FIRST DATE WITH A DISCUSSION ABOUT YOUR MIDDLE SCHOOL NARUTO PHASE. * HIRE HANNIBAL LECTER AS YOUR CATERER. * PANTS A MOBSTER. * PAY BACK LOAN SHARKS WITH BUCKETS OF CHUM.

BAD IDEA #1811: PLAY "THE FLOOR IS LAVA" WITH VOLCANOLOGISTS.

PRACTICE KARATE CHOPS AND KICKS ON BEEHIVES. * MAKE YOU CRY, SAY GOODBYE, TELL A LIE, AND HURT YOU. * TAKE A VACATION ON ALDERAAN. * GUIDE SLOTHS. * GO IN AGAINST A SICILIAN WHEN DEATH IS ON THE LINE. * BETTING ON INCHWORM RACES.

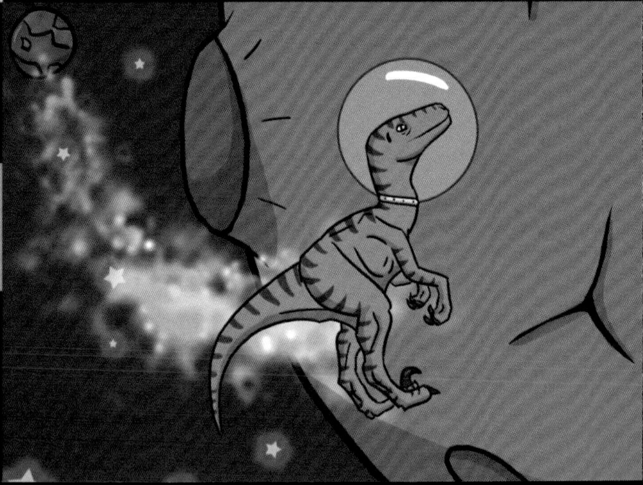

SWIRLY-STRAW COLONOSCOPY. * WALK ON HOT COALS. * HOLD UP AN ATM. * MOBIUS DONUTS. * EXTERNAL COMBUSTION ENGINE. * T-SHIRT CANNON GRAPESHOT. * TRUST YOUR SPELLCHECKER TO KNOW WHAT YOU MEAN. * BOWLING WITH PLANETS.

BAD IDEA #1870: MOOSE MITTENS. MITTENS FOR MOOSE.

USE THE SAME PASSWORD FOR EVERYTHING. * SERVE A LOAN SHARK A SHARK FIN SOUP. * T.V. DINNER PARTIES. * DESIGN A SADDLE FOR YOUR BATHTUB AND RIDE IT INTO BATTLE. * HAGGLE WITH AN AUTOMATIC CHECK-OUT. * PRANK GENGHIS KHAN.

SHARK HERDING. * HIPPO-SKYDIVING. * BUILD A POTASSIUM SUBMARINE. * SEAL-FLAVORED POLAR BEAR REPELLANT. * CORKSCREW TREPANATION * WEAR ACHILLES HIGH HEELS WHEN YOU VISIT PARIS. * GO BACK TO SCHOOL AS A 27-YEAR-OLD.

BAD IDEA #1895: FENCELESS WILDLIFE PARK.

CONFUSE "AVIARY" AND "APIARY." * LEECHING. * "IRISH" UP YOUR MORNING COFFEE ONE COMMUNAL OFFICE COFFEE POT AT A TIME. * PERFORM AN AUTOPSY ON A BEACHED WHALE. * PLAY TAG WITH A PSYCHOPATHIC KILLER.

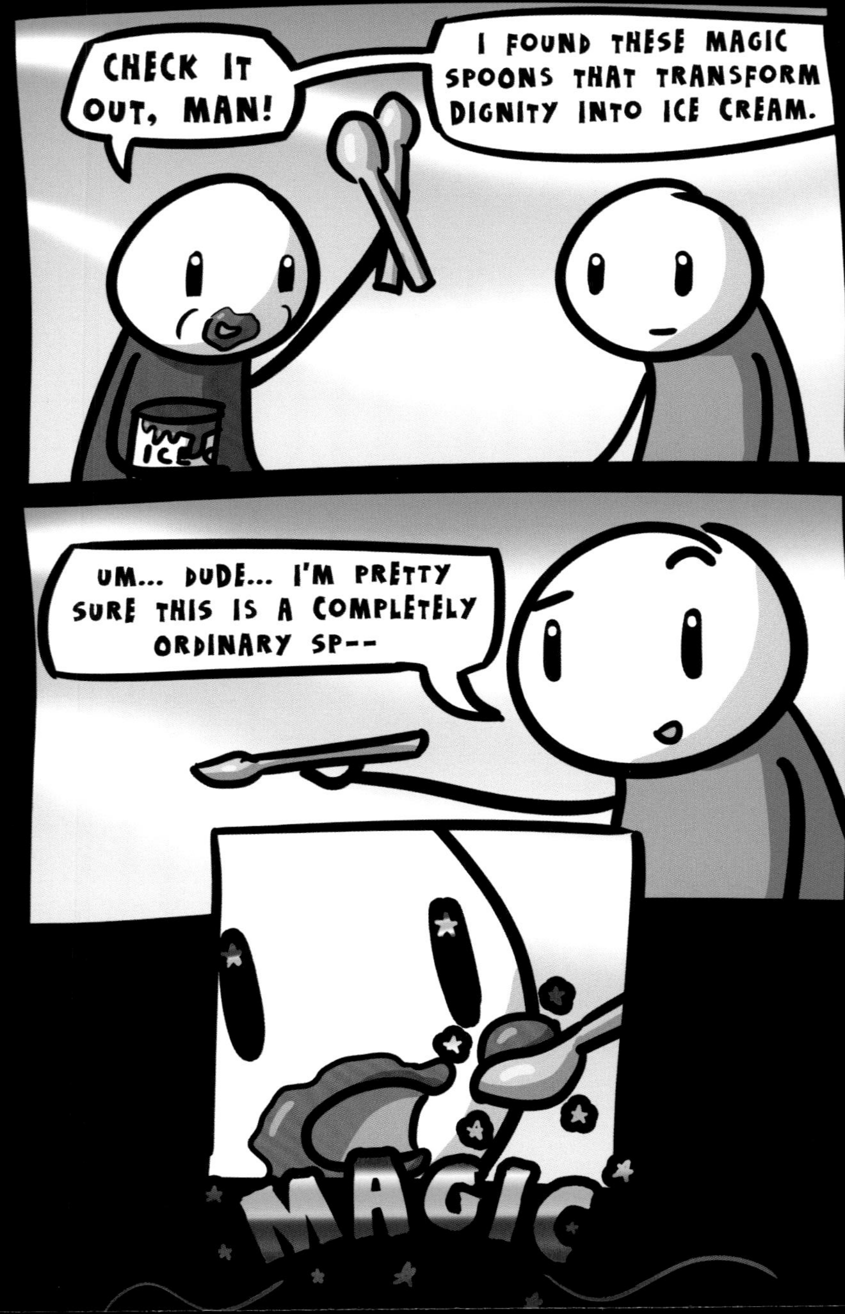
CHECK IT OUT, MAN!
I FOUND THESE MAGIC SPOONS THAT TRANSFORM DIGNITY INTO ICE CREAM.
ICE
UM... DUDE... I'M PRETTY SURE THIS IS A COMPLETELY ORDINARY SP--
MAGIC

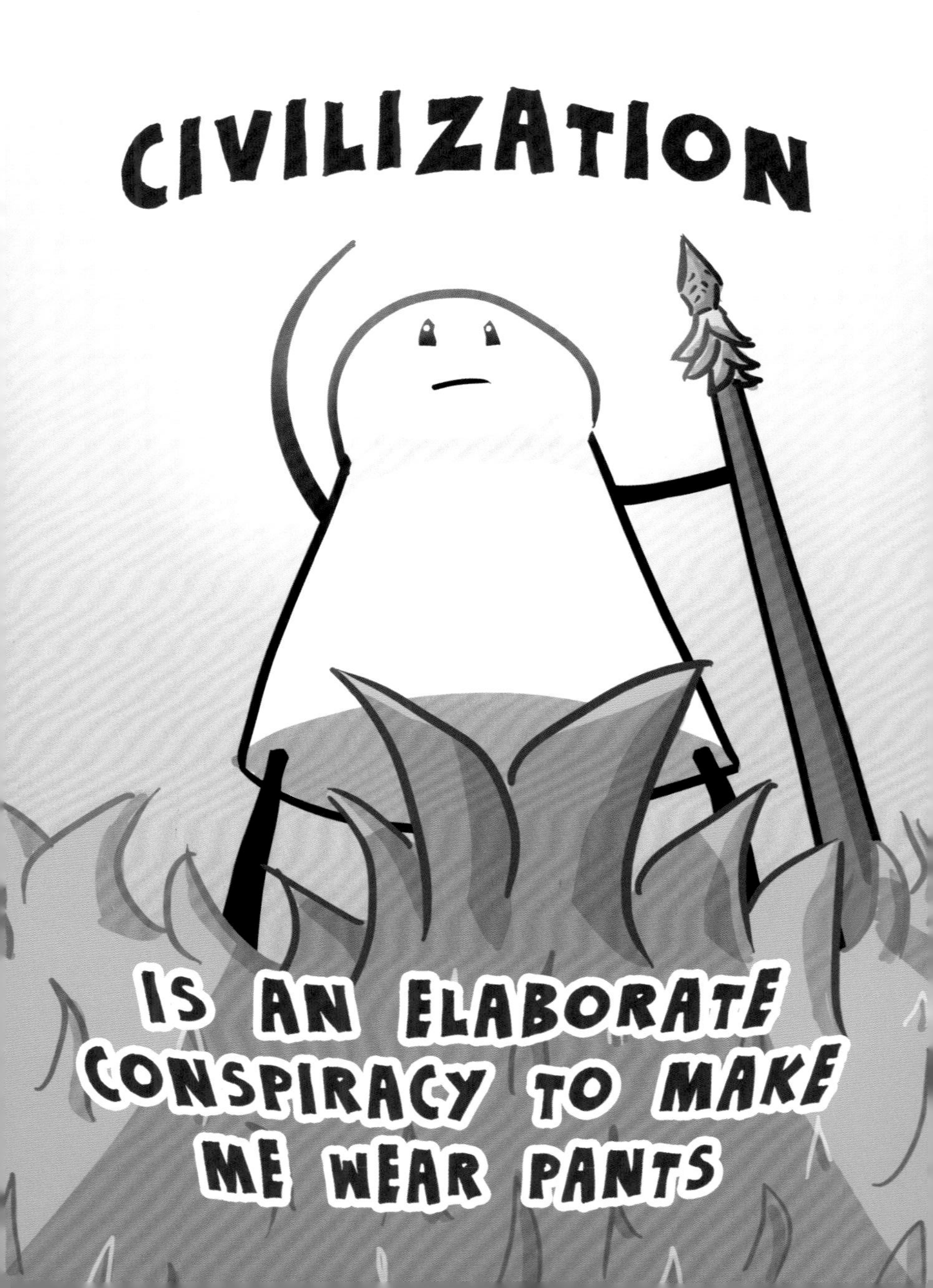
CIVILIZATION
IS AN ELABORATE CONSPIRACY TO MAKE ME WEAR PANTS

NO, CHEM 2202 ISN'T USEFUL FOR MY DEGREE

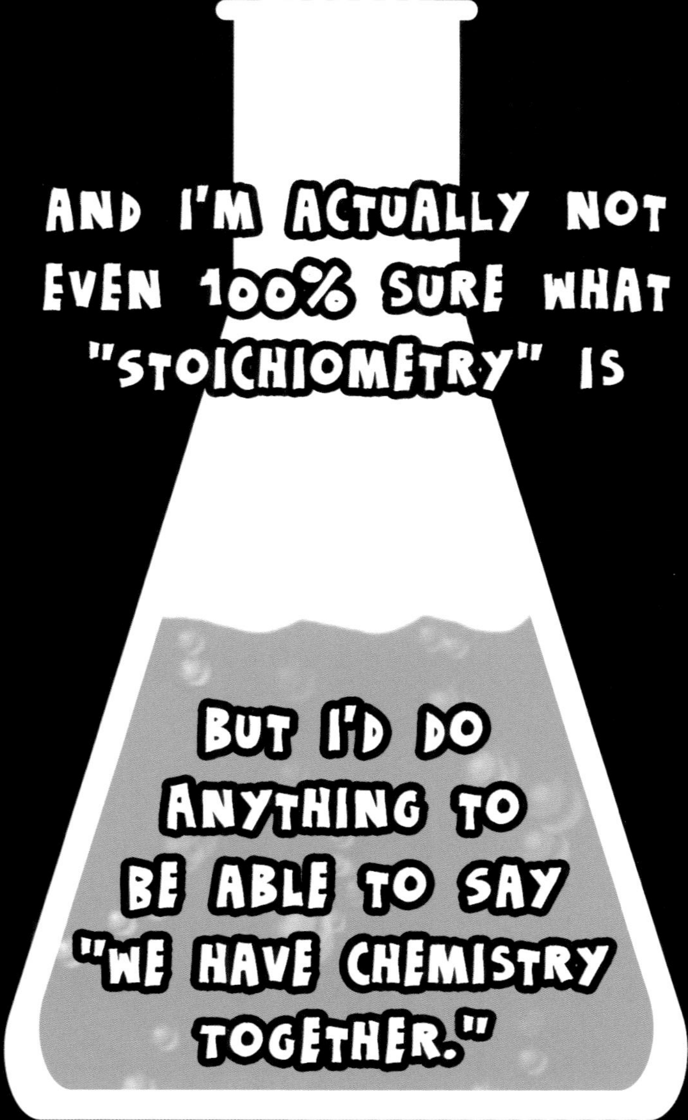
AND I'M ACTUALLY NOT
EVEN 100% SURE WHAT
"STOICHIOMETRY" IS
BUT I'D DO
ANYTHING TO
BE ABLE TO SAY
"WE HAVE CHEMISTRY
TOGETHER."

ENVIRONMENTAL SUSTAINABILITY NINJA

LEAVES NO FOOTPRINT

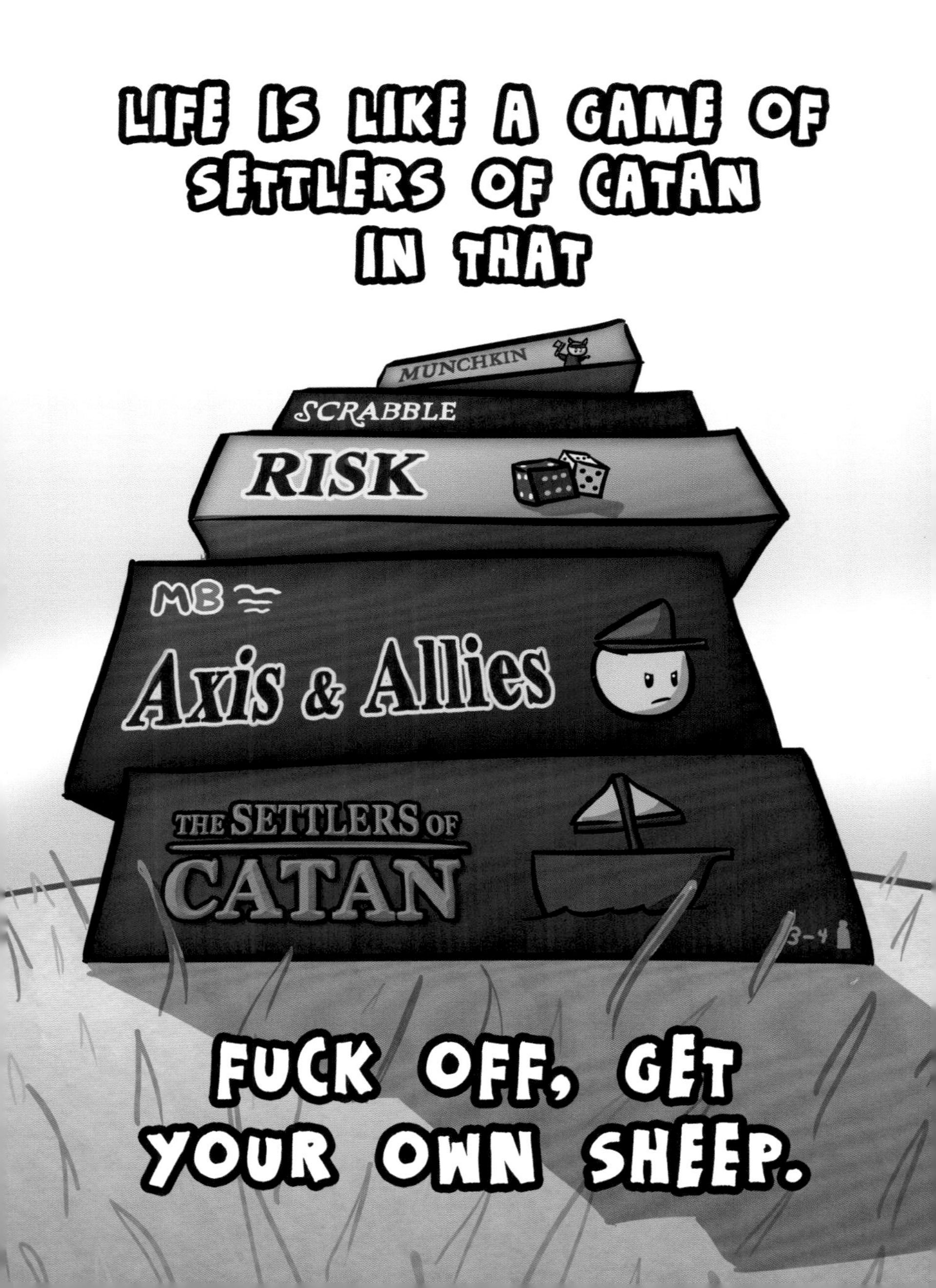
LIFE IS LIKE A GAME OF
SETTLERS OF CATAN
IN THAT
MUNCHKIN
SCRABBLE
RISK
MB
Axis & Allies
THE SETTLERS OF
CATAN
3-4
FUCK OFF, GET
YOUR OWN SHEEP.

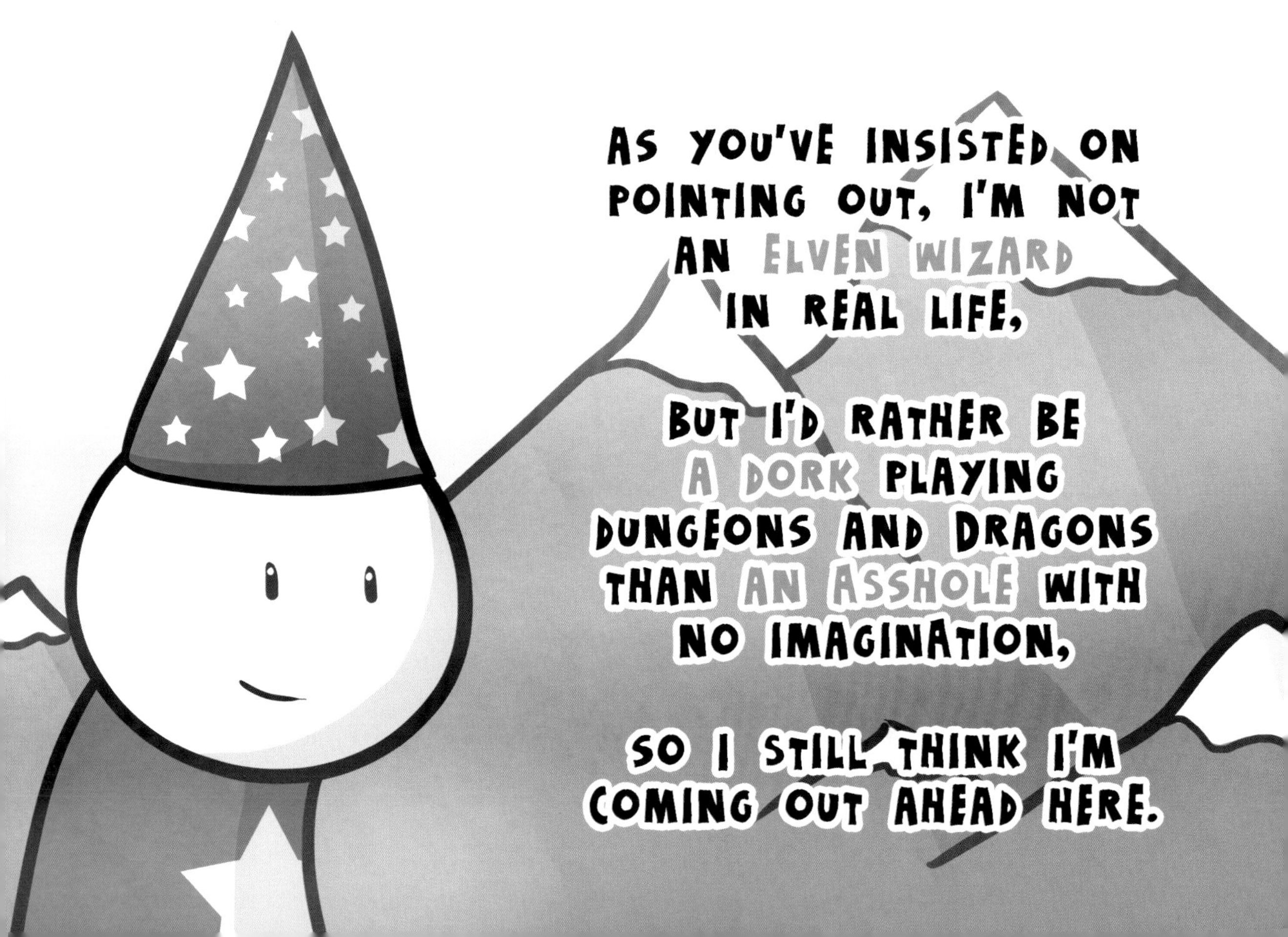
AS YOU'VE INSISTED ON POINTING OUT, I'M NOT AN ELVEN WIZARD IN REAL LIFE,
BUT I'D RATHER BE A DORK PLAYING DUNGEONS AND DRAGONS THAN AN ASSHOLE WITH NO IMAGINATION,
SO I STILL THINK I'M COMING OUT AHEAD HERE.

WEARING A MONOCLE

PERCEPTION
HOLY MOLY! AN AWESOME MONOCLE!
REALITY
HOLY MOLY! AN AWESOME MONOCLE!

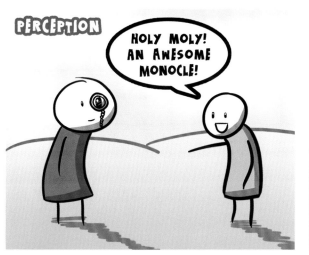

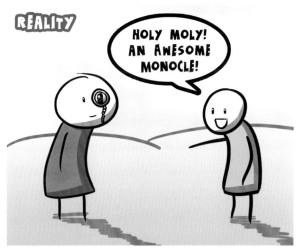

CONCLUSION: JUST GO FOR IT

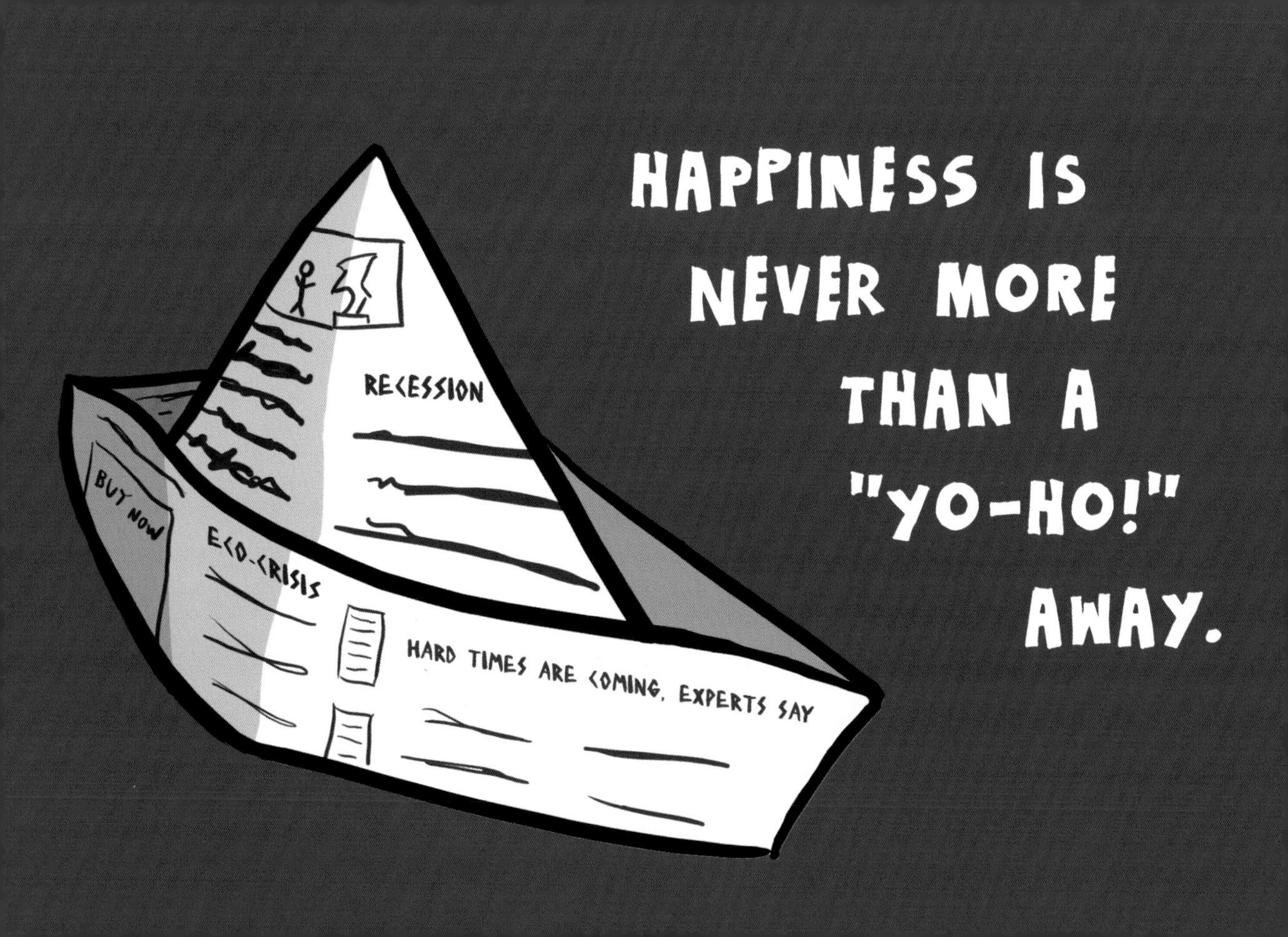
RECESSION
BUY NOW
ECO-CRISIS
HARD TIMES ARE COMING, EXPERTS SAY

HAPPINESS IS NEVER MORE THAN A "YO-HO!" AWAY.

ZAMBURAK ⟨N.⟩: A COMBAT CAMEL WEARING A
SWIVEL-MOUNTED CANNON
ON ITS BACK*

IT IS UTTERLY AMAZING AND YET TOTALLY BONKERS
THAT WE LIVE ON A PLANET THAT HAS A WORD FOR
CAMELS THAT SHOOT PEOPLE.

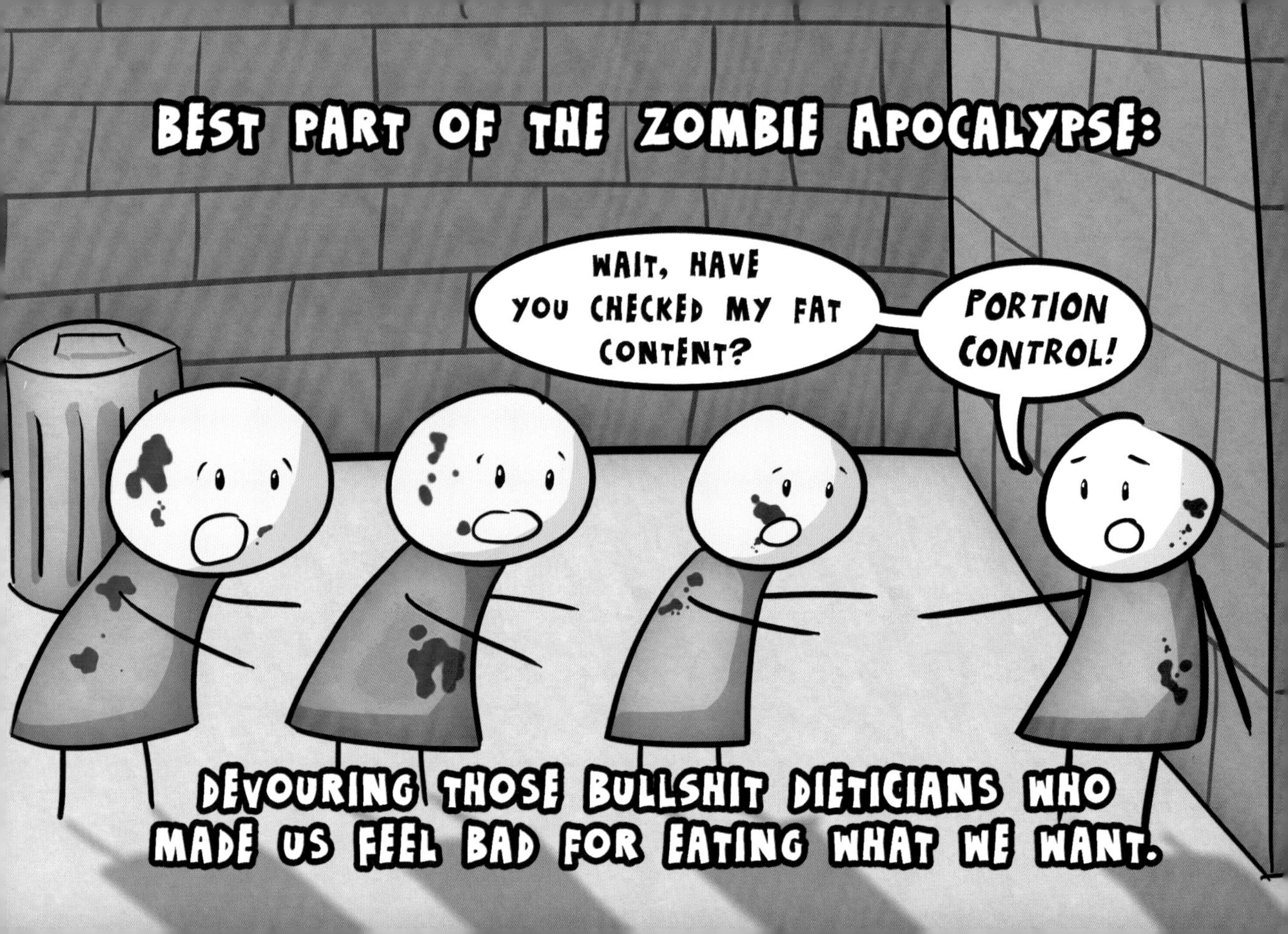
BEST PART OF THE ZOMBIE APOCALYPSE:
WAIT, HAVE YOU CHECKED MY FAT CONTENT?
PORTION CONTROL!
DEVOURING THOSE BULLSHIT DIETICIANS WHO MADE US FEEL BAD FOR EATING WHAT WE WANT.

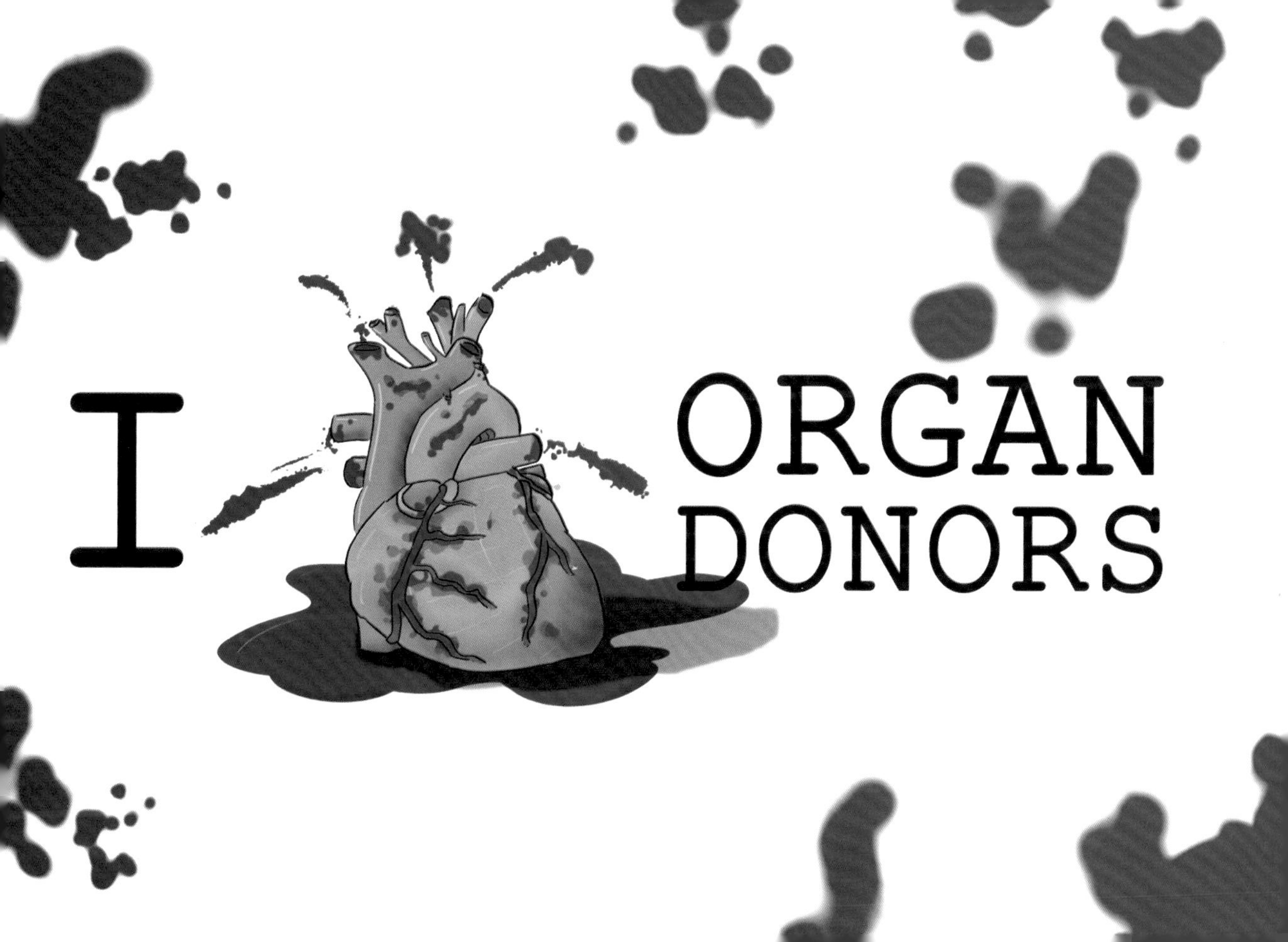
I
ORGAN
DONORS

THE ONLY RESPONSIBLE USE OF PHYSICS

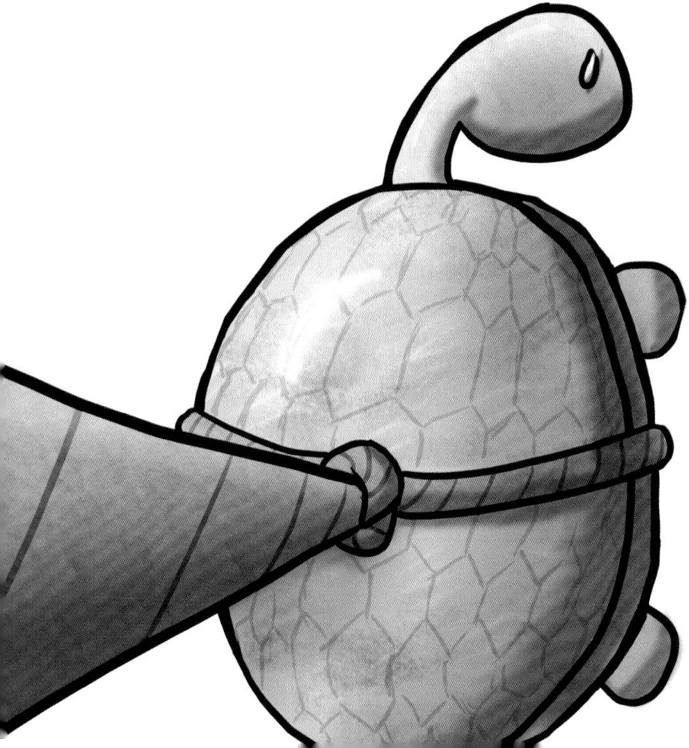

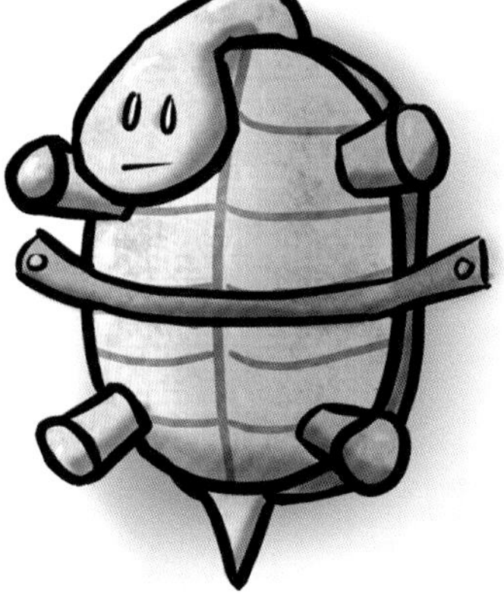

IS HELPING TURTLES HUG.

10 PERFECTLY REASONABLE STEPS FOR CLEANING OUT YOUR FRIDGE

1. WRITE DOWN THE DATE WHENEVER YOU PUT FOOD INTO YOUR FRIDGE.

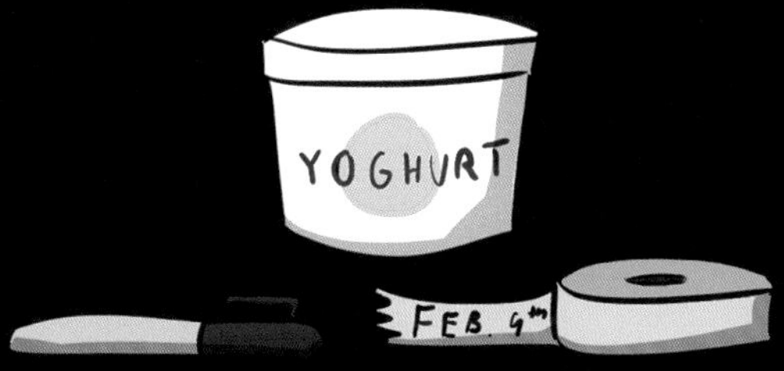
YOGHURT
FEB. 9th

2. AT THE END OF THE MONTH, IDENTIFY ANY FOOD THAT MIGHT BE STARTING TO TURN.

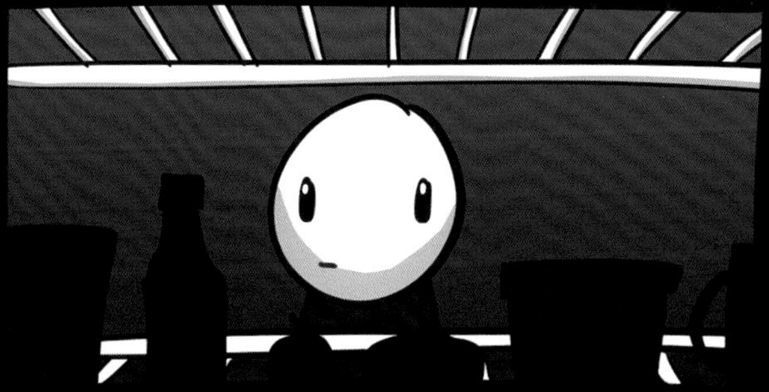

3. IGNORE IT.

4. AVOID FRIDGE AT ALL COSTS. IF YOU YOU MUST ACCESS IT, ASSERT DOMINANCE BY AVOIDING EYE CONTACT.

5. IN TIME, YOUR FRIDGE WILL COME TO RESPECT YOU, MAYBE EVEN LOVE YOU.

6. LET IT SMELL THE BACK OF YOUR HAND. SEE HOW IT GROWS COMFORTABLE WITH YOUR SCENT?

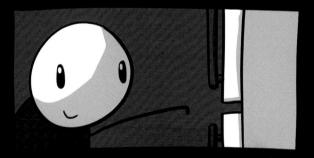

7. NOW THAT YOU HAVE EARNED ITS TRUST, YOU KNOW WHAT YOU MUST DO.

8. YOU KNOW.

9. WHAT YOU

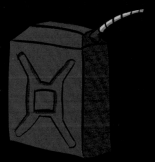

10. MUST DO.

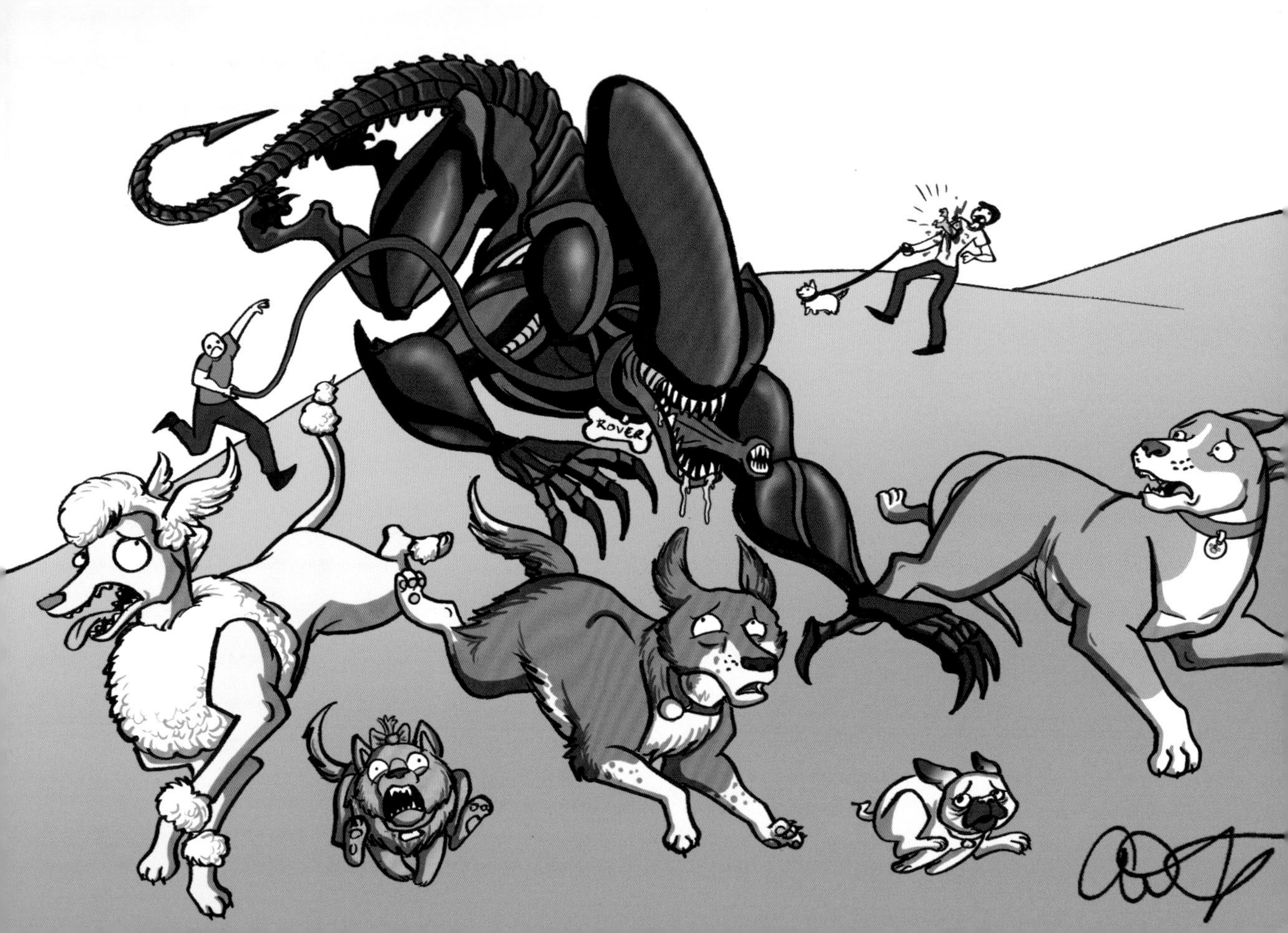
ROVER

EXPECT A ZOMBIE NOT TO BITE THE HAND THAT FEEDS. * GET DRUNK OFF MOLOTOV COCKTAILS. * OPEN THE DOOR MARKED "DRAMATIC IRONY," ESPECIALLY IF YOU'RE IN A HORROR MOVIE. * SING THE BLUES TO A COMMUNIST. * STUDY AGNOSTICISM RELIGIOUSLY. * TAKE A PUNCH FROM A MANTIS SHRIMP. * ACCEPT HANNIBAL'S "FACE BOOK" INVITATION. * GO CANOEING WITH CHARGED DEFIBRILLATOR PADDLES.

BAD IDEA #1945:
TAKE YOUR PET XENOMORPH TO PLAY AT THE LOCAL DOG PARK.

HUMP A BEEHIVE. * SWIM WITH PIRANHAS. * BUY A MINI COOPER AND MAKE FRIENDS WITH TRAVELING BAND OF CLOWNS. * CHECK A GUN BY LOOKING INTO THE BARREL. * DETOX INTERVENTION FOR A COMMUNITY OF JUNKIE KOALAS. SEE WHAT HAPPENS FIRST: STARVATION, OR SPONTANEOUS EVOLUTION INTO AN APEX PREDATOR. * WEAR A SUIT OF MEAT INTO A CAGE FULL OF HUNGRY TIGERS. * LEGO-LINED SANDALS

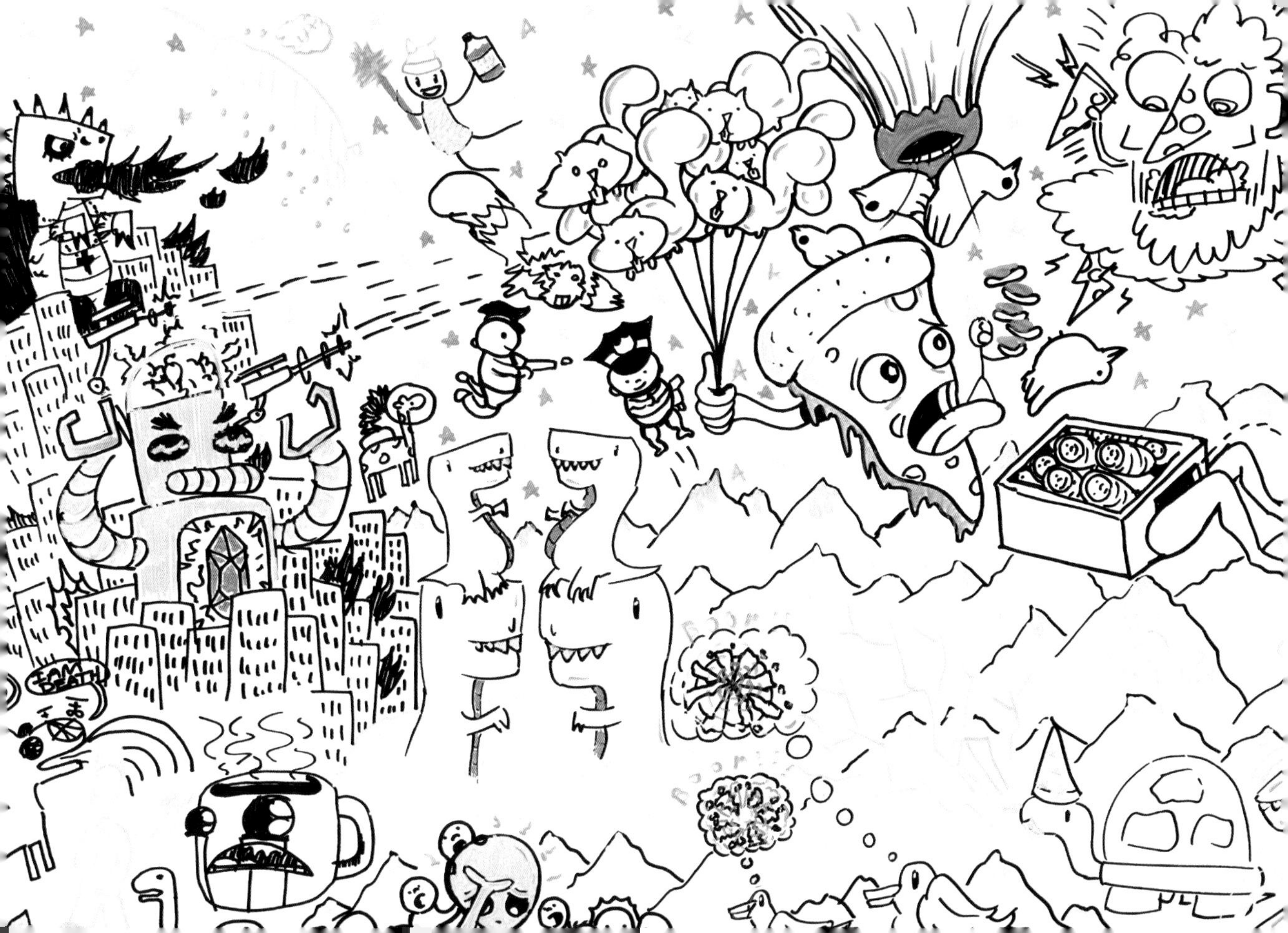
I AM DEATH

PLAY SNAKES AND LADDERS WITH ACTUAL SNAKES AND LADDERS. * RIDE A HORSE TO YOUR FIRST WATER POLO MATCH. * TELL YOURSELF THAT YOU'LL DO SOMETHING "LATER." * TEACH A CHIMPANZEE ADVANCED TAE KWON DO. * WAIL AT A WHALE WHILE WHALING IN A WELL. * TWERK AS THE FIRST DANCE AT YOUR WEDDING. * MAKE GUACAMOLE WITH WASABI INSTEAD OF AVOCADO. * TURTLE GUILLOTINES. * POTATO-POWERED TASERS.

BAD IDEA #2010: GIVE ALCOHOL TO CARTOONISTS.

GET YOURSELF INTO A "WHY"-"BECAUSE" QUESTION-AND-ANSWER LOOP. * HAVE YOUR DEAD GRANDMOTHER STUFFED AND MOUNTED WHILE IN MOURNING. * GET AS MANY X-RAY SCREENINGS AS POSSIBLE, JUST TO BE REALLY SURE. * ESTELLE GETTYSBURG: THE BLOODIEST BATTLE OF THE GOLDEN GIRLS. * PLACE A BLIND TRAFFIC COP AT THE INTERSECTION NEAR A GRADE SCHOOL. * DRESS UP AS A COW TO TOUR AN ABATTOIR.

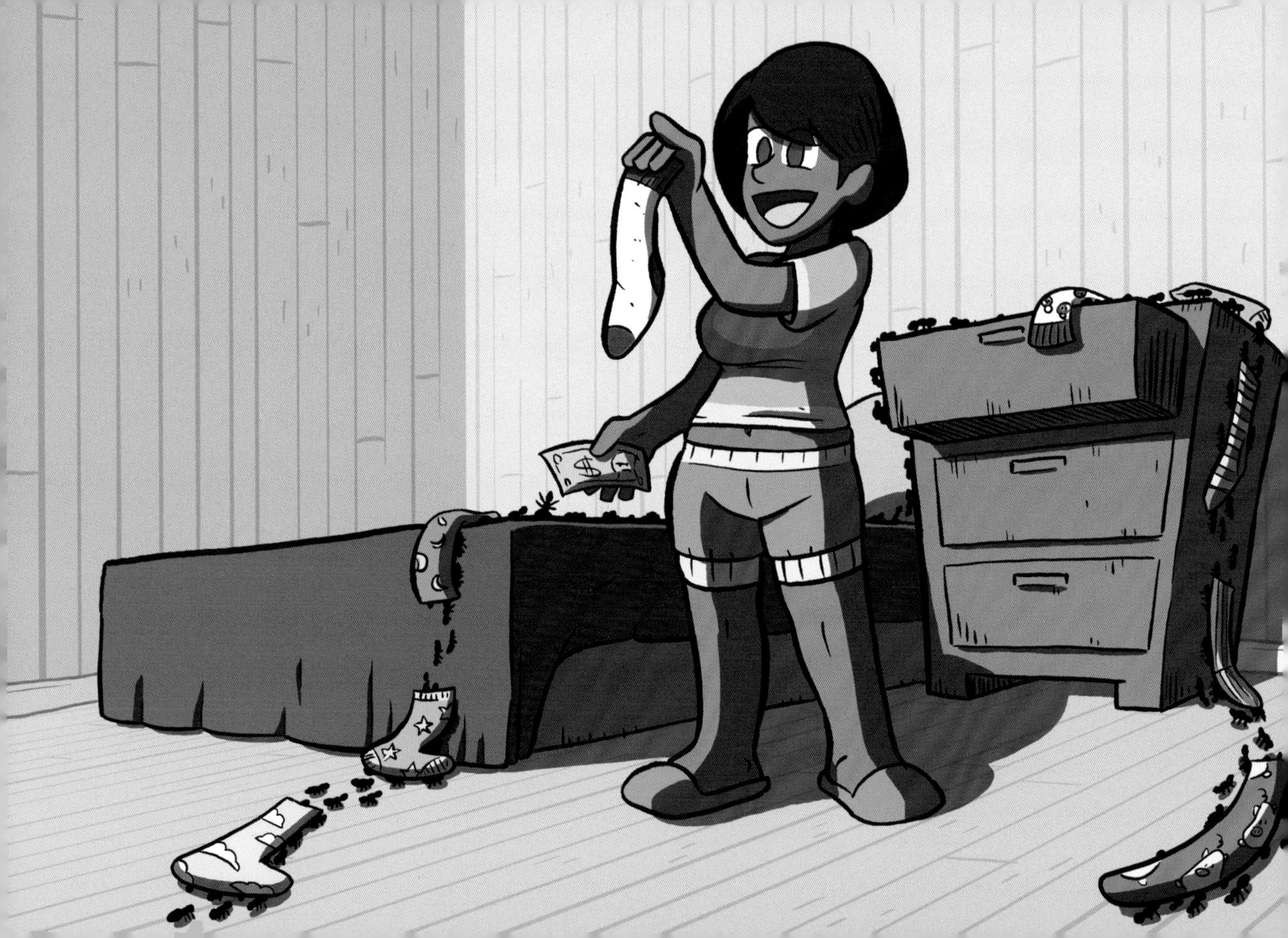

TREADMILL. * TIME-TRAVEL TO THE EXACT MOMENT OF THE BIG BANG.

BAD IDEA #2121:
HIRE SMALL BUT CORRUPT TEAMS OF ANTS TO FIND YOUR MISSING SOCKS.

TAKE UP THE HOBBIES OF CARPENTRY AND ARSON AT THE SAME TIME. * SET UP A "ROCK, PAPER, SCISSORS" CAGE MATCH BETWEEN EDWARD SCISSORHANDS AND THE THING. * ATTEND A WRESTLING EVENT, JUMP THE BARRIER, CLIMB INTO THE RING, AND DECLARE YOURSELF CAPTAIN

GERBIL LAUNCHERS. * "PIMP MY TRIREME." * SQUEEZE BLOOD FROM A STONE. * POISON ONLY THE COCONUT-FLAVORED CHOCOLATES IN THE BOX OF SWEETS YOU LEAVE ON YOUR ENEMY'S DOORSTEP * LET YOUR DRIVER'S LICENSE EXPIRE.

BAD IDEA #2208: DRAW COPYRIGHT-INFRINGING SUPERHEROES WITH YOUR MOUTH.

DECLARE "I AM INVINCIBLE" AND LAUGH MANIACALLY. * TAKE COVER BEHIND A RED BARREL IN A VIDEO GAME. * EXITING WITHOUT SAVING. * BECOME THE LEADER OF GERMANY AND START A WORLD WAR. * HAVE A WATER FIGHT WITH BRICKS.

Mouth Batman

SWING FROM A VINE FOR LONGER THAN SIX SECONDS. * SIGN YOUR DOG UP FOR TWITTER. * SUBTERRANEAN WINDMILL POWER. * TACO-FLAVORED COFFEE. * SMUGGLE DRUGS IN A BASSET HOUND'S WRINKLES. * MAKE A SOLAR-POWERED FLASHLIGHT.

BAD IDEA #2236: TURN A HOMEMADE SLINGSHOT INTO A D.I.Y. AMUSEMENT PARK RIDE.

INFANT SURGEONS. * NAME THE BIRD "TURKEY" AFTER A PLACE IT DOESN'T EVEN COME FROM. * ANYTHING A 16-YEAR-OLD TEXAN BOY SAYS. * SRIRACHA OREOS. * COMPETITIVE NOSE PICKING. * DECLARE SPANK-BANKRUPTCY. * HOLD UP A FOODBANK.

IDEA
ANGRÉ BÖRDS

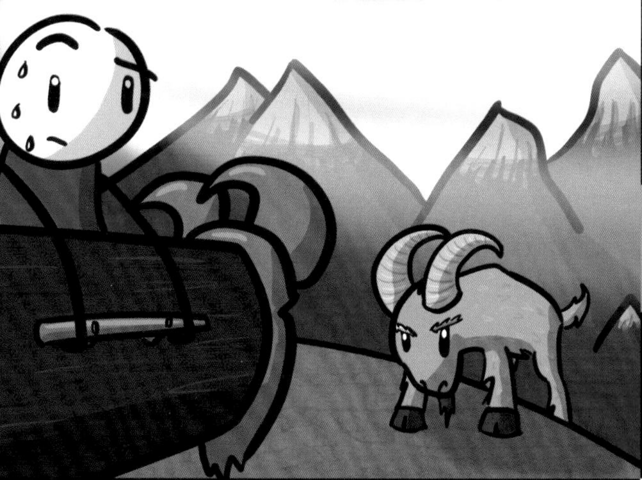

LEAVE THE HERO ALONE TO MEET HIS OR HER "CERTAIN" DOOM. * DROP YOUR KEYS IN A HORROR MOVIE. * STEAL FOOD FROM A GORILLA. * ATTEMPT A SPEED RUN OF DESERT BUS. * STOP BELIEVIN'. * WIN A STARING CONTEST USING AN ACTUAL DEATH STARE.

BAD IDEA #2260: BATTER A RAM WITH A BATTERING RAM.

SELL YOUR DIGNITY ON CRAIGSLIST. $50 O.B.O. * ATTEMPT TO INSEMINATE A VENUS FLYTRAP. * CONFUSE AN AMBUSH AND A BACON TREE. * RUB A SHARK THE WRONG WAY. * RIDE A BIKE WEARING ROLLERBLADES. * TOSS A DWARF. * KNIFE-BATONS.

BATTLE MIMES. * INTERVENTION: THE DRINKING GAME! * BUDGIE JUMPING. * EAT AN APPLE A DAY AS DOCTOR REPELLENT. * UNDERESTIMATE THE NUMBER OF BAD IDEAS REQUIRED TO FILL A BOOK. * JUMP A SHARK. * SAY "NEVER." * SNAIL MAIL ARMOR.

BAD IDEA #2291: REPLACE THE PIRATE CAPTAIN'S STASH OF GROG WITH NON-ALCOHOLIC BEER.

POWER A CITY WITH RANDY ELECTRIC EELS. * WRITE A PARODY OF A WEIRD AL SONG. * WINDOW PANE ORIGAMI. * PLAY "MARCO POLO" WITH A PARROT. * CURSE THE DAY YOU WERE BORN. * BELIEVE IN YOURSELF. * QUIT YOUR DAY JOB.

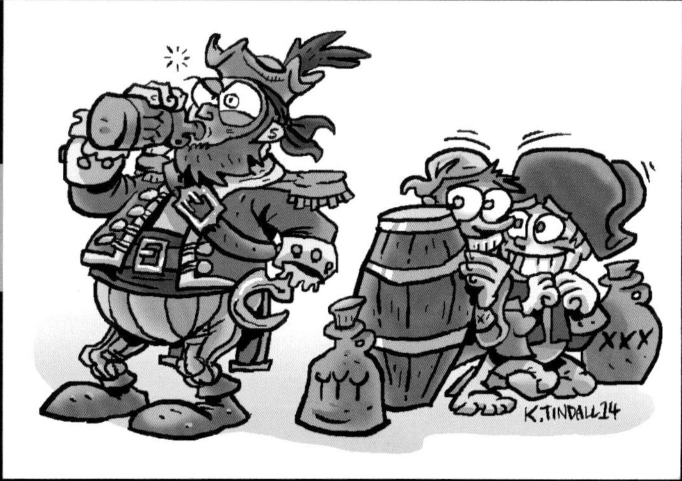
K.TINDALL14

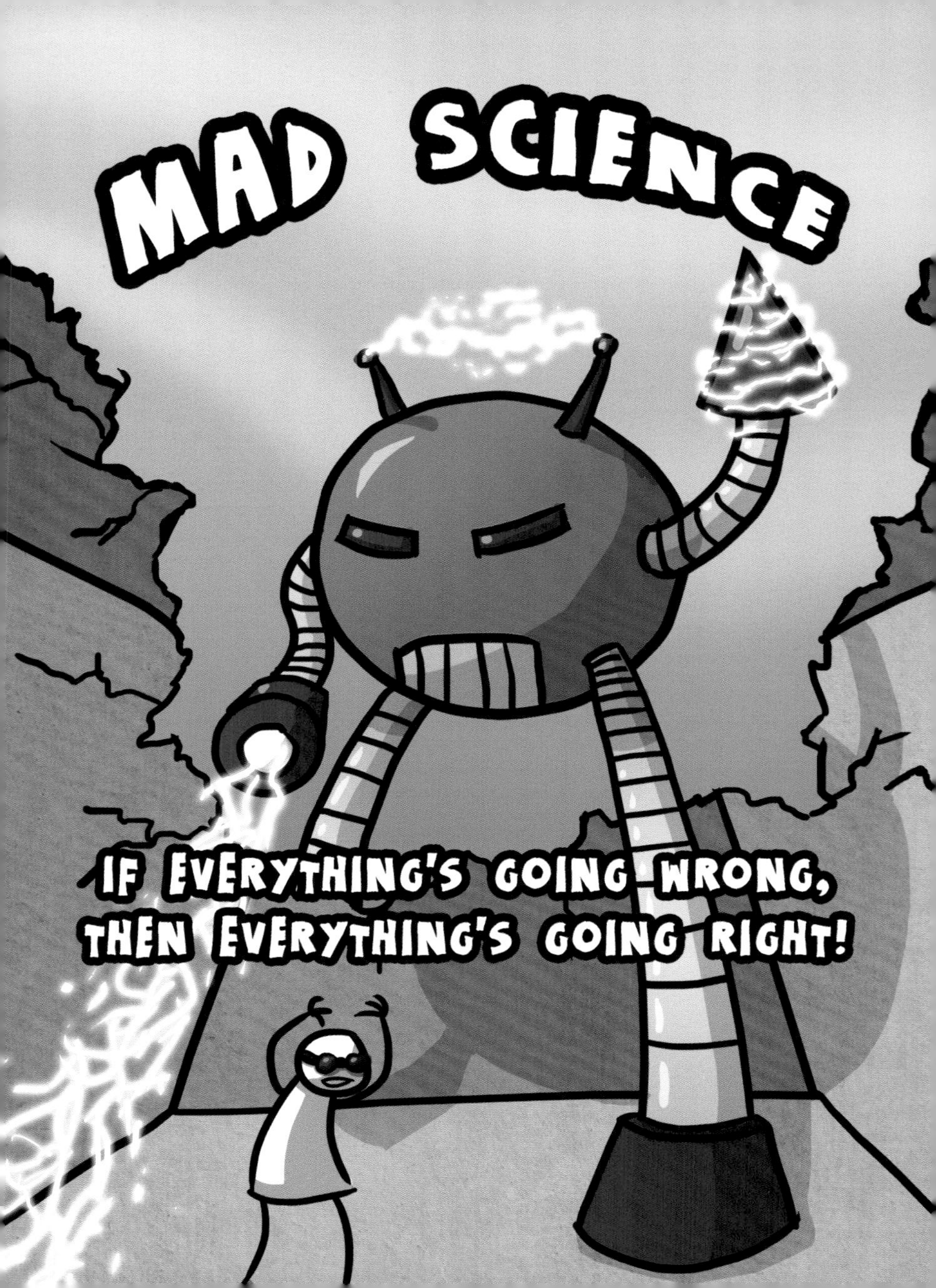
MAD SCIENCE
IF EVERYTHING'S GOING WRONG,
THEN EVERYTHING'S GOING RIGHT!

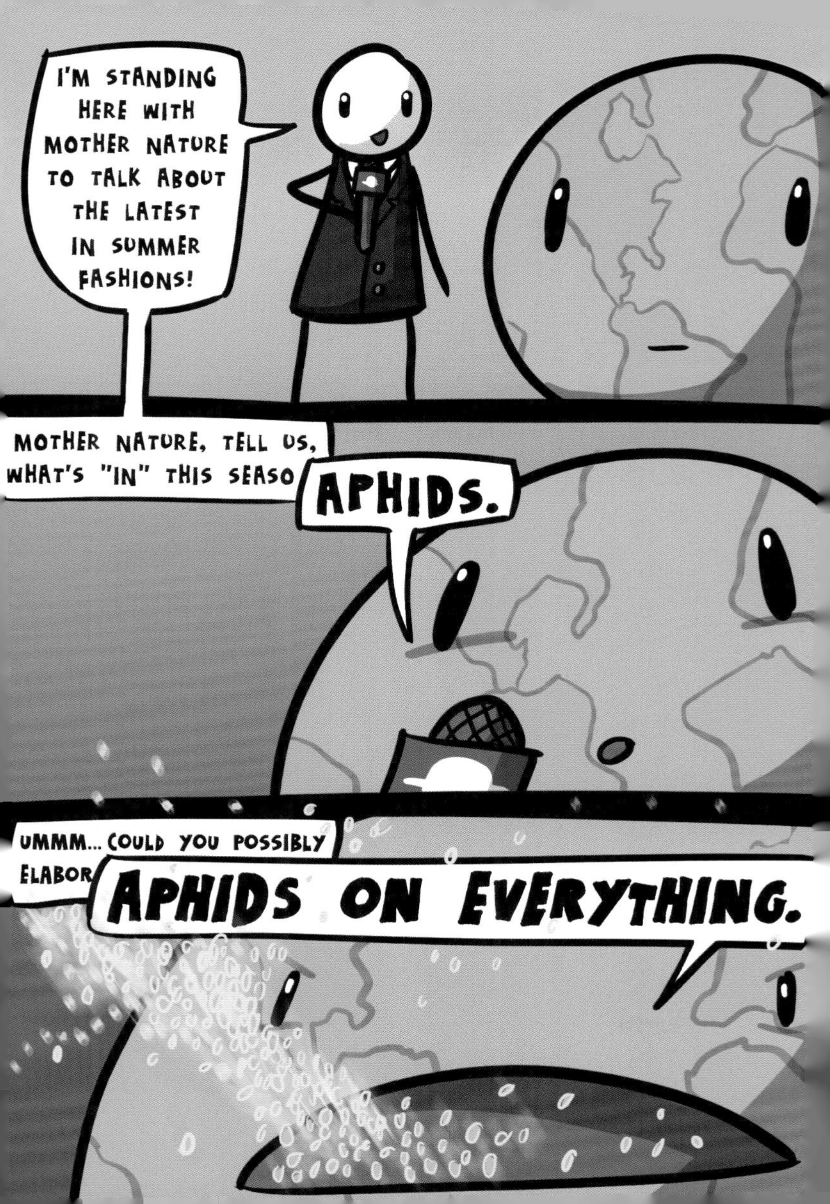
I'M STANDING HERE WITH MOTHER NATURE TO TALK ABOUT THE LATEST IN SUMMER FASHIONS!
MOTHER NATURE, TELL US, WHAT'S "IN" THIS SEASO
APHIDS.
UMMM... COULD YOU POSSIBLY ELABOR
APHIDS ON EVERYTHING.

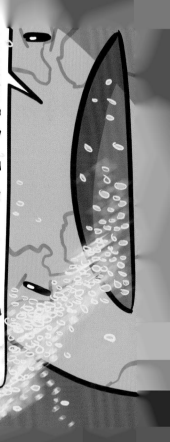

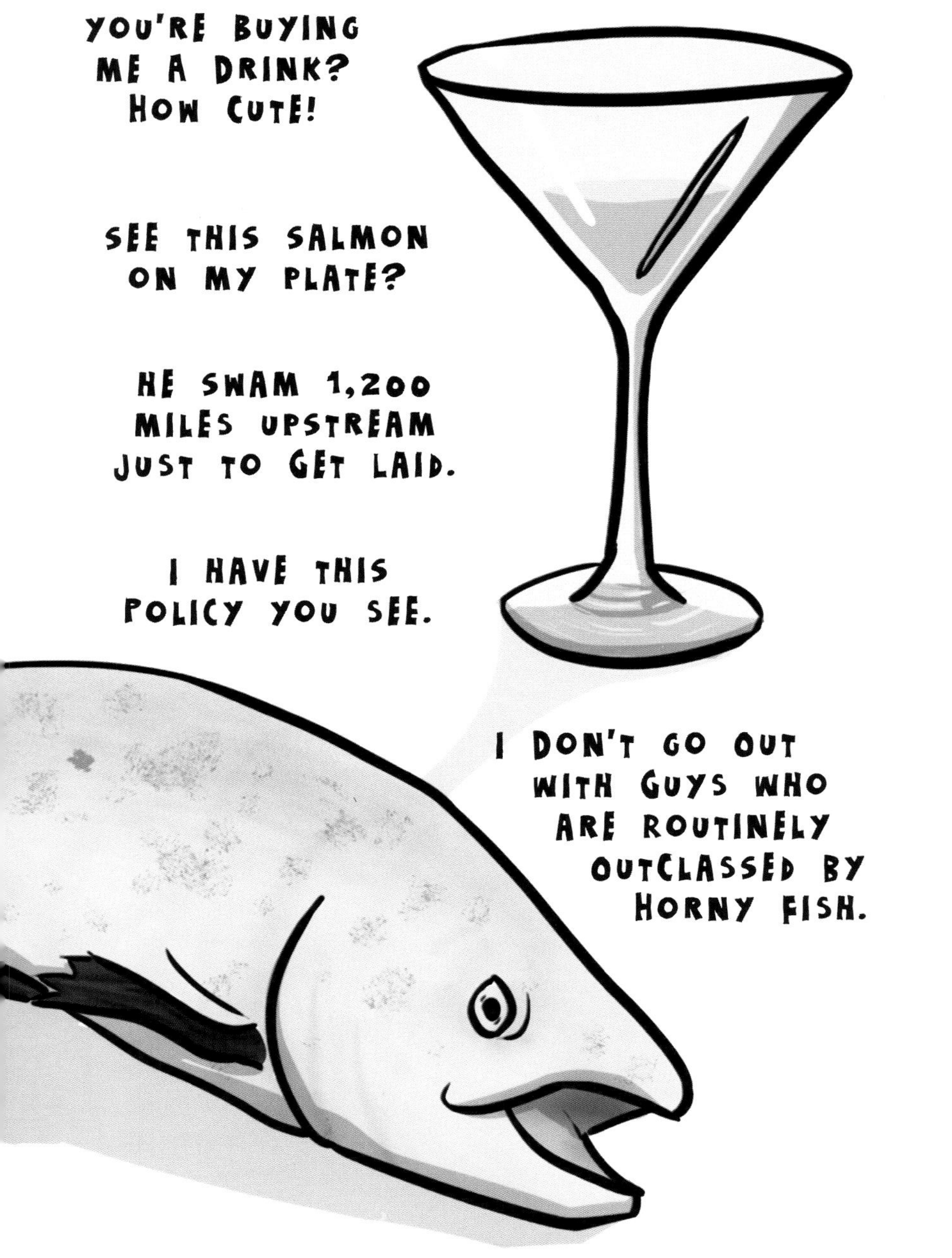
YOU'RE BUYING ME A DRINK? HOW CUTE!
SEE THIS SALMON ON MY PLATE?
HE SWAM 1,200 MILES UPSTREAM JUST TO GET LAID.
I HAVE THIS POLICY YOU SEE.
I DON'T GO OUT WITH GUYS WHO ARE ROUTINELY OUTCLASSED BY HORNY FISH.

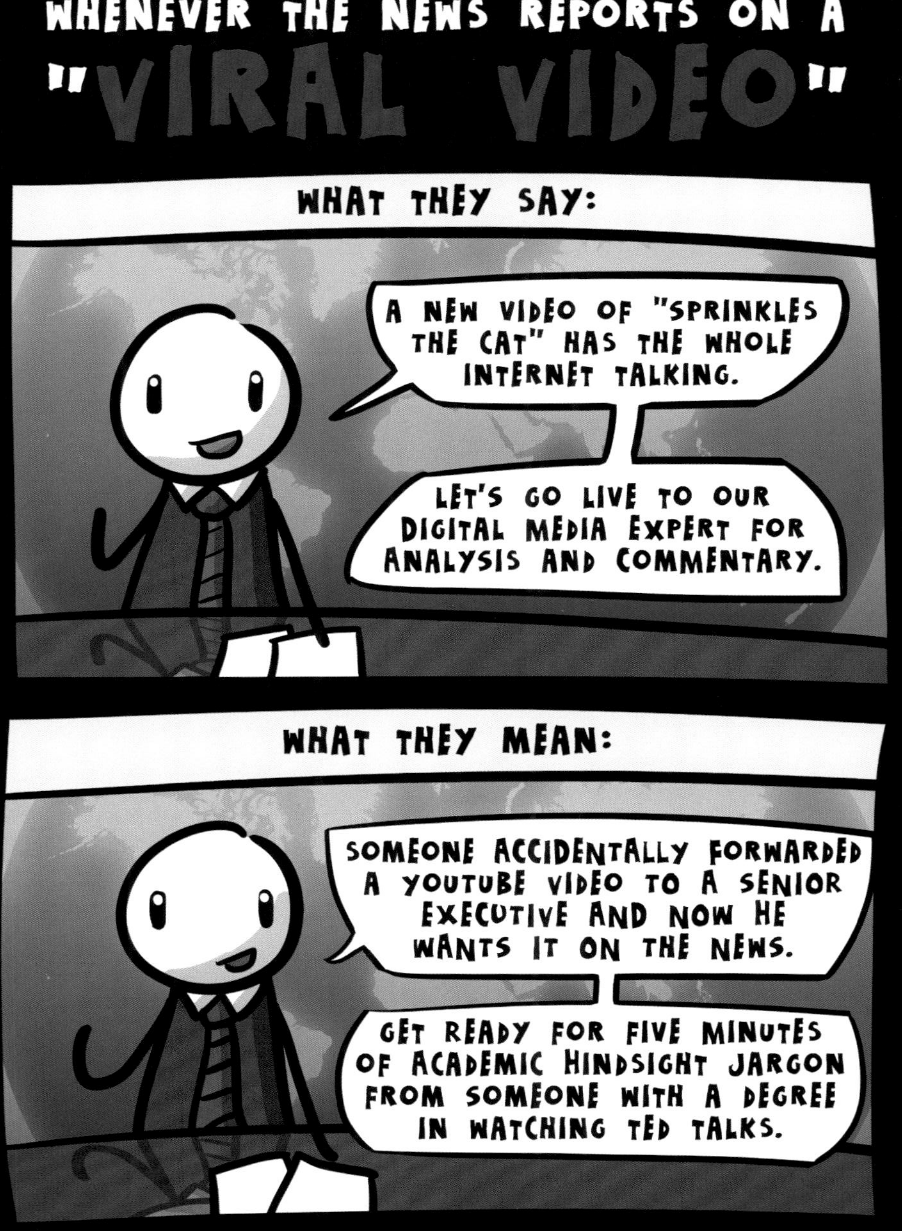
WHENEVER THE NEWS REPORTS ON A
"VIRAL VIDEO"
WHAT THEY SAY:
A NEW VIDEO OF "SPRINKLES THE CAT" HAS THE WHOLE INTERNET TALKING.
LET'S GO LIVE TO OUR DIGITAL MEDIA EXPERT FOR ANALYSIS AND COMMENTARY.
WHAT THEY MEAN:
SOMEONE ACCIDENTALLY FORWARDED A YOUTUBE VIDEO TO A SENIOR EXECUTIVE AND NOW HE WANTS IT ON THE NEWS.
GET READY FOR FIVE MINUTES OF ACADEMIC HINDSIGHT JARGON FROM SOMEONE WITH A DEGREE IN WATCHING TED TALKS.

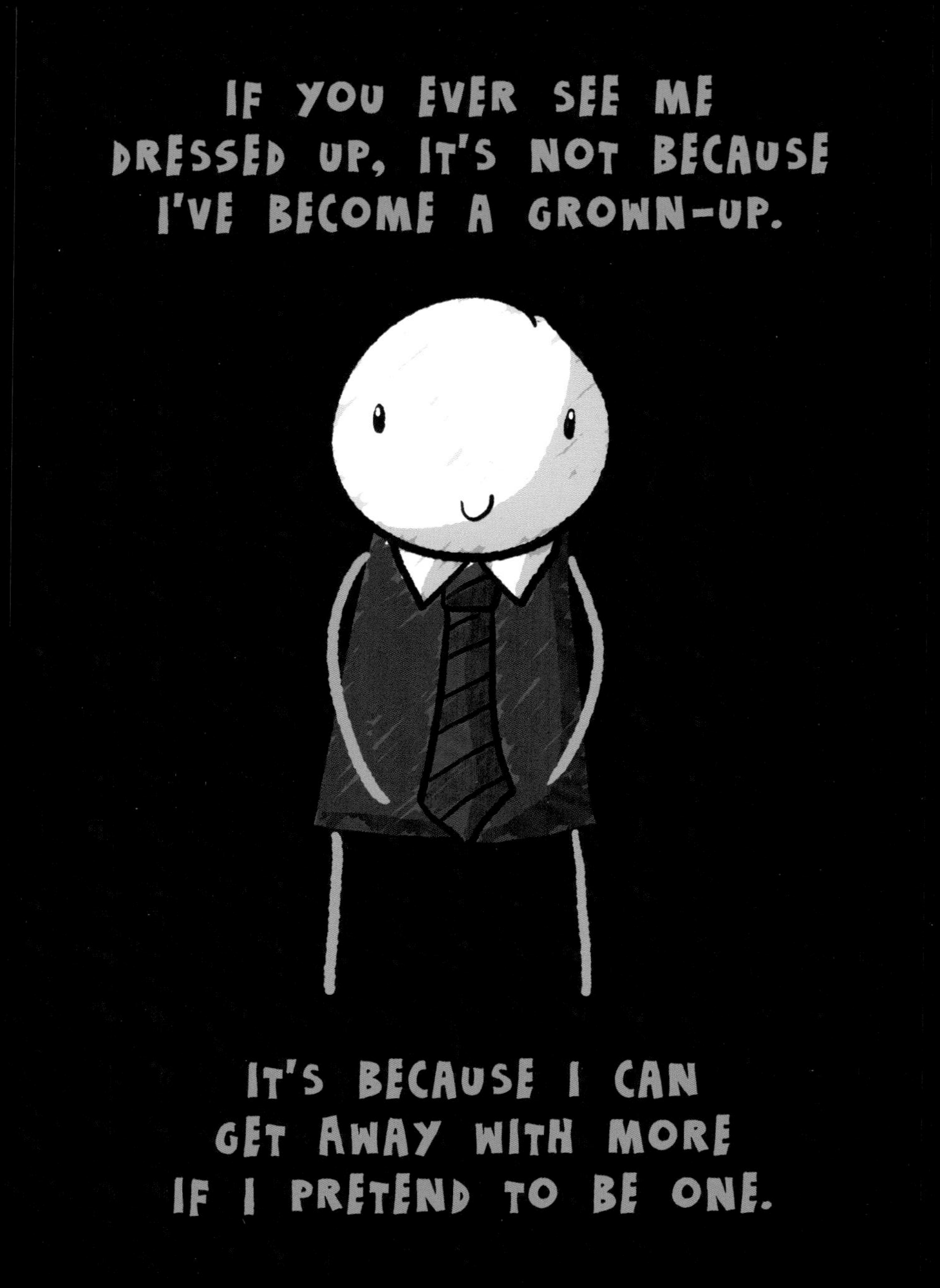
IF YOU EVER SEE ME DRESSED UP, IT'S NOT BECAUSE I'VE BECOME A GROWN-UP.
IT'S BECAUSE I CAN GET AWAY WITH MORE IF I PRETEND TO BE ONE.

IN A WORLD WHERE ZOMBIES ARE BITING EVERYONE,

ONE MAN FINDS THE COURAGE TO BITE BACK.

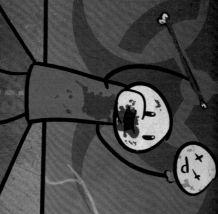

ZOMBIE-BITER
THE GUY WHO BITES ZOMBIES

"SOUNDS LIKE A TERRIBLE IDEA FOR A MOVIE."

—EVERYONE, EVERYWHERE

"I DON'T UNDERSTAND, HE BITES THE ZOMBIES?"

—THE DIRECTOR'S MOM

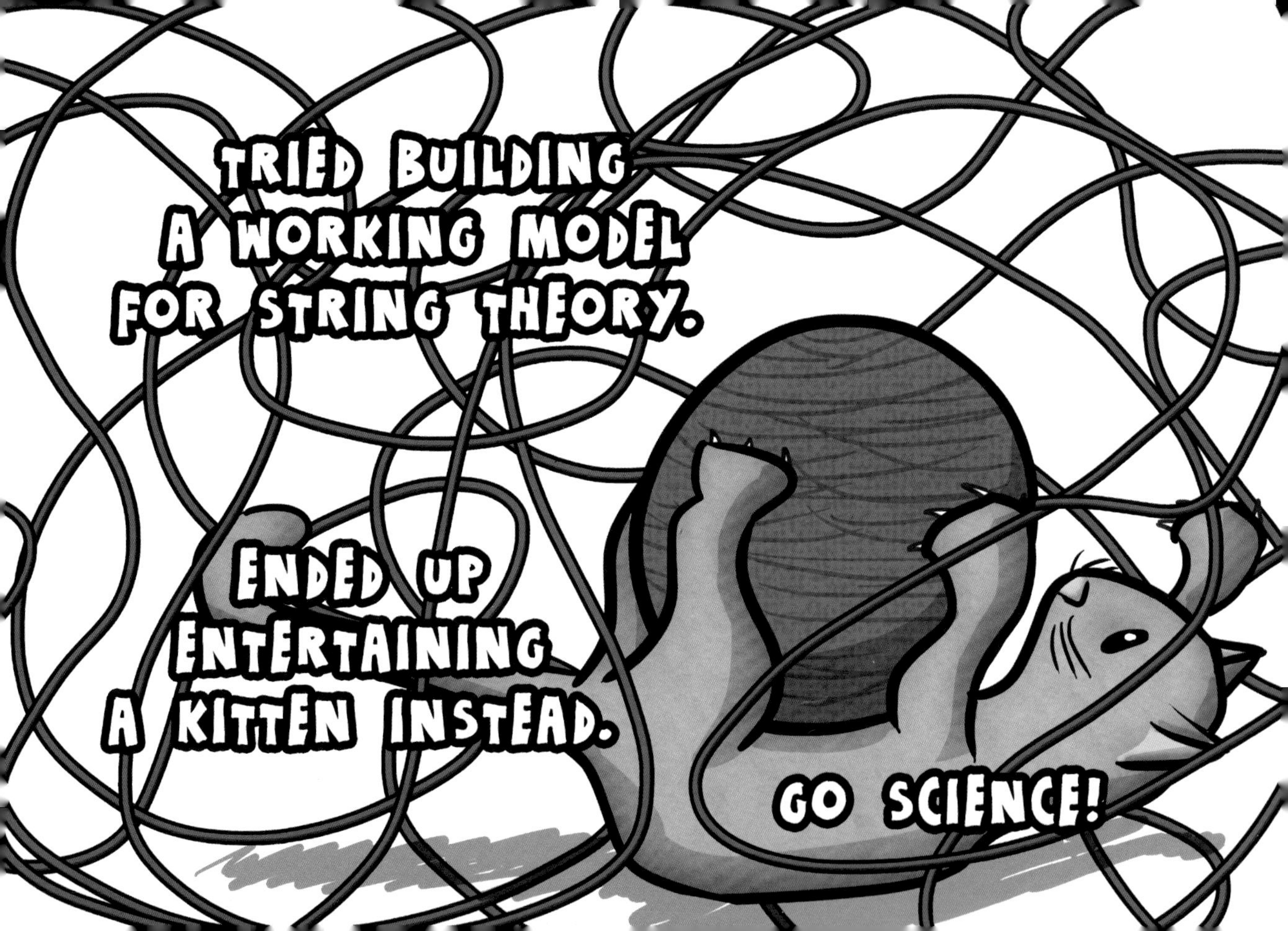
TRIED BUILDING A WORKING MODEL FOR STRING THEORY.
ENDED UP ENTERTAINING A KITTEN INSTEAD.
GO SCIENCE!

THE ONLY WAY TO DEAL WITH PEOPLE WHO DON'T BELIEVE IN UNICORNS

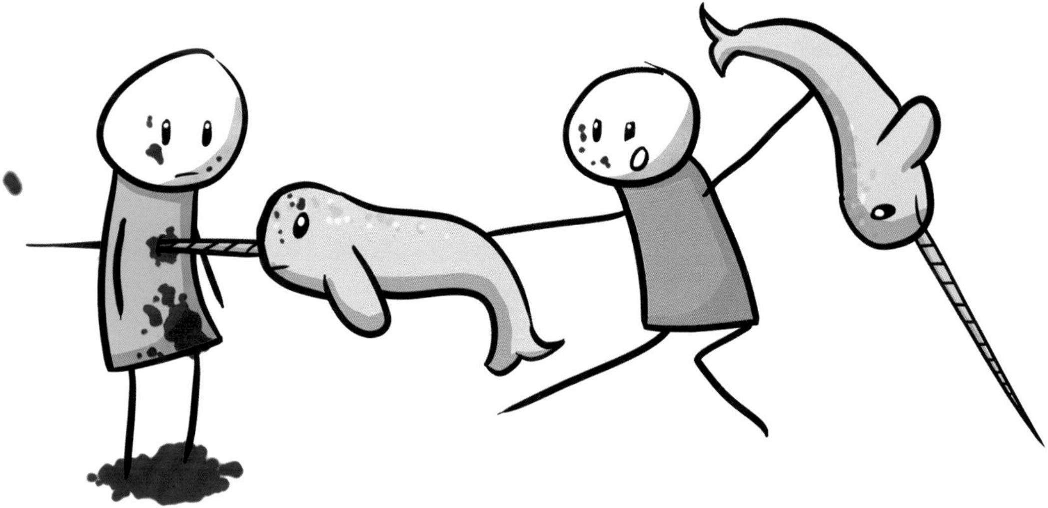

IS TO STAB THEM WITH NARWHALS.

TO OPEN YOUR ACCOUNT ON THIS WEBSITE, YOU MUST CHOOSE YOUR PASSWORD.

PASSWORD: | CHOOSEYOURPASSWORD |

❌ SORRY, YOUR PASSWORD MAY NOT CONTAIN THE WORD "PASSWORD."

PASSWORD: | CHOOSEYOUR |

❌ SORRY, YOUR PASSWORD MUST CONTAIN AT LEAST ONE NON-LETTER CHARACTER.

PASSWORD: | CHOOSEYOUR13 |

❌ SORRY, YOUR PASSWORD MUST CONTAIN AT LEAST ONE SCANDINAVIAN RUNE.

PASSWORD: | CHOOSEYOUR13 |

SORRY, YOUR PASSWORD MUST CONTAIN THE TRUE NAME OF AT LEAST ONE ANCIENT ENTITY OF COSMIC POWER.

PASSWORD: CHOOSEYOUR13CTHULHU

 SORRY, YOUR PASSWORD MUST CONTAIN AT LEAST ONE PASSAGE FROM THE BOOK OF REVELATION.

PASSWORD: CHOOSEYOUR13CTHULHUHISWRATHISCOME

 SORRY, YOUR PASSWORD SUMMONED THE DARK LORD CTHULHU, DEVOURER OF HOPE, SCOURGE OF SPIRITS.

PLEASE WAIT AS YOUR SOUL IS TORN FROM YOUR BODY.

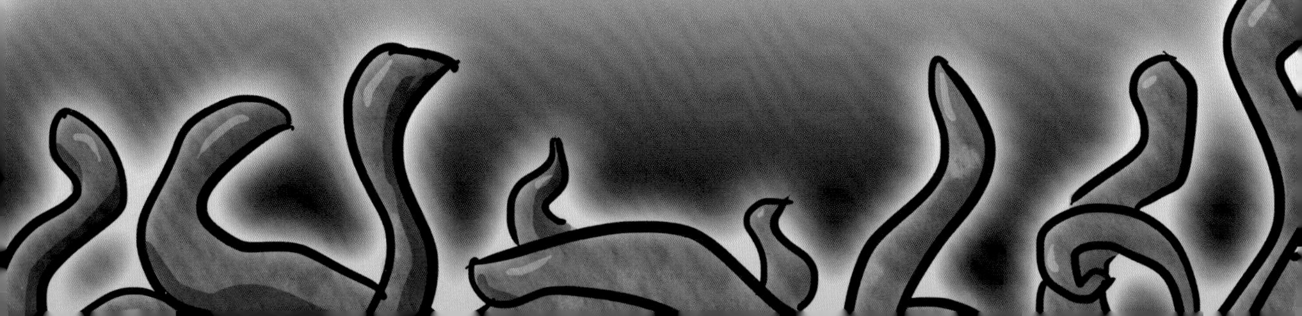

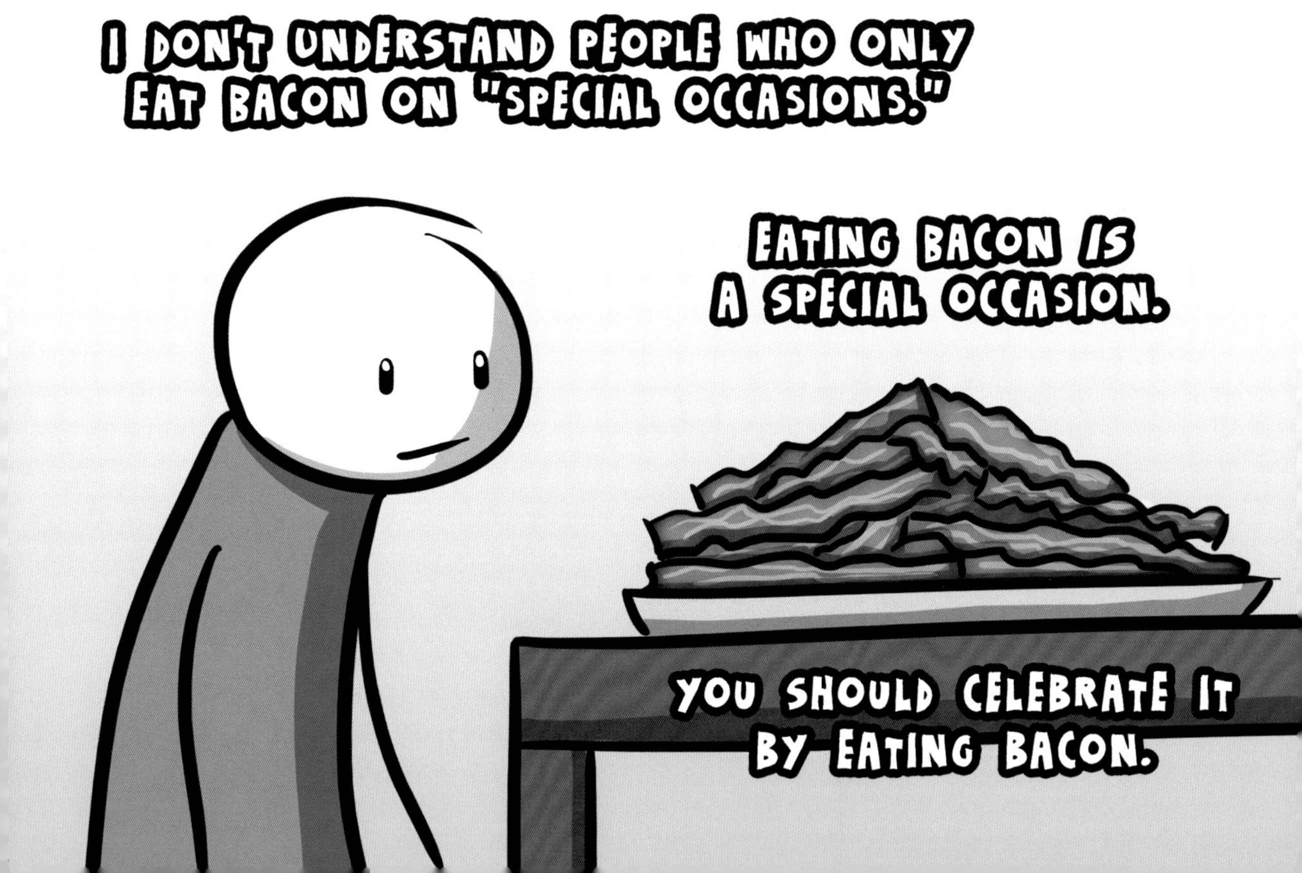
I DON'T UNDERSTAND PEOPLE WHO ONLY EAT BACON ON "SPECIAL OCCASIONS."
EATING BACON IS A SPECIAL OCCASION.
YOU SHOULD CELEBRATE IT BY EATING BACON.

I KNOW MONEY CAN'T BUY HAPPINESS.

BUT IT CAN BUY ICE CREAM,

AND I'M NOT READY TO LIVE IN A WORLD WHERE THERE IS A DIFFERENCE.

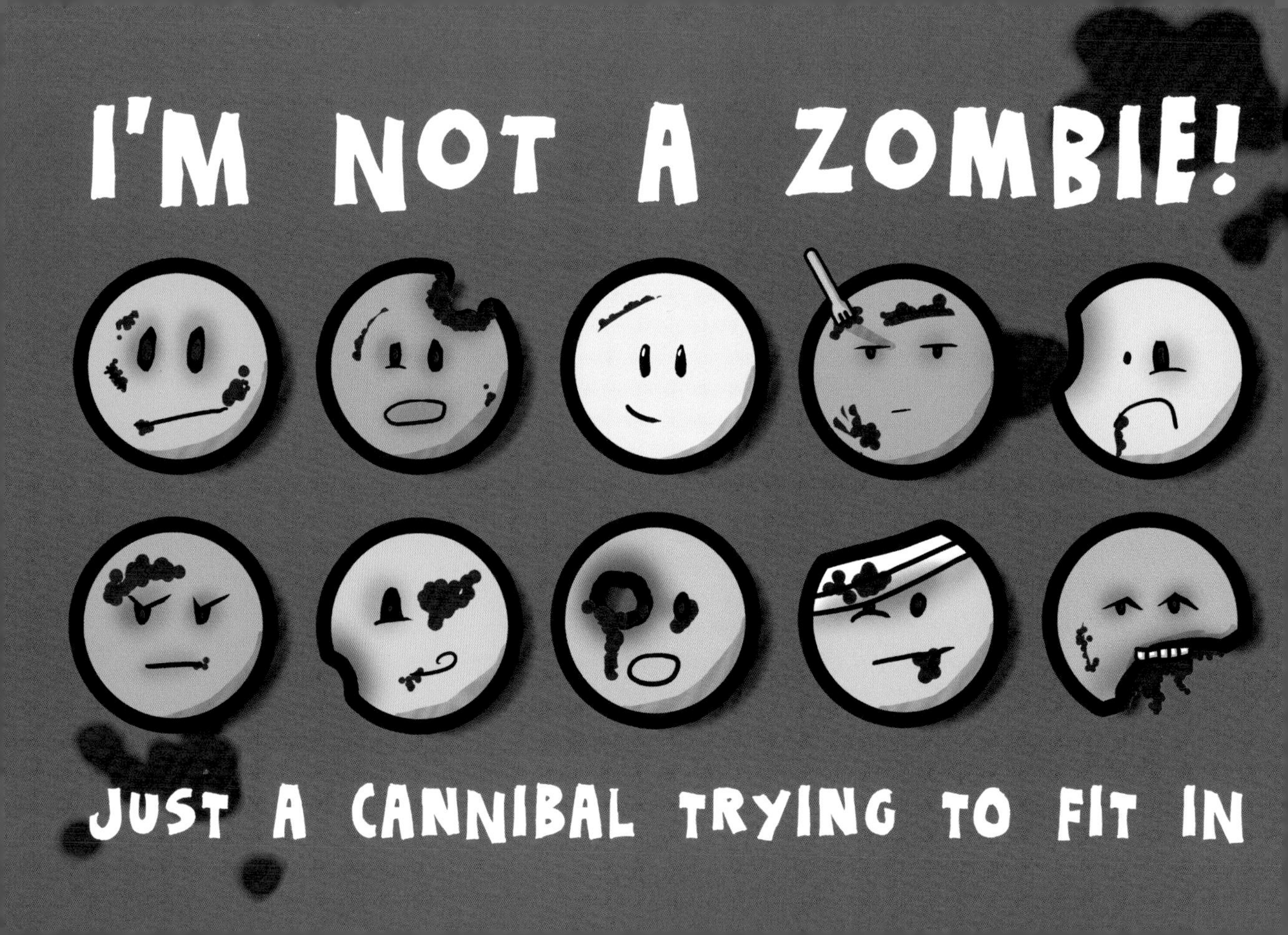
I'M NOT A ZOMBIE!
JUST A CANNIBAL TRYING TO FIT IN

THINGS THAT ARE ALWAYS AWESOME

- ✓ BEST FRIENDS
- ✓ DINOSAURS
- ✓ READING

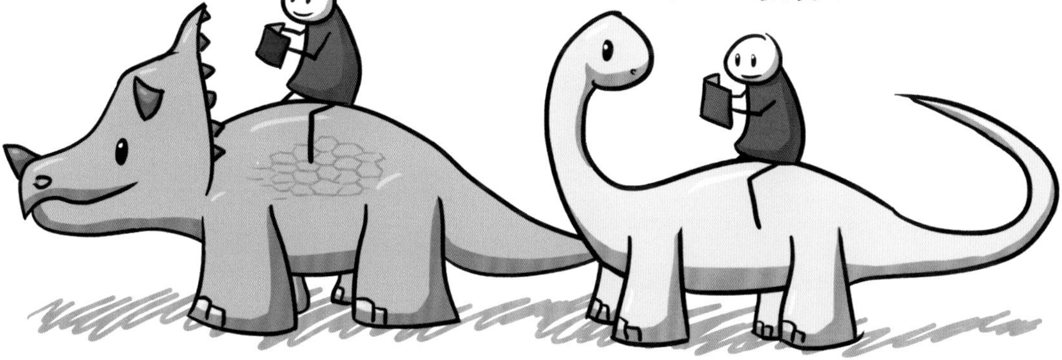

LIVIN' THE GOOD LIFE

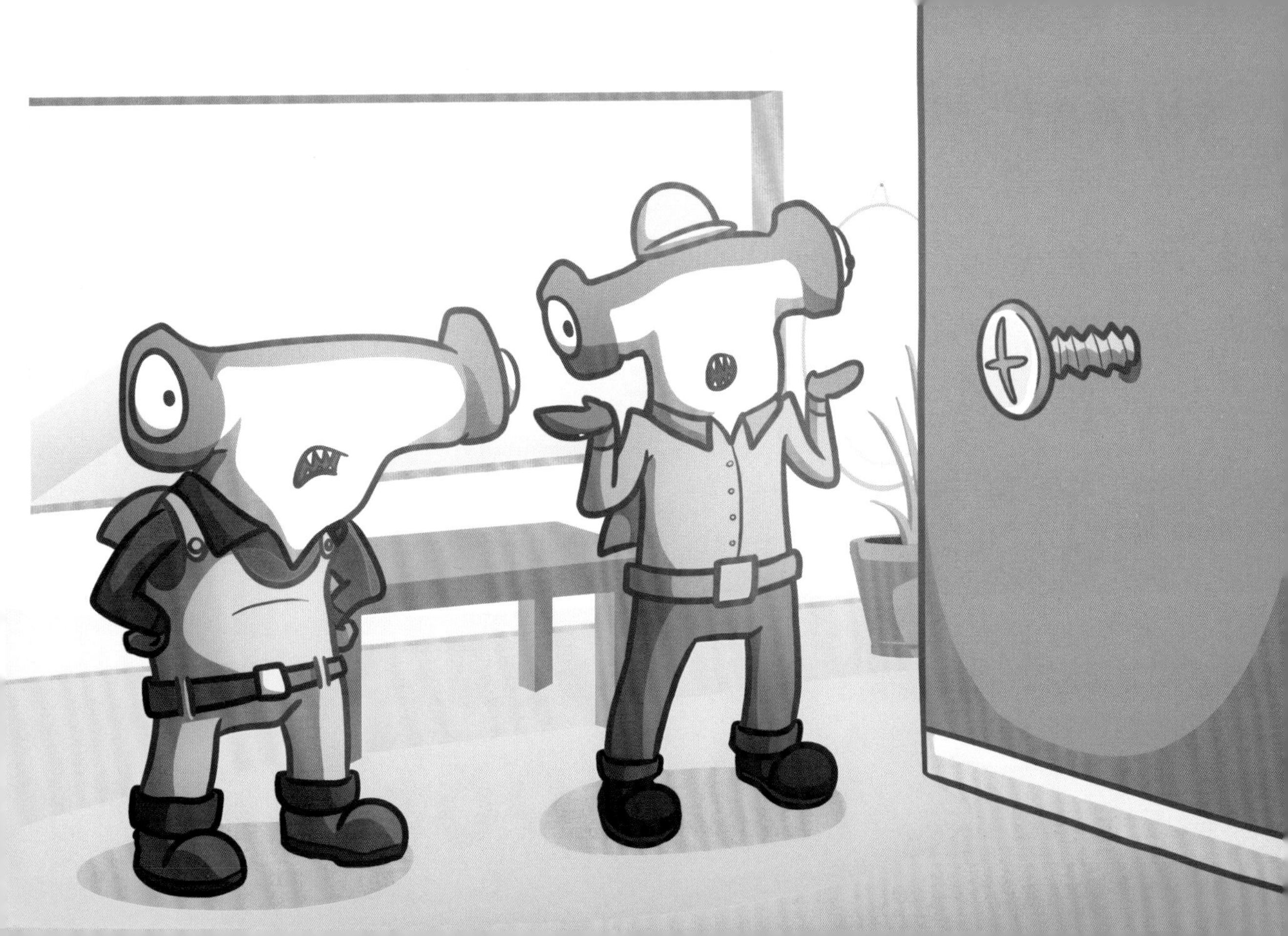

FART IN A TIME CAPSULE. * ORANGE JUICE-FLAVORED TOOTHPASTE. *
DRESS UP AS A PINATA FOR HALLOWEEN. * TRY TO MAKE YOUR
SMALLPOX INFECTION GO VIRAL. * COLLECT LIVE LANDMINES. * DRAGONS'
DEN WITH REAL DRAGONS. * TAKE THE ADVICE TO "LIGHT A FIRE UNDER
SOMEONE" LITERALLY. * LET A BEAR MOW YOUR LAWN. * TELL YOUR
TEENAGE DAUGHTER THAT TWILIGHT VAMPIRES AREN'T REAL VAMPIRES.

BAD IDEA #2343: HAMMERHEAD SHARK HANDYMEN.

SCORPION JUGGLING. * YOU + RAW STEAK + TENT + BEAR COUNTRY. * PAY
YOUR PARKING METER BY CHECK. * PORCUPINE ACUPUNCTURE. * TALK
LOUDLY ON YOUR PHONE ABOUT HOW YOU PLAN TO INVITE SOME FRIENDS
FOR PUBLIC MASTICATION IN THE PARK. DON'T FORGET THE WIENERS! *
START A LUCRATIVE ARMS RACE IN THE EPIC BATTLE OF DOG VS. SQUIRREL.
* HUMAN BATTLE CHESS. * HANG-GLIDE NAKED IN A SNOWSTORM.

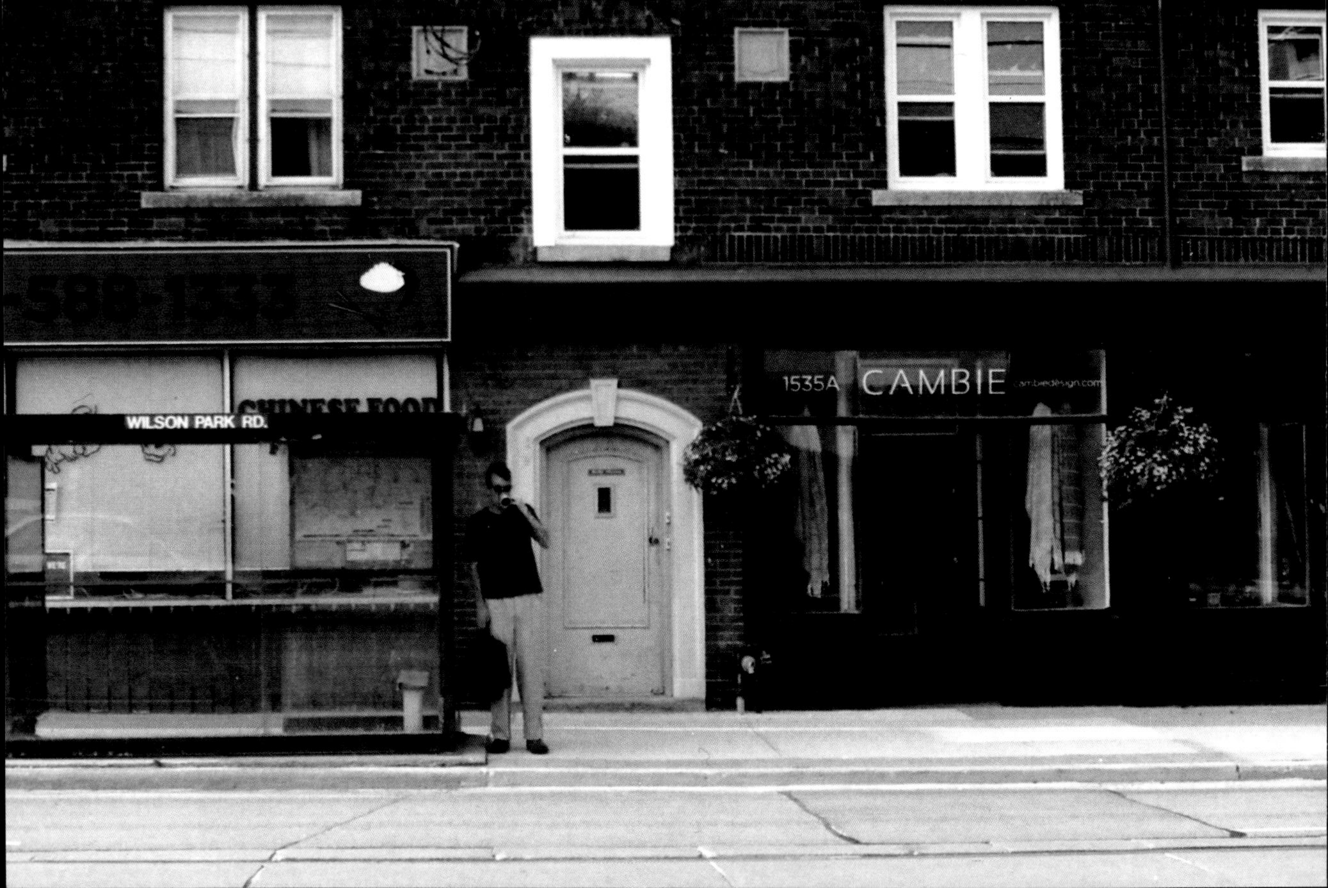

WILSON PARK RD.
CHINESE FOOD
1535A
CAMBIE
cambiedesign.com

NAME YOUR CHILD ANONYMOUS. * TELL SECRETS TO YOUR PARROT. * PLAY PAINTBALL IN AN ART GALLERY. * SUBURBAN GUARD DRAGONS. * BRING A NERF GUN TO THE ZOMBIE APOCALYPSE. * GOOGLE "FREE SCREENSAVERS" WITHOUT ANTIVIRUS INSTALLED. * FIGHT THE ROCK WITH A ROCK. * TOUT THE BENEFITS OF HABANERO EYE DROPS. BREAK A JAWBREAKER EMOTIONALLY. * STRIP-DANCE FOR PENNIES.

BAD IDEA #2498: "WEAR WHAT YOU SLEEP IN TO WORK" DAY.

BUBBLEWRAP BODY ARMOUR. * RECORD "GET ON THE GROUND! THIS IS A ROBBERY!" AS YOUR RINGTONE. * GROUP SEX WITH THE LIGHTS OFF. * GROUP SEX WITH THE LIGHTS ON. * TAKE THE PHRASE "KILL 'EM ALL AND LET GOD SORT THEM OUT" AS YOUR PERSONAL GOAL IN LIFE. * SERVE ABSINTHE DAIQUIRIS AT AN INTERNATIONAL PEACE TALK. * GIVE IRON MAN ANEMIA. * HAVE A RACIST-THEMED WEDDING. * NARWHAL FIGHT

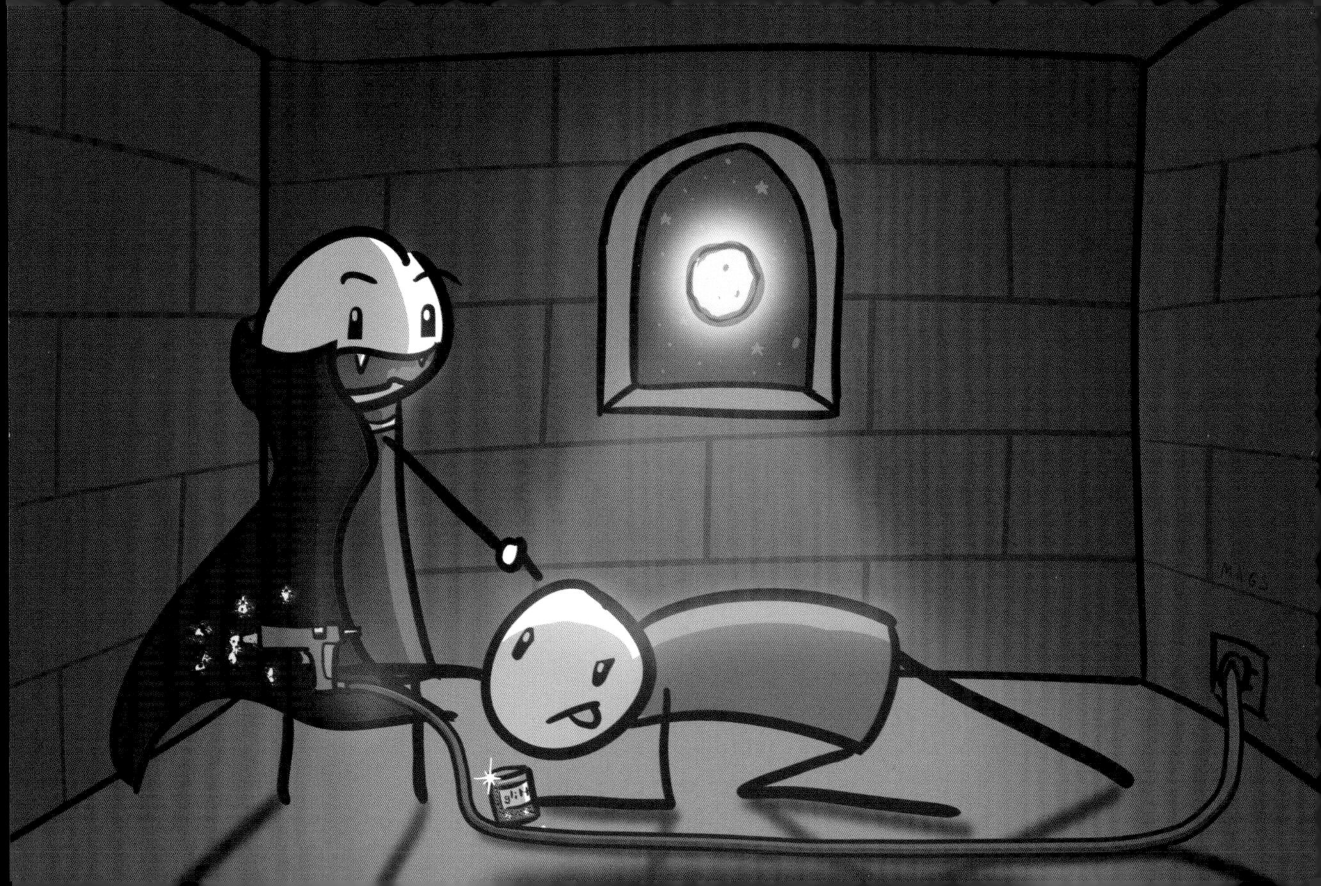

READ THE COMMENTS SECTION OF ANYTHING, EVER. * "TRY THIS AT HOME." * SELL YOUR BONES ON EBAY. * CLEAN ELECTRONICS WITH WATER. * REPLACE YOUR LIVER WITH A NOVELTY FLASK. * BUILD A PORTABLE TELEPORTER THAT ONLY USES EUROPEAN OUTLETS. * PLAY H.O.R.S.E. WITH MARVEL'S TASKMASTER. * GO BACK IN TIME TO DRAW SATANIC GRAFFITI ON PLYMOUTH ROCK BEFORE THE PILGRIMS LAND. *

BAD IDEA #2583: GLUE SPARKLES TO A VAMPIRE.

RESCUE AND ADOPT A BATTLE ORANGUTAN. * KILL THYME. * DISOBEY THE ROBOT OVERLORDS. * BREAK UP THE BAND. * DEEP-SEA DIVE WITHOUT OXYGEN. * DECEPTIVE DIVORCE CONDITIONS: "PARTNER AGREES TO PAY $2,000 IN ALIMONY PER MONTH IN EQUIVALENT CANS OF EXPIRED TUNA." * GO BANKRUPT IN DUBAI "FOR THE LOLZ." * PADDLE A CHOCOLATE CANOE THROUGH HOT SPRINGS FULL OF PIRANHAS. * FULL-CONTACT PATTICAKE.

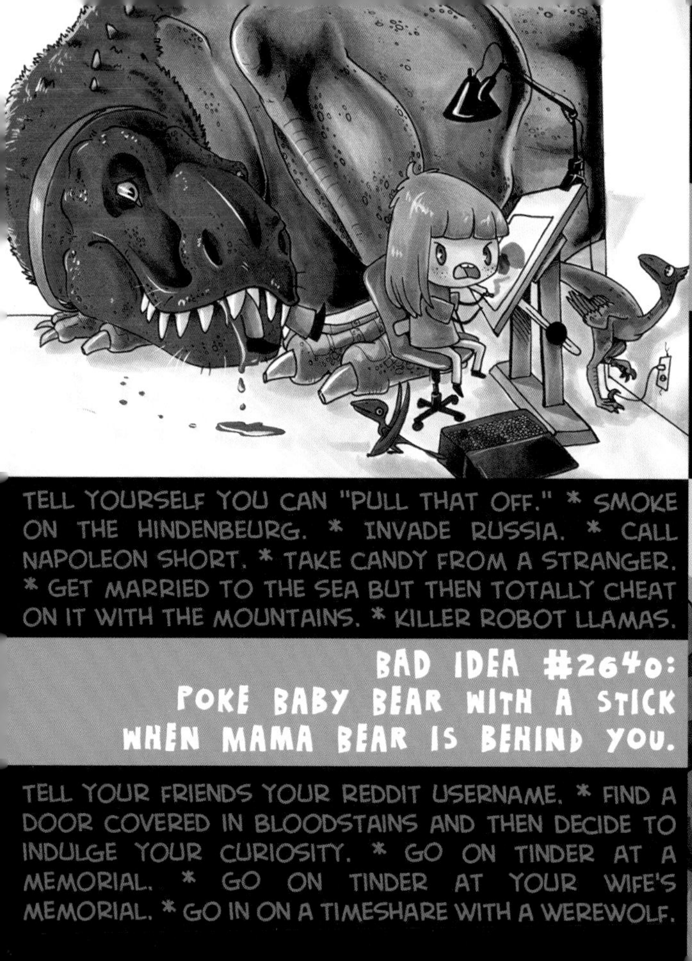

TELL YOURSELF YOU CAN "PULL THAT OFF." * SMOKE ON THE HINDENBEURG. * INVADE RUSSIA. * CALL NAPOLEON SHORT. * TAKE CANDY FROM A STRANGER. * GET MARRIED TO THE SEA BUT THEN TOTALLY CHEAT ON IT WITH THE MOUNTAINS. * KILLER ROBOT LLAMAS.

BAD IDEA #2640: POKE BABY BEAR WITH A STICK WHEN MAMA BEAR IS BEHIND YOU.

TELL YOUR FRIENDS YOUR REDDIT USERNAME. * FIND A DOOR COVERED IN BLOODSTAINS AND THEN DECIDE TO INDULGE YOUR CURIOSITY. * GO ON TINDER AT A MEMORIAL. * GO ON TINDER AT YOUR WIFE'S MEMORIAL. * GO IN ON A TIMESHARE WITH A WEREWOLF.

JELLYFISH DODGEBALL. * TELL YOURSELF YOU'LL FINISH THAT ESSAY "IN THE MORNING." * GET ADVICE FROM THE INTERNET. * SELF-DIAGNOSE CANCER. * STARE INTO THE SUN. * SOCKS AND SANDALS. * CASUAL HOOK-UPS AT THE D.M.V.

BAD IDEA #2615: "BRING YOUR DINOSAUR TO WORK" DAY.

JELLYFISH WIGS. * PICK-UP HOCKEY ON THE SUBWAY TRACKS. * IGNORE THE ORACLE AT DELPHI. * TATTOO THE NAME OF EVERY TINDER MATCH ONTO YOUR BODY. * PISTOL DUEL AFTER A NIGHT OF HEAVY DRINKING. * NAP-TIME AT THE CREMATORIUM.

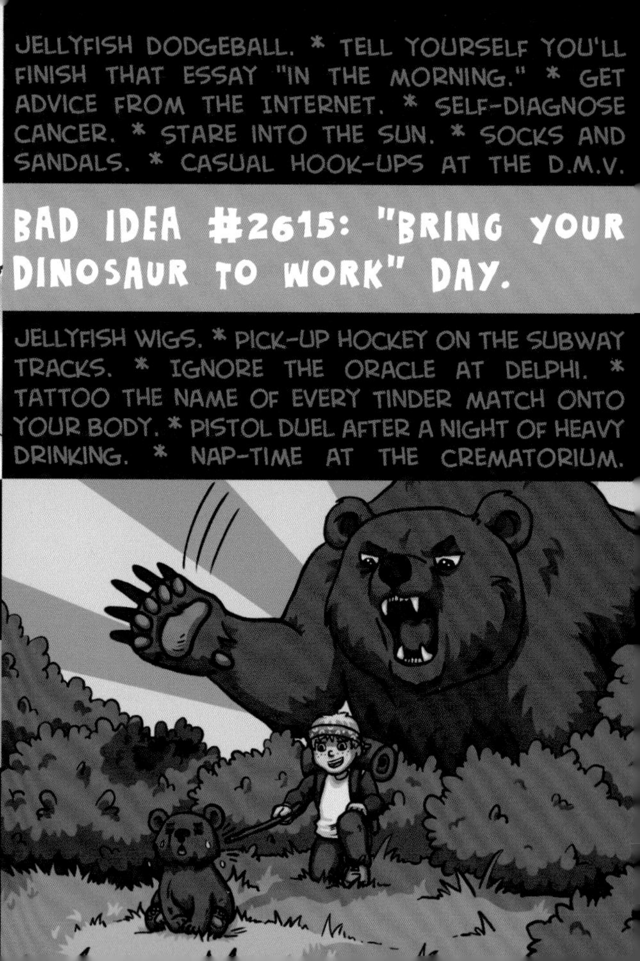

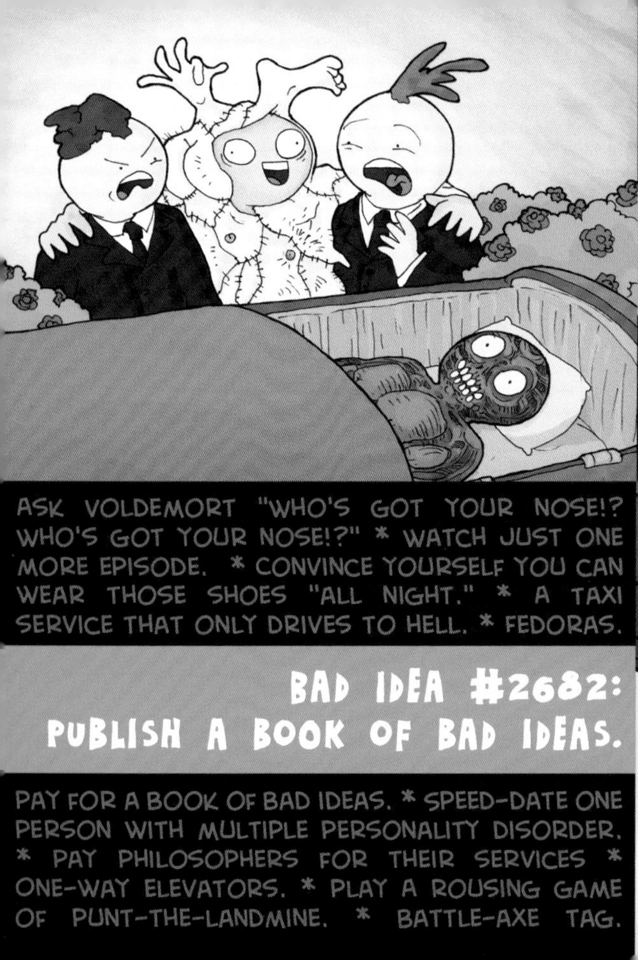

ASK VOLDEMORT "WHO'S GOT YOUR NOSE!? WHO'S GOT YOUR NOSE!?" * WATCH JUST ONE MORE EPISODE. * CONVINCE YOURSELF YOU CAN WEAR THOSE SHOES "ALL NIGHT." * A TAXI SERVICE THAT ONLY DRIVES TO HELL. * FEDORAS.

BAD IDEA #2682: PUBLISH A BOOK OF BAD IDEAS.

PAY FOR A BOOK OF BAD IDEAS. * SPEED-DATE ONE PERSON WITH MULTIPLE PERSONALITY DISORDER. * PAY PHILOSOPHERS FOR THEIR SERVICES * ONE-WAY ELEVATORS. * PLAY A ROUSING GAME OF PUNT-THE-LANDMINE. * BATTLE-AXE TAG.

HOLD A NARCOTICS ANONYMOUS MEETING IN AN OPIUM DEN. * WEAR A TURKEY COSTUME THE WEEK BEFORE THANKSGIVING. * PHOTOSHOP GANDALF INTO YOUR ONLINE DATING PROFILE PICTURE. * EAT UNCOOKED CENTIPEDE. * GET A SPRAY-ON SUNBURN.

BAD IDEA #2651: TURN UP TO A FUNERAL IN THE SKIN OF THE DEPARTED.

GENETICALLY ENGINEER A MONSTER THAT ATTACKS A STARBUCKS EVERY TIME SOMEONE SAYS "CAN'T EVEN." * EAT A SPOONFUL OF CINNAMON. * GIVE YOUR MOTHER THE KEYS TO YOUR APARTMENT. * GET AN MD IN FAITH HEALING. * BUY MAGIC BEANS.

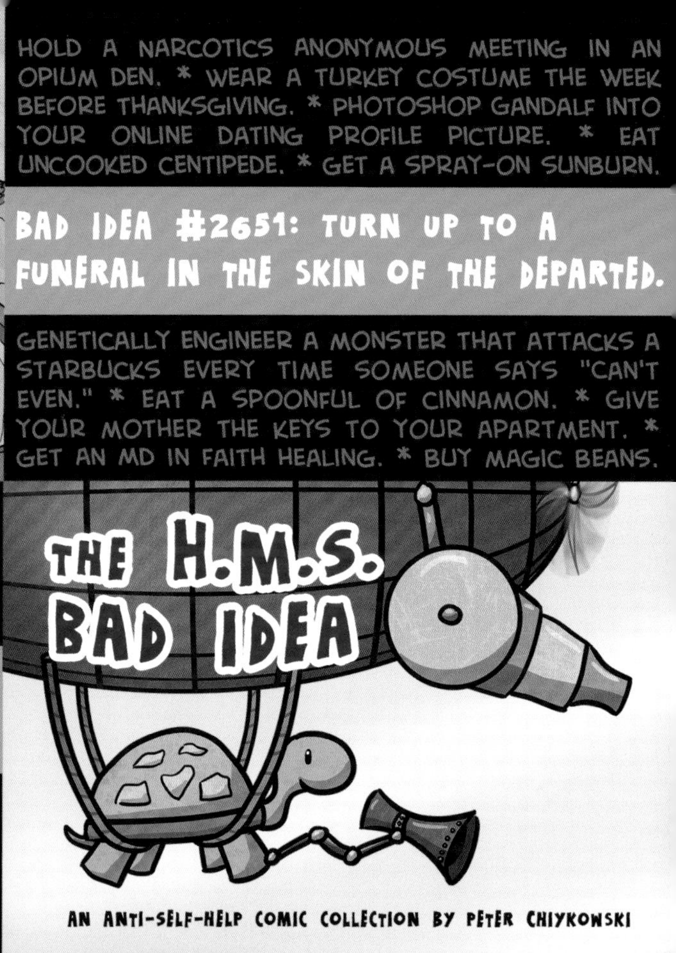
THE H.M.S.
BAD IDEA
AN ANTI-SELF-HELP COMIC COLLECTION BY PETER CHIYKOWSKI

THE END

GUEST ARTISTS AND BAD IDEA CONTRIBUTORS

BAD IDEA #1 WRITTEN BY NICHOLAS BRUCE AND ILLUSTRATED BY PETER CHIYKOWSKI.

BAD IDEA #285 WRITTEN BY KERI AND ILLUSTRATED BY KATIE TIEDRICH.

KATIE TIEDRICH MAKES *AWKWARD ZOMBIE*, A WEBCOMIC ABOUT VIDEOGAMES AND THE THINGS THAT HAPPEN IN THEM. WHEN SHE'S NOT DOING THAT, SHE'S USUALLY AT HER DAY JOB AS A MECHANICAL ENGINEER, BUILDING SPACESHIP PARTS. AWKWARDZOMBIE.COM

BAD IDEA #363 WRITTEN BY JOSH HAIWORONSKY AND CHANTEL REITER AND ILLUSTRATED BY CHRISTOPHER STEININGER.

CHRISTOPHER STEININGER WRITES AND ILLUSTRATES *DEAD HEAVEN*, A CHARACTER-DRIVEN, POST-APOCALYPTIC DARK FANTASY HORROR SERIES. DEADHEAVEN.NET

BAD IDEA #414 WRITTEN BY CRAIG LAWRIE AND ILLUSTRATED BY DOUG SAVAGE.

DOUG SAVAGE IS THE CREATOR OF *SAVAGE CHICKENS*, A COMIC DRAWN ENTIRELY ON STICKY NOTES. HIS WORK HAS BEEN PUBLISHED BY PENGUIN USA AND ANDREWS MCMEEL PUBLISHING. SAVAGECHICKENS.COM

BAD IDEA #421 WRITTEN BY MICHAEL LINN AND ILLUSTRATED BY PETER CHIYKOWSKI.

BAD IDEA #451 WRITTEN BY JOE MOLINOSKI AND ILLUSTRATED BY SUZE SHORE.

SUZE IS A FREELANCE ILLUSTRATOR AND BACKGROUND COLORIST WORKING IN OTTAWA. SHE DIVIDES HER TIME BETWEEN WORKING ON SUPERHERO COMIC *MY SO-CALLED SECRET IDENTITY* AND IMMORTALIZING THE ANTICS OF HER CAT ON TUMBLR. SMUZE.NET

BAD IDEA #463 ILLUSTRATED BY ROB DENBLEYKER.

ROB DENBLEYKER IS CO-CREATOR OF THE WEBCOMIC *CYANIDE AND HAPPINESS*. HE IS A MAN'S BODY TRAPPED IN A MAN'S BODY. FOREVER STUCK IN A DOG KNOT. EXPLOSM.NET

BAD IDEA #517 WRITTEN BY AMBREA JOHNSON, ILLUSTRATED BY CHRISTOPHER HASTINGS, AND COLORED BY ANTHONY CLARK.

CHRISTOPHER HASTINGS IS A CARTOONIST, WRITER, AND COMEDIAN LIVING IN BROOKLYN WITH HIS WIFE, CARLY MONARDO, AND DOG, COMMISSIONER GORDON. BEST KNOWN FOR *THE ADVENTURES OF DR. MCNINJA*, HE WRITES OTHER COMICS TOO--MOSTLY A LOT OF DEADPOOL. YOU CAN USUALLY FIND HIM PERFORMING WEEKLY IMPROV COMEDY AT THE MAGNET THEATER. DRMCNINJA.COM

BAD IDEA #690 WRITTEN BY "TURCK3" AND ILLUSTRATED BY ZACH WEINER.

ZACH WEINERSMITH, CREATOR OF THE POPULAR COMIC *SATURDAY MORNING BREAKFAST CEREAL*, HAS A DEGREE IN LITERATURE AND 3/8'S OF A DEGREE IN PHYSICS. HE ENJOYS READING ABOUT MATH, LOGIC, SCIENCE, HISTORY, FICTION, AND PHILOSOPHY. HIS HOBBIES ARE SPACE TRAVEL, DINOSAUR RIDING, AND WISHFUL THINKING. SMBC-COMICS.COM

BAD IDEA #706 WRITTEN BY HUSEIN PANJU AND ILLUSTRATED BY AARON LENK.

AARON LENK IS A TORONTO-BASED WRITER/ARTIST WHO LIKES TO THINK ABOUT HIS EXISTENCE IN HIS SPARE TIME. HE MAKES COMICS, DRAWS PICTURES, AND HE MADE *DAVE'S WURLD*, A STORY ABOUT GOD, BUT ALSO NOT GOD. HE LIKES GUMMY BEARS. BIGSIMPLECOMICS.COM

HUSEIN PANJU IS A TORONTO-BASED CARTOONIST, WHO JOINED THE COMIC SCENE IN SEPTEMBER 2013. HIS WEEKLY WEBCOMIC, *HIGH COMEDIC VALUE*, PUTS A SPIN ON EVERYDAY LIFE AND IS ACCESSIBLE TO NERDS AND NON-NERDS ALIKE. ALTHOUGH HE IS A LAWYER BY PROFESSION, HUSEIN'S ACTUALLY A PRETTY DECENT HUMAN BEING. HIGHCOMEDICVALUE.COM

BAD IDEA #725 WRITTEN BY SOLEGO AND ILLUSTRATED BY PETER CHIYKOWSKI.

BAD IDEA #756 WRITTEN BY FANBOAT AND ILLUSTRATED BY CHRIS "LUNARBABOON" GRADY.

LUNARBABOON IS MARRIED AND HAS ONE CHILD. HE WORKS AS A SCHOOL TEACHER AND LIVES A LIFE SIMILAR TO MOST NORTH AMERICAN HUMANS. LUNARBABOON.COM

BAD IDEA #780 WRITTEN BY ARMOND NETHERLY AND ILLUSTRATED BY ANDREW GREGOIRE.

ANDREW GREGOIRE IS A TORONTO-BASED CHARACTER ANIMATOR AND ILLUSTRATOR BEST KNOWN FOR HIS WEBCOMIC, *I AM ARG!*--A "SLICE OF LIFE" NERD HUMOR COMIC ABOUT A YOUNG COUPLE COMING TO TERMS WITH THEIR IMPENDING ADULTHOOD. ANDREW PLAYS PRINCESS PEACH IN SUPER SMASH BROS. IAMARG.COM

BAD IDEA #800 WRITTEN BY NIELS NELLISSEN AND ILLUSTRATED BY VITALY S. ALEXIUS.

VITALY S. ALEXIUS WORKS AS A PHOTOGRAPHER/ FREELANCE ILLUSTRATOR AND PAINTS THE ONLINE GRAPHIC NOVEL *ROMANTICALLY APOCALYPTIC*. ROM.AC

BAD IDEA #912 WRITTEN BY ROBIN ESS AND ILLUSTRATED BY ANTHONY CLARK.

ANTHONY IS A COMPUTER PROGRAM DESIGNED FOR THE EXPRESS PURPOSE OF DRAWING GOOFY COMICS. HE WRITES *NEDROID PICTURE DIARY* AND DOES THE COLORS ON *THE ADVENTURES OF DR. MCNINJA*. NEDROID.COM

BAD IDEA #1032 WRITTEN BY "LORD OF THE HONEY BADGERS" AND ILLUSTRATED BY RYAN NORTH.

RYAN NORTH IS A PRETTY OKAY DUDE WHO LIVES IN TORONTO. HE HAS TWO DEGREES IN THE COMPUTER

SCIENCES, IF YOU CAN BELIEVE THAT! GIVING AWAY COMICS FOR FREE ON THE INTERNET IS WHAT PAYS HIS RENT, AND HE'S REALLY HAPPY ABOUT THAT. RYAN HAS KISSED, BY HIS COUNT, AT LEAST FOUR DIFFERENT WOMEN, AND THEY ALL TOTALLY CAME BACK FOR MORE. QWANTZ.COM

BAD IDEA # 1107 WRITTEN BY TESS HOLMQUIST AND ILLUSTRATED BY ALEX WRONSKI.

ALEX WRONSKI PONDERS QUESTIONS OF LIFE AND HAPPINESS IN HIS EXISTENTIALIST WEBCOMIC, *1111 COMICS*. HIS COMICS HAVE TWO SIDES AND CAN BE BOTH DARK AND HILARIOUS, DEPENDING ON WHICH PERSPECTIVE YOU CHOOSE TO VIEW THEM FROM. 1111COMICS.ME

BAD IDEA #1120 WRITTEN BY SHENG WANG AND ILLUSTRATED BY SARA ZIMMERMAN.

UNEARTHED COMICS IS CREATED BY ARTIST/ DESIGNER, SARA ZIMMERMAN. IT IS A WEBCOMIC THAT UPDATES SEVERAL TIMES A WEEK, FEATURING COMICS ABOUT SCIENCE, PARENTING, BUSINESS, THE ENVIRONMENT, AND HEALTH. IT IS OFTEN CURATED BY AN ANTHROPOMORPHIC MARILYN EARTH CHARACTER AND IS DOUSED IN DOUBLE ENTENDRES, WORD-PLAY, AND MORE. UNEARTHEDCOMICS.COM

BAD IDEA #1175 ILLUSTRATED BY ANDREW GRIEVE.

ANDREW GRIEVE IS A WEBCOMIC ARTIST OPERATING OUT OF CALGARY, ALBERTA. ANDREW ATTENDED THE ART INSTITUTE FOR VIDEO GAME ART AND DESIGN IN 2005, BUT HAS SINCE LEFT THE VIDEO GAME INDUSTRY TO FOCUS ON HIS COMIC SERIES, *TEAM STRYKER*. TEAMSTRYKERCOMIC.COM

BAD IDEA #1191 WRITTEN BY KARI MAAREN AND ILLUSTRATED BY STEVEN ROSIA.

STEVEN ROSIA IS A CANADIAN RABBLE-ROUSER BENT ON BURSTING FULL FORCE INTO THE COMIC BOOK INDUSTRY. CURRENTLY OPERATING OUT OF OKOTOKS, ALBERTA, HE IS ENJOYING A POSITIVELY DROLL LIFE WITH HIS WONDERFUL AND MOST ELOQUENT FIANCEE AND THEIR FEISTY PUP. WITHOUTATITLE.COM

BAD IDEA #1201 ILLUSTRATED BY PETER CHIYKOWSKI.

BAD IDEA #1248 WRITTEN BY SCOTT CORNEAU AND ILLUSTRATED BY LAR DESOUZA.

LAR DESOUZA IS AN AWARD-WINNING CARTOONIST KNOWN FOR *LEAST I COULD DO* AND *LOOKING FOR GROUP*. LEASTICOULDDO.COM

BAD IDEA #1355 WRITTEN BY MAESON HAUFFEN AND ILLUSTRATED BY ABBY HOWARD.

ABBY HOWARD IS THE CARTOONIST BEHIND *JUNIOR SCIENTIST POWER HOUR* AND *THE LAST HALLOWEEN*. JSPOWERHOUR.COM

BAD IDEA #1419 WRITTEN BY JOSE LUIS CASILLAS AND ILLUSTRATED BY JERI WEAVER.

JERI WEAVER CREATES HER OWN COMICS, WHICH SHE PUBLISHES UNDER THE SHARED NAME GURUKITTY STUDIOS. GURUKITTY.COM

BAD IDEA #1431 WRITTEN BY BART WALLS AND ILLUSTRATED BY KARI MAAREN.

KARI MAAREN IS RESPONSIBLE FOR A COMPLETED WEBCOMIC CALLED *WEST OF BATHURST*, AN ONGOING WEBCOMIC CALLED *IT NEVER RAINS*, A NUMBER OF CHEERFUL UKULELE SONGS ABOUT DISMEMBERMENT, AND THE CAREFUL SHAPING OF YOUNG MINDS, FOR SOME REASON. ITNEVERRAINSCOMIC.COM

BAD IDEA #1461 WRITTEN BY LUCA ROSE AND ILLUSTRATED BY ZACH SCHUSTER.

ZACH SCHUSTER IS FROM CALGARY, ALBERTA, AND IS CURRENTLY ATTENDING THE ALBERTA COLLEGE OF ART AND DESIGN. HE HOPES TO ONE DAY EITHER BE A RENOWNED SPACE PIRATE OR A PROFESSIONAL COMIC ARTIST. ZACH'S CURRENT PROJECT IS A WEBCOMIC CALLED *MEAT LOVER'S SPECIAL*. MLS.THECOMICSERIES.COM

BAD IDEA #1488 WRITTEN BY STEPHANIE POTVIN AND ILLUSTRATED BY DAVIE CAHILL.

DAVIE WRITES AND ILLUSTRATES THE WEBCOMIC *PICTURES IN BOXES*. PICTURESINBOXES.COM

BAD IDEA #1571 WRITTEN BY MICHAEL EPSTEIN AND ILLUSTRATED BY REZA FARAZMAND.

REZA WRITES DRAWS COMICS AND WRITES THINGS. POORLYDRAWNLINES.COM

BAD IDEA #1678 WRITTEN BY ANDREAS "DANZI" DANZEBRINK AND ILLUSTRATED BY ARTHUR "LAZERHORSE" DOYLE.

"LAZERHORSE" IS THE ALIAS OF ILLUSTRATOR ARTHUR DOYLE. WHILE HE CURRENTLY RESIDES IN TORONTO, ARTHUR LIVED MOST OF HIS LIFE IN HALIFAX, NOVA SCOTIA, WHERE HE SPENT HIS FORMATIVE YEARS PLAYING TOO MANY VIDEO GAMES. LAZERHORSE.COM

BAD IDEA #1702 WRITTEN BY ROB SKENE, DEDICATED TO FINLAY, AND ILLUSTRATED BY GREGOR CZAYKOWSKI.

AFTER A BRIEF QUARTER-LIFE CRISIS, GREGOR CZAYKOWSKI STARTED A WEBCOMIC CALLED *LOADING ARTIST* AND CONTINUES TO WORK ON IT IN HIS SPARE TIME, HOPING TO EVENTUALLY ACHIEVE CRAZY AMOUNTS OF FAME AND FORTUNE. LOADINGARTIST.COM

BAD IDEA #1811 WRITTEN BY NATHAN WOOD AND ILLUSTRATED BY JUSTIN BOYD.

JUSTIN BOYD IS A PROGRAMMER AND THE CREATOR OF THE WEBCOMIC *INVISIBLE BREAD*. INVISIBLEBREAD.COM

BAD IDEA #1825 ILLUSTRATED BY PETER CHIYKOWSKI.

BAD IDEA #1870 WRITTEN BY LESHIA DOUCET AND ILLUSTRATED BY ANGELA MELICK.

ANGELA MELICK IS A COMICKER FROM VANCOUVER, CANADA. SHE IS BEST KNOWN AS THE CREATOR OF THE WEBCOMIC *WASTED TALENT*. WASTEDTALENT.CA

BAD IDEA #1895 WRITTEN BY NIELS NELLISSEN AND ILLUSTRATED BY SHAWN DALEY.

SHAWN DALEY IS A CANADIAN CARTOONIST AND CREATOR OF *TERRAQUILL*, AN ONGOING SHORT STORY COMIC. HE SPENDS THE DAYS WRITING AND DRAWING, COMPOSING 8-BIT BAD RELIGION COVERS, AND DEARLY MISSING COUNT CHOCULA CEREAL. SHAWNDALEY.CA

BAD IDEA #1945 WRITTEN BY ZEB S. AND ILLUSTRATED BY ALINA PETE.

ALINA PETE WRITES AND ILLUSTRATES THE WEBCOMIC *WEREGEEK*. WEREGEEK.COM

BAD IDEA #2010 WRITTEN BY TWITTER CONTEST PARTICIPANTS AND ILLUSTRATED BY JASON ANARCHY, PETER CHIYKOWSKI, CHRIS "LUNARBABOON" GRADY, AND AARON LENK.

JASON ANARCHY IS A MCRIB-EATING GAME DESIGNER WITH HULKING BICEPS. HE LIKES TO OCCASIONALLY HAVE A DRINK AND MAKE POP CULTURE REFERENCES. HE IS THE CREATOR OF THE *DRINKING QUEST* GAMES, AND A PARTY FOR HIRE. DRINKINGQUEST.COM

BAD IDEA #2121 WRITTEN BY "VICE-ADMIRAL G BANHAMMER" AND ILLUSTRATED BY SAM LOGAN.

VANCOUVER-BASED COMIC ARTIST SAM LOGAN IS BEST KNOWN AS THE AUTHOR OF *SAM & FUZZY*, THE ONGOING SERIALIZED COMEDY ADVENTURE THAT HAS CHRONICLED MASSIVE TALES OF WARRING NINJA MAFIOSOS, SECRET UNDERGROUND SOCIETIES AND LOVESICK STALKER VAMPIRES FOR OVER TEN YEARS, ONLINE AND IN PRINT. SAMANDFUZZY.COM

BAD IDEA #2208 ACTED OUT AND ILLUSTRATED BY JAY PAULIN.

JAY PAULIN LAUNCHED INK'D WELL COMICS IN 2009, AND HAS SINCE BUILT IT INTO A SMALL PRESS. IN ADDITION TO PUBLISHING HIS OWN WORK, HE GIVES OTHERS A CHANCE TO SHINE--MOST NOTABLY IN HIS THREE CHARITY ANTHOLOGIES THAT HAVE RAISED OVER $3,000 FOR CHILD'S PLAY AND FREE THE CHILDREN. INKDWELLCOMICS.COM

BAD IDEA #2236 WRITTEN BY C-J BOHLE AND ILLUSTRATED BY CRAIG FERGUSON.

CRAIG FERGUSON IS AN INDEPENDENT ARTIST TRYING TO BREAK INTO THE COMICS AND GAMING INDUSTRIES. HE CAN OFTEN BE FOUND LURKING IN ARTIST ALLEY AT COMIC/ANIME CONVENTIONS. REBELRABBITART.BLOGSPOT.CA

BAD IDEA #2260 WRITTEN BY NEYBOR AND ILLUSTRATED BY PETER CHIYKOWSKI.

BAD IDEA #2291 WRITTEN BY CAROLYN W. AND ILLUSTRATED BY KELLY TINDALL.

MR. TINDALL IS A FORMER BIRTHDAY PARTY CLOWN FROM MARSDEN, SASKATCHEWAN. FOR MORE PIRATE COMICS, READ HIS WEBCOMIC *STRANGEBREARD*. STRANGEBEARD.COM.

BAD IDEA #2343 WRITTEN BY ARMOND NETHERLY AND ILLUSTRATED BY RAYNATO CASTRO AND ALEX CULANG.

RAYNATO CASTRO'S LIFELONG GOAL IS TO SOMEDAY MASTER THE ONE-INCH PUNCH. HE CAN PERFORM THE TWO-INCH PUNCH. HOWEVER, THE DENSITY OF AIR AND THE DISTANCE OF THE EARTH FROM THE SUN LIMITS ITS EFFECTIVENESS IN MOST PRACTICAL CASES. IN THE MEANTIME, RAY SPENDS HIS DAYS AT THE FOOT OF A WATERFALL, TRAINING. BUTTERSAFE.COM

ALEX CULANG IS A RUSTY BUTTON. BUTTERSAFE.COM

BAD IDEA #2498 WRITTEN BY TIM WILDE AND ILLUSTRATED BY EMILY HORNE.

EMILY HORNE HAS BEEN THE DESIGNER AND PHOTOGRAPHER FOR THE WEBCOMIC *A SOFTER WORLD* SINCE THE DARK OLD DAYS OF 2003. SHE ALSO WRITES BOOKS SOMETIMES, MOST RECENTLY *THE INSPECTION HOUSE: AN IMPERTINENT FIELD GUIDE TO MODERN SURVEILLANCE* FROM COACH HOUSE BOOKS. ASOFTERWORLD.COM

BAD IDEA #2583 WRITTEN BY MAGS STOREY AND ILLUSTRATED BY PETER CHIYKOWSKI.

BAD IDEA #2615 WRITTEN BY BONNIE SEIDEL AND ILLUSTRATED BY JAYLEEN WEAVER.

JAYLEEN IS A COMIC ARTIST AND VANCOUVER FILM SCHOOL GRADUATE FROM VANCOUVER. HER PASSIONS INCLUDE COPIC MARKERS, DINOSAURS, CHICKENS WITH PANTALOONS, AND CATS. GURUKITTY.COM

BAD IDEA #2640 WRITTEN BY ERIC "AWESOME" FIRTH AND ILLUSTRATED BY ARIEL MARSH.

ARIEL MARSH SPENDS MOST OF HER TIME DRAWING, PLAYING VIDEO GAMES AND HANGING OUT WITH HER HUSBAND AND CAT. SHE HAS DRAWN MANY COMIC BOOKS IN THE PAST FEW YEARS: *INFANTASY*, *SCI-FACT COMICS*, *SUPER GALACTIC SPACE EXPLORERS*, AND THE WEBCOMIC, *EMMA AWESOME*. AW, YEAH! SWEETLOOTS.COM

BAD IDEA #2651 WRITTEN BY TOMMY C. AND ILLUSTRATED BY DAN MARTIN.

DAN IS THE CREATOR OF THE WEBCOMIC *DEATHBULGE*. OUTSIDE OF DRAWING, HE ENJOYS VIDEO GAMES, BOARD GAMES AND GOING OUTSIDE SOMETIMES. HE ALSO HAS A MASTER'S DEGREE IN FINE ART FOR SOME REASON. DEATHBULGE.COM

BAD IDEA #2682 WRITTEN BY GREG WONG AND ILLUSTRATED BY PETER CHIYKOWSKI.

BLAME & ACKNOWLEDGMENTS

IF I WAS A BETTING MAN, I WOULDN'T HAVE BET ON THIS BOOK GETTING FINISHED. HECK, I WOULDN'T HAVE BET ON ME GETTING *ROCK, PAPER, CYNIC* TO LAST LONGER THAN A WEEK.

FORTUNATELY, I KNOW SOME IRRESPONSIBLE GAMBLERS WHO BELIEVE IN MY BAD IDEAS. THERE WERE THE 365 BACKERS WHO DECIDED, "YES, THIS LUDICROUS BOOK DESERVES TO GET MADE" AND PUT MONEY DOWN ON THE KICKSTARTER AND DREAMED UP ALL OF THE BAD IDEAS THAT FILL THESE PAGES.

MY TWO UNREASONABLY GENEROUS PUBLISHERS, SANDRA KASTURI AND BRETT SAVORY, DECIDED TO TAKE A CHANCE ON THIS WEIRD LITTLE BOOK WHILE SIMULTANEOUSLY TRYING TO LAUNCH A GRAPHIC NOVEL LINE. OLD FRIENDS LIKE LAUREN GROVES, AARON LENK, DANIELLE PACEY, JAY PAULIN, MICHAEL SANSREGRET, BEN THOMPSON AND CKHYAMOJ TOWNSEND HAVE FILLED MY LIFE WITH THE RICH CONVERSATIONS AND ODD THOUGHTS THAT INSPIRED MOST OF MY EARLY COMICS.

I'D LIKE TO THANK: MEGAN HARRIS, KATE LANE-SMITH, JASMINE MINOZA, JAY PAULIN, AND SAM ZUCCHI, WHO PROOFREAD THE BOOK; INNA YASINSKA, WHO CUT TOGETHER A PHENOMENAL VIDEO FOR THE CAMPAIGN; MEGAN HARRIS, HUSEIN PANJU, JAMES STEVENSON, AND SAM ZUCCHI, WHO WROTE DOZENS OF EXTRA BAD IDEAS TO FILL OUT THE TEXT; AND BEVERLY BAMBURY AND ANDREA MAGEE, TWO ALL-CAPABLE SOCIAL MEDIA MAVENS WHO HELPED ME GET THROUGH THE KICKSTARTER WITHOUT CHEWING OFF A LIMB.

AND OF COURSE THIS BOOK STRAIGHT-UP WOULDN'T EXIST WITHOUT THE INCREDIBLE GUEST ARTISTS WHO TOOK THE BAD IDEA PROMPTS AND NEVER STOPPED RUNNING WITH THEM.

I OWE A RIDICULOUSLY BIG THANK YOU TO MY FIANCEE, JASMINE, WHO HAS BEEN IMPOSSIBLY PATIENT DURING THE FIVE (GOING ON SIX YEARS) I'VE BEEN WRITING THIS COMIC, WHO GUIDED ME THROUGH DRAWING MY FIRST RPG-STYLE TURTLE, AND WHO HAS ALWAYS CHALLENGED ME TO DITCH THE LOW-HANGING FRUIT AND REACH FOR RIPER PUNCHLINES. I'VE ALSO STRAIGHT-UP STOLEN A GOOD HANDFUL OF HER JOKES.

FINALLY, I OWE THANKS (AND APOLOGIES) TO MY DOGS, ROXY AND TOMMY, WHO HAVE MISSED MORE THAN A FEW WALKS AS I PORED OVER GUEST ARTIST EMAILS, BUDGETING SPREADSHEETS, AND PAGE LAYOUTS. I PROMISE I'LL PAY YOU BACK IN SALMON TREATS AND... OH SHIT, THEY'RE GIVING ME THE SAD EYES LIKE RIGHT NOW. I GUESS THEY'RE GETTING SOME HUMAN FOOD.

WITH IMPOSSIBLE GRATITUDE,

PETER CHIYKOWSKI

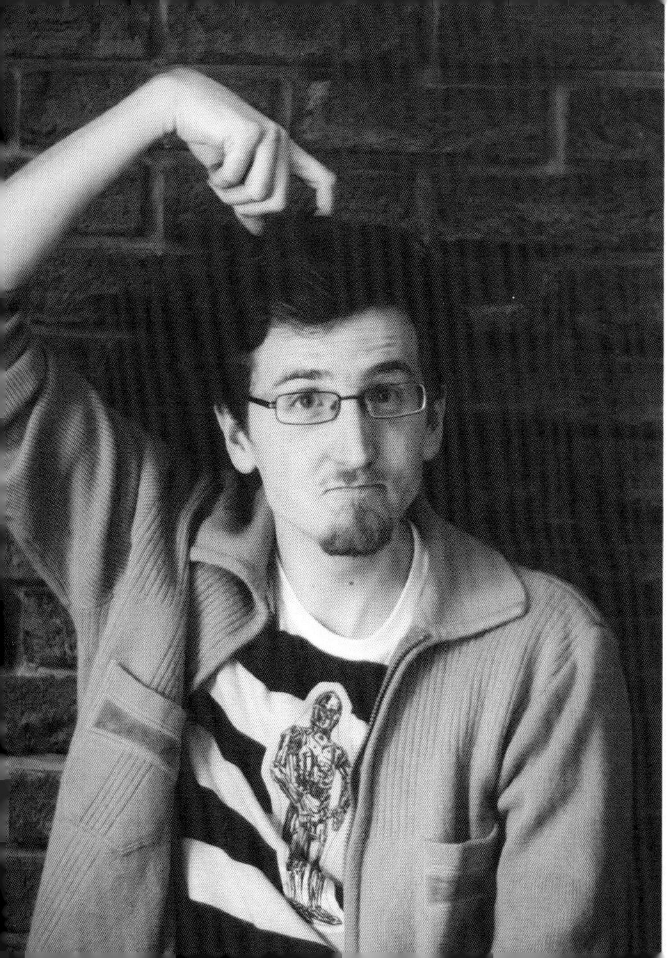

ABOUT THE AUTHOR

PETER CHIYKOWSKI IS THE AUTHOR OF *ROCK, PAPER, CYNIC*, A WEBCOMIC CURRENTLY NOMINATED FOR BEST GRAPHIC NOVEL BY THE CANADIAN SCIENCE FICTION AND FANTASY ASSOCIATION.

HE'S ALSO A LIFETIME MEMBER OF THE HALF-CAT FIELD RESEARCH ORGANIZATION. HIS COLLABORATIVE RESEARCH ON HALF-CATS HAS BEEN PUBLISHED IN THE STAFF-PICKED KICKSTARTER BOOK *HALF-CAT: A PARTIAL HISTORY*, AS WELL AS PRESENTED AS A TEDX TALK AND PRESENTED AT THE KICKSTARTER HEADQUARTERS IN NEW YORK.

HE PUBLISHES NEW COMICS ONLINE EVERY WEEK AT ROCKPAPERCYNIC.COM.

NEW COMICS
EVERY WEEK AT:

ROCKPAPERCYNIC.COM